ALSO BY THE MOTLEY FOOL

THE
MOTLEY FOOL
INVESTMENT
WORKBOOK

COMPLETELY REVISED AND UPDATED

DAVID and TOM GARDNER

WITH BILL BARKER, BRIAN LUND, BILL MANN,

DAVID MARINO-NACHISON, AND RICK MUNARRIZ

A FIRESIDE BOOK

PUBLISHED BY SIMON & SCHUSTER

New York   London   Toronto   Sydney   Singapore

FIRESIDE
Rockefeller Center
1230 Avenue of the Americas
New York, NY 10020

FIRESIDE and colophon are registered trademarks
of Simon & Schuster, Inc.

The Motley Fool and the jester logo are registered trademarks
of The Motley Fool, Inc.

For information about special discounts for bulk purchases,
please contact Simon & Schuster Special Sales:
1-800-456-6798 or business@simonandschuster.com.

Designed by Katy Riegel

Manufactured in the United States of America

5   7   9   10   8   6   4

ISBN 0-7432-2998-3

For our nieces and nephews

CONTENTS

ACKNOWLEDGMENTS

As you read and work through this updated and revised edition of *The Motley Fool Investment Workbook,* please join us in thanking the many Fools who helped give it a new lease on life.

First a big thank-you to our home team of talented editors and writers. For helping research, advise, and write this edition we thank Bill Mann, Bill Barker, Rick Munarriz, Brian Lund, and David Marino-Nachison. Uh, guys, which one of you still has the big pencil? Also, cheers go to our publishing managing duo of Jonathan Mudd and Alissa Territo who oversee all the fine points of getting the book from our home to yours. Also to our legal eagle, Marthe LaRosiliere, for her help in, well, ensuring we're always saying legal things! And doing so with a smile befitting our company logo.

Also to our friends in New York—our long-time agent, Suzanne Gluck, who makes publishers shiver when we walk into offices with her, and, of course, our long-time publishers, Simon & Schuster! In particular, we extend our appreciation to Doris Cooper and Isolde Sauer for their guidance and keen attention to detail to ensure that all the words we present to you are indeed actual words and make sense.

And finally we thank you, our reader, and the many members of our Fool community. Your own personal investing stories, your contributions, and your questions keep us fueled and energized . . . and have a wonderful habit of creeping into our books! Through good markets and bad, we'll continue to work hard to bring you financial education, amusement, and enrichment to help you make better decisions, and (what counts most of all) to improve your quality of life. Fool on!

THE
MOTLEY FOOL
INVESTMENT
WORKBOOK

CHAPTER 1

GETTING STARTED

WHY ARE YOU HERE?

Turn on any investing show on television. Just keep clicking until you see tickers racing across the bottom of your screen. Perfect. You found one! Well, chances are that at some point in the next half hour you'll see a person looking quite knowledgeable make a prediction about the direction of the stock market. He or she might say something like: "As you know, Bob"—for some reason, they're always named Bob—"the market is entering a 'push-pull' phase, as evidenced by the inverse parabolic formation that is occurring in the advance-decline line. The Dow will drop 342 points over the next two months, starting Monday." The interviewer nods gravely and sympathetically. The guest goes on to predict that some guy in Wichita will get sick after eating a bowl of spoiled chicken salad casserole on Thursday and that an Alice Munson of Sacramento should check the air pressure on her left rear tire over the weekend. "I can't compete with that," you think. You keep clicking until you find your favorite bass fishing program.

Is it any wonder that for decades, most Ameri-

cans haven't thought they could handle investing on their own?

The good news is that, despite how intimidating investing might seem, never before has information been so readily available to individuals. These days millions of people are managing their own investments, using the Internet to research companies, listening in on corporate discussions to which we never had access in the past. A lot of us are successfully directing our own retirement money through things like 401(k) plans and investment retirement accounts (IRAs). And most of us expect that in our lifetimes we'll save enough to buy a house, put children through school, and cover unexpected expenses without ever having to learn about inverse parabolic formations.

But did any of us think that we could expect some Foolish fun along the way, too? Hopefully, you've realized that managing your money can be as entertaining and enlightening as it is empowering.

For all the success we've had with people taking control of their financial lives, our work is far from done. Millions have not yet taken to saving and investing—either because the stock market seems indecipherable or because they consider "money watching" a petty, self-interested pastime. Oddly enough, because of their failure to save or invest, they tend to be the very same people who have the most to worry about later on as they close in on a retirement for which they have made no preparations. For them, the stock market is a bugaboo, because they know that, unlike interest in a savings account, making money through investing in the stock market is not a sure thing. They are right, to a certain extent. There is no FDIC-insured 3.621 percent ironclad return waiting at the other end of the year.

Markets rise. Markets fall.

It's a common worry. It's an understandable worry. Risk and reward are sorority sisters. Any near-term analysis will be ripe with extremes. Bull or bear? Feast or famine? Expand your time frame and the feasts become reasonable meals. The famine takes on the characteristics of a diet. You can do this! Really. Granted, watching financial "experts" on television probably does little to put one's mind at ease, and in fact, we think that people can do plenty of damage to their financial futures by following the hot stock picks that each expert seems to have in large supply. The impenetrability also turns off the very people who need basic financial help the most—people genuinely bored by it all. But once you begin to realize that the experts know a lot less than they let on, you can quickly come to the point where you know a lot more than you'd ever have believed.

Thanks to the recent and unprecedented spread of education about money, it's easier and more rewarding than ever to take a do-it-yourself approach in building your financial fortitude. Financial services are no longer the domain of the upper crust. Information is now there for the taking, or made available at fair and reasonable costs. Want proof? Look in the mirror. Lift up this workbook so we can see it, too. You are our latest indicator! Welcome to the revolution, which, in the words of Gil Scott-Heron, will not be televised. It is particularly important to recognize that our collective interest in managing our own money is a direct threat to Wall Street institutions, which have a strong financial incentive to make investing seem like Newtonian physics. After all, much of Wall Street exists to manage other people's money. The Manhattan rent, the dry cleaning, and those Carnegie Deli lunches don't come cheap. Their livelihood revolves around their ability to convince you that managing your money is just too difficult to do on your own. Instead, they'd like you to simply buy their high-load mutual funds. Better yet, turn over your portfolio to an investment broker and let him manage it for you. But as we'll demonstrate in this Foolish guide, investing is not Newtonian physics. It's more like financial Darwinism, and you're about to realize the full potential of how money savvy you really are.

Professional money management, in fact, contradicts the normal way things work in business. Most professions exist to translate or reduce complex things into simpler forms more accessible and helpful to the rest of us. An accountant sifts through difficult tax laws and reams of financial data to tell a corporation how much it owes in taxes. A doctor takes advantage of years of research and education to prescribe a drug that will help your hay fever. An engineer makes use of physics and material science to design the office building you work in. However, professionals in the investing world generally try to make everything more difficult, for the reason already elaborated. They make your investing decisions sound dicey so that you contract them to guide you. Convenient, eh?

While you may not want to perform brain surgery on yourself, are you ready to submit yourself to wallet surgery? No one will ever know the answers to your financial questions if you fail to ask them. It's the twenty-first century: do you know where your money is?

This workbook is designed to show you that while investing may be hard work, it isn't as difficult as you thought. What do you know about investing? We'll say it again: you know more than you think. Everybody knows something about something. Did you know that the stock market makes it possible for you to buy shares in companies that are involved in almost any facet of your life?

Do you have a car, or know someone who does? Chances are, you know which companies make the best parts. Do you play sports? You probably know which companies make the best-selling gear. If you are a doctor, you probably know which pharmaceutical companies are coming out with the most promising drugs. Successful investing primarily involves just looking around you, scratching your head a bit, and saying stuff like, "Uhh, that makes sense."

The Motley Fool Investment Workbook has been carefully designed to provide a roll-up-your-sleeves interactive learning experience. Scratch your head here. Scratch your pencil there. The aim is to have *you* take control of *your* financial future. Absolutely no preexisting knowledge of any kind about personal finance or the stock market is required— though we guarantee that you'll have it by the time you've completed this book.

Quiz #1

Do you know what variable-ratio option writing is?

   a. Yes   *b.* No

If you circled *b*, you're in the right place. Read on.

   One of our hopes with this book is that whether you have $500,000 to invest or $57 in pocket change, you'll learn enough to avoid using overpaid middlemen (brokers, managed mutual funds, you name it) and have more control, more satisfaction, and more fun on the way to a more prosperous retirement. But at a minimum we hope you take these three things about investing with you:

   • Hey, I can do this.
   • It will require some perseverance.
   • If I'm patient I can reap substantial rewards.

Finally, lest we sugarcoat our efforts too much, learning to invest can be a lot of fun, but it's also going to require some work on your end. This is fun work. This is important work. But this is work, nonetheless. That's why what you're holding in your very hands right now is called a workbook. You can enjoy the investing process. We sure do.
   Let's begin.

WHERE, EXACTLY, ARE YOU?

The first step, taking stock of where you are, is the simplest but the most often overlooked of all the 593 steps we'll be covering. Too many people make their first stock trade without understanding what sort of disposition they have or what financial position they're in. If you want to dive in the deep end of the public pool, it's important to learn how to swim first. At the very least, remember to wear a swimsuit.

   To get a little perspective on your own financial situation, it often helps to look at some others, to see how they're doing. So let's go on a field trip. Let's head out to our local mega bookstore and see who we can find. Don't worry, we're not that far. We're just a paragraph away.

ERIC AND CAROL AGEE

As we pull into the parking lot, amazed to find a choice space just steps away from the entrance door, we see Eric and Carol Agee flipping through the books on sale out in front of the store. Who are the Agees? They're a married couple with two young, rambunctious sons, Mike and John. The Agees moved into a renovated Victorian house on Oak Street about two years ago. Both have good jobs; Carol inherited a little money from a great-aunt she never knew; and the two of them have successfully budgeted their money. While they've taken out a mortgage on the house and have monthly car payments, they don't have any other debt.

   Eric looks kind of bored as his wife pages through a book on the evolution of the English language. His eyes wander over to the cover of some personal finance book. Boy, those things are everywhere these days. This one's priced to sell at 80 percent off, too! Eric hasn't thought a lot about investing. He thinks investing is something that really rich people do, and he certainly isn't rich. He has seen the market rise. He has seen the market fall. Carol reads the finance pages now and then, but only just started investing some of her salary into mutual funds. They are both aware that in the future they'll need significant sums of money to send their boys to college. And the Agees will need plenty of money left over in the wake of all that schooling, to comfortably retire as empty-nesters.

Eric and Carol haven't neglected their retirement planning. Both contribute 6 percent of their salaries to their employers' 401(k) plans (which allow employees to park a portion of their salaries in tax-deferred investments—more on that later, of course). Their employers match those investments with 2 percent of their salaries.

Where is that money invested? The Agees aren't entirely sure. When Eric's employer started the plan, there was a presentation by the company that handles the 401(k), and they offered a choice of three mutual funds. Eric has no idea how well these funds have actually done; all he vaguely remembers is that one was "high return, high risk," the other was "low risk, less return," and the last was something that promised "fixed income." What do those terms mean? He doesn't know. He just remembers that he chose the low-risk one, because he didn't want to take chances with his money.

Carol's employer offers three mutual funds, too. One is an "index fund" that invests in the five hundred companies that make up the Standard & Poor's 500—many of the largest companies in America. Another is a government bond fund, and the last is a corporate bond fund. Carol wanted to put all of her contribution in the S&P 500 fund. However, Eric talked her out of that, because he thought it was much too risky. So she put her money in the government bond fund, which Eric feels is the best place.

Where does Eric get his approach to investing? Perhaps from his mother—who watched her uncle's fortune disintegrate during the Great Depression. Even though Eric is taking one of the safest routes possible—a fund comprising largely government-issued bonds—his mother still considers him a high roller. "Those corrupt politicians in Washington might be lining their pockets with your savings right now!" she says.

Money has definitely gotten in the way of familial relations in the Agee family. It's sad, but Carol has been ignoring her mother-in-law lately because of her constant meddling in her family's financial affairs. She recently calculated how much she and Eric need to retire. It's a lot of money, and with the performance of their investments to date, it doesn't look like they'll be able to save enough for their sons to get to college and for themselves to retire at sixty-five.

Carol insists that Eric sit down with her and just take a look at the numbers. She wants Eric to find out exactly what options are available in his 401(k), and to consider more seriously where he is putting his contribution. She wants to move her funds into the index fund in her plan, and contribute more. And Carol would love it if she could just get Eric to read one or two books about investing. But he won't. It's just easier for him to avoid the subject since every time his mother hears of their plans she starts talking about how Uncle Nim lost his shirt in 1929. "You're going to be ruined like poor Nimmy," she warns. "And I'm not going to be the one to bail you out, you hear?"

Let's leave Eric and Carol to enjoy their time *away from relatives*, and head into the store to see who else we can find.

JIM DONATELLO

Over by the magazine rack, we find Jim—lanky, pensive, and sporting a goatee this week. He's looking at some music magazines. Jim plays a guitar, not well enough to quit his day job, not poorly enough to give up the thought of doing so. About two years ago, he graduated from college with a B.A. in medieval history. He's single and has a job driving a delivery van for UPS. It's not exactly what he wanted, but it's a start. (We guess medieval history companies aren't hiring these days.)

Jim grew up on a farm twenty minutes southwest of Bradford, Pennsylvania. His family raised horses and dairy cattle, and farmed oats. Growing up on a farm gave him a love of the outdoors, a willingness to work hard, and an intense fear of the dreaded desk job. Jim now lives in an apartment in the metropolis of McKeesport, Pennsylvania, which is located at the confluence of the Monongahela and Youghiogheny Rivers. Enjoying an active social life, he dates a woman in the apartment across the hall, another who lives back at home in Bradford, and one who lives in Mine Hill, West Virginia. What a dog! When he is not working or dating, he can be found rolling over the Pennsylvania hills on a mountain bike.

Despite his active life, Jim is actually quite thrifty with his finances. His car is paid for, and he's almost paid off the loan he took out for the guitar. Other than his Dell computer, he doesn't have any other luxuries, nor does he see the need for them. This leaves him with a significant amount of extra money, which he has stashed in an account at the local savings and loan.

So far, Jim's investments have been twofold. On the advice of one of his girlfriends' brother ("It's a sure thing!" he said), he speculated in a penny stock—a gold mining company listed on something called the "pink sheets." The company was named Quick Pay Goldmines (ticker: QPGM) and used a new electromagnetic device to mine gold out of magnetic black sands in western Canada.

Jim was skeptical about this whole gold mining venture. But his girlfriend Alison reassured him; her brother Wade knew what he was talking about. Wade told Jim that the company was run by Trapshooter Reilly, renowned to be a human fountain of liquid gold. Jim had heard of Reilly somewhere, but if he remembered correctly, the story wasn't good. Still, at the urging of Alison, he invested $1,700. Besides, Wade said to him, "At 43 cents a share, how can you go wrong?"

Two weeks after he bought it, the thing was trading at 61 cents per share, and Jim began entertaining the idea of a biking tour of the Northeast. But a week later, CNBC ran a story that Quick Pay Goldmines was under investigation by the Royal Canadian Mounted Police. The gold mine turned out to be nothing more than a money laundering operation. That evening, Jim brought up a picture of Trapshooter Reilly on the Internet—with Reilly in

handcuffs and leg irons, on his way to court. That was the first time Jim saw him, and all he could think was, Holy cow, I invested my money in *that* guy? Trading in the company was halted overnight, and Jim's investment became worthless.

Jim's second investment was in a savings account down at the local bank. He still knows very well that the 3 percent interest he's getting on his account at the savings and loan in McKeesport isn't adding to his wealth at all. In time, he'd like to move out of his apartment in McKeesport and into a house. That won't happen solely on the proceeds from promotions at UPS and a savings account. But Jim knows it's better to have money than to lose it in the market. He just doesn't have a clue about where to go next.

RONALD AND SANDY WASHINGTON

Let's leave Jim at the magazine rack and step into the coffee shop. My, what fancy blends they have here! Sitting at one of the tables is a well-dressed couple. They don't look too happy. In fact, they're pretty stressed out. Travel magazines are spread out all over the table, but something's ruining their dreams of a walking tour through the west of Ireland. Ronald and Sandy Washington are doing well professionally. They both earn high salaries and drive new luxury cars. They have two children, but the live-in nanny, Bridget, does most of the work of raising them. Their house is decked out like an Ethan Allen showroom and the state-of-the-art home entertainment center is to die for. They belong to the local country club and a health club. And Ronald just bought a fifty-five-foot yacht. They're living large!

Everything must be fine, right?

Nope. Opulence comes with a bill at the end of every month. Salary checks are racing out the door—for tuition, for all the stuff that they believe their kids need, for insurance, for hefty mortgage payments, for those huge car and boat payments, and for Ronald's Synchro-Satellite Fish Tracker 3000, which his yacht dealer sold him on as a last-minute add-on. ("Come now, Ronald. What you going to do—just *float* out there?")

Commensurate with all that consumption, the bills are getting worse and Ronald is afraid of incoming mail. Yet their debts aren't limited to those mentioned. They have more plastic than a toy factory, in the form of several credit cards and numerous store charge cards. Each card has exorbitant fees, and paying the minimums isn't helping shrink the debt load. They also have overdraft protection on their checking accounts. Every time they write a check for more than the balance of the account, money is kicked into the account by their bank, in $100 increments. This makes it impossible to keep track of their accounts.

There have been a number of warnings that they were getting in trouble, but it really has just hit home, here, over the maps at the bookstore. When they bought their latest cars, the Schnauzer 900ZX and the Manatee Coupe, the dealer told them they owed more on the trade-ins than they were worth. He said they were "upside down." So to get the loans on the new cars, they had to borrow more than the cars were worth. Sandy had some doubts about whether they should buy those automobiles, but as a salesman, Ronald was worried about what business partners would think if he and his wife drove old cars.

Ronald does realize that a lot of the purchases he made on credit weren't necessary. He wonders if he needs all the different suits he has in his closet. Some he hasn't worn more than once. The home entertainment center is another thing they probably shouldn't have bought. The only one who seems to use it is Bridget (she enjoys it a lot, though). Also, why do they have three camcorders? No one watches the videos they shoot, anyway. The country club membership is nice, but Sandy never gets a chance to get over there. Same for the health club— they just can't find the time to put their membership to use.

We stumbled on this pair today just as they began confessing and reasoning their way through the giant knot of their financial state. The trip is certainly off. Sandy is now so worried about the payments that the thought of going away seems insane.

The interest accumulating on their debt boggles the mind. After making payments each month, they have almost no cash left over. They are also arguing more now with each other than ever before.

To top it all off, neither of them feels total job stability. Ronald's firm has seen business drop off recently, and he worries he may be reduced to consultant status. Sandy's company is telling her that she is not a team player, and she's concerned that they might ask her to leave. Both have been quietly and constantly on the lookout for other jobs, but they fear they may experience periods of unemployment. That could be a real disaster for them. Ronald just turned to Sandy and said, "We may look wealthy, but we're essentially broke."

JOANNE KURTZ

Before we leave the bookstore, let's go downstairs again. This store has a fireplace with comfortable furniture placed around it so that customers can relax while paging through one book after another. Sitting on the couch immediately in front of the fireplace is Joanne. She's in her mid-fifties and divorced. Several years ago, her husband left her for a young model. It was a devastating shock, but Joanne didn't waste any time feeling sorry for herself. She went out and got a job. She had been out of the workforce for many years raising children, which meant that getting a traditional job would be difficult. So she decided to sell real estate. She obtained her license, and after a few lean months she started selling.

Joanne succeeded in the real estate business because she spent time with customers to determine what they really needed, and she knew her sales area thoroughly. She was careful to bring clients only to homes that fit their financial needs. Other agents habitually showed clients houses that sold $10,000 to $20,000 higher than what they'd requested, hoping to squeeze out some extra commission. Joanne knew better. If a client wanted a $100,000 house, she showed the client a $100,000 house. The consequence? She sold a lot of houses.

It wasn't long before Joanne accumulated a fair amount of cash from her sales. Plus, the divorce settlement gave her a lump sum. She set up an account with a full-service broker, tried that for a short while, but quickly became disillusioned. First, as a salesperson, she knew her product. But her stockbroker didn't seem to know anything about the investments he sold. He only offered memorized responses to her questions. And he was just flat-out uncooperative. Once, she had wanted to buy stock in a company that performed relocation services. A number of her clients used them and it seemed their business was booming. Her broker blew off her suggestion. He also never bothered speaking to her about her specific investment needs, which disturbed her even more.

What's worse, he was constantly calling her with recommendations of what to buy or sell, talking down to her about unknown and unproven companies. She'd buy a stock that he insisted was hot, and two weeks later he'd urge her to sell it because "it isn't making earnings." One day he called her with his latest recommendation, and she had the nerve to ask him why. "It's on my company's recommended list," he answered.

"So?" she asked. "Is that the reason I should buy it? What if it 'misses earnings'? Do I sell it in two weeks?"

Her broker steamed. "Look," he stammered at her, "if you want me to be your broker, you should go with what I say!" It didn't take Joanne more than a second to think about that. "Leave my money alone. I'm transferring my account." She's always been thankful that she said those words.

Where did she go with her money? Joanne set up an account with a discount broker, joined an investment club of friends, and began doing her own research. This worked for real estate—why shouldn't it work for the stock market? She went to the library and asked the librarian which books she should read on investing. "The Peter Lynch books tend to be pretty popular," the librarian suggested. Joanne went ahead and checked out *Beating the Street* and started to read it that night. Lynch's ideas were inspiring, and the guy actually seemed to be having fun with all this. And the idea that she might be smart enough to pick stocks fascinated her. On her next trip to the bookstore, she picked up *The Mot-*

ley Fool Investment Workbook and at this very moment is reading about herself. Hey there, Joanne!

Armed with knowledge and confidence, she started investing in stocks. How did she and the club choose which ones to buy? Just by focusing on companies she knew and checking out to make sure they were profitably run. When she found a product or a company she liked, she would call the company for its financials and read up at the official websites.

Overall, Joanne's investments have done quite well—some big winners, some average, others just plain dawgs. To her surprise, she has learned that business is more full of stories and science and mystery and history and philosophy and arts than common fools could ever have imagined. She's empowered. Her lone regret is waiting so long before telling her first broker to get his grubby hands out of her portfolio.

OK, we've done our survey of a few bookstore patrons. Let's walk over to the lemonade stand, grab three cups of juice, ask the merchant how business is, and then sit down on the nearest bench and reflect on what we've learned.

WHY SHOULD THESE PEOPLE INVEST?

The people we've just met illustrate widely varied financial situations. One might have hit close to home in your case, but that's not entirely important at this point. Each has a different reason for investing, although, obviously, one couple needs to get their debt under control before they should even think about investing. Here are some reasons that our bookstore friends should be investing—perhaps one or more will strike a chord with you. Check any reasons that apply to you.

Why Should I Invest?

___ To accumulate money for retirement because I have no retirement plan where I work.

___ To supplement retirement income from a pension fund.

___ To save enough money for a large expense I can foresee, such as sending children to college, buying a house, or starting a business.

___ To have resources for an unforeseen future emergency.

___ To make one hell of a lot of money and become master of the universe.

___ To learn more about the company at which I work.

___ To have something to talk to Dad about.

If you checked at least one box, you're going to get your money's worth out of this—or we're going to die trying.

Now let's debunk some commonly shared misconceptions:

1. You *need* to be rich to invest.

No, you don't. There are investment strategies appropriate to all income levels.

2. You *need* to put a lot of time into investing.

No, you don't. You can put in as much or as little time as you want—anywhere from a few minutes a month to as much of your day as you're willing to commit will work. Some people make a hobby of investing and regularly read about companies, financial news, and the latest in fashion wear. Others make a hobby of mountain biking or newts, and *still* invest by using strategies that require little effort and only periodic checks of their investment performance.

3. You *need* to know a lot about stocks.

Nope, you don't need this, either. You just need to know about what you are investing in, or the strategy you are using. Some strategies, like index investing, require no knowledge at all. Others, like investing in small-cap growth stocks, require more time to learn the nuances of market mechanics and valuation. Don't worry, we've got you covered a few chapters down.

4. Investing is *deadly* boring.

Again, no, it doesn't have to be—unless you're an MBA student assigned to follow the utility industry by a mammoth investment firm. Otherwise, it's good, clean, educational fun. We still can't believe the subject isn't a required course in high school. (If you have or know a teenager, may we recommend our recently published *Investment Guide for Teens* to get them started investing?)

Make a hobby of investing and you can learn what forces drive industry, the economy, and nations themselves. You learn how companies are run, how they treat their people, and how they continue to grow. Learning about investing gives you a useful new way to look at the world around you.

For some people, the word *learning* conjures up images of no. 2 pencils filling out bubbles, algebraic word problems, or ill-timed pop quizzes. Hey, that was then and this is now. At Fool Global HQ, we make it our business to ensure that you hardly notice how much you're learning.

Now, going back to the beginning of this chapter, remember what the talking head was saying on television? We'll quote him again: "The market is entering a 'push-pull' phase, as evidenced by the inverse parabolic formation that is occurring in the advance-decline line. The Dow will drop 342 points over the next two months, starting Monday."

Let's pull that apart word by word and analyze what he meant.

OK, we're done.

You see, he said absolutely nothing useful. Sadly, the above quote is a compilation of actual statements made by "experts" on financial television. The business of Wall Street, and the Wise men and women who populate it, is to speak a language you don't understand, to convince you that you don't have the necessary intelligence to do well investing. We already explained the reason for this: *their livelihoods depend on being able to charge you enormous amounts to manage your money.* Fools that we are, we aim to convince you that you don't need the self-promoting ways of the Wise. With a little education and self-discipline, you can make your own decisions, invest your own money, and significantly improve your returns.

TAKING STOCK: WHERE YOU ARE

It's time to pull the Foolmobile over to the side of the road and ask: "Hey, who the heck *are* you?" In the pages just ahead we'll be pulling back from actually getting into the mechanics of investing—that's later—and instead we'll concentrate on your personality, your preferences. Get ready for a mix of Myers-Briggs, Stuart Smalley, and our syndicated *Ask the Fool* column.

WHAT KIND OF FOOL AM I?

Who am I?

If you know the answer to "Who am I?" you probably don't need this workbook. Having solved man's existential dilemma, you'll have already made millions and given it all away to those around you. Good for you! Most of the rest of us are always trying to figure out what sort of person we are—and for the purposes of this book, what type of investor we are.

There are literally dozens of ways to invest successfully in stocks; we'll be identifying as many of them as we have space for here. But you're going to have to know thyself, because if you select an otherwise great approach that is wrong *for you*, you likely won't be pleased with the results. Even if you make money, your stomach lining won't be there to thank you. And it's also quite likely that you won't make any money. George Soros, a great trader, and Warren Buffett, a masterful investor, have entirely different ways of approaching the equity markets. Each has made billions, and each has profoundly affected the world around him. But force one into the other's shoes and you have the recipe for a small disaster, for failure and discontentment.

Figuring out who you are is critical to the art of investing. Let's start by asking a few questions:

How much risk are you willing to take?

How much time can you really devote to investing?

Are you the sort of person who loves taking the dog for a walk in the evening, or prefers buzzing around town to every cocktail party?

How do you feel about prosperity?

What has your family taught you about investing?

Do public companies inspire, frighten, bore, or disgust you?

And how about your personal finances—do you balance your checkbook, or do your monthly statements and ATM machine receipts always surprise you with their contents?

Are you a saver, a spender, or both?

Answering the above questions plays a role in your ability to invest successfully. Do you want to excel at it almost without effort? If so, you'll need a plan. But not just any plan. You will need a specific plan of what you want to achieve, the tools and skills to put your plan into motion, and for just a short period of time here, a take-no-prisoners attitude to get through the initial research.

Begin to formulate your vision by filling in the following list. Heck, this stuff may seem sappy. But if you ponder it for a second, isn't it incredible that so many of us ramble through our lives without penciling down what it is we're hoping to gain out of all this? Perhaps this simple exercise will unleash your desire to home in on global goals throughout your life! Wouldn't that be great? But you know what? You only paid us to teach you how to invest. So let's get back to the task at hand. It's time to find out a few of your financial goals.

Ten Things I Would Like to Be, Do, or Have

1. _____

2. _____

3. _____

4. _____

5. _____

6. _____

7. _____

8. _____

9. _____

10. _____

Skim through the above list. We started out by posing the question "Why are you here?" Now the more appropriate question is, "Why aren't you there?" Some of your goals are quite ambitious. Are you sure about number 7? Well, anyway, let's go over these now. Are there any dreams requiring some money that you don't have? You want to be a master magician? You'll need the tools and a marketing budget. You'd like to sail the Tyrrhenian Sea? The boat, the crew, the food, the cellular linkup to Fool.com—these aren't free. Oh, you want to open up local homes for struggling teenagers? Federal and state grants won't carry the full load of expenses. You'll need to come up with some of this money on your own.

Take a second and circle the items on your list that will require capital. Voilà! You now know why you hold this book and why you're giving up an entire afternoon to the scrutiny of your finances. Refer back to this page often. We're working toward giving you the independent wealth to achieve your goals. Today this is a wish list. Tomorrow it can be a checklist.

Now let's look to the root of some of your dreams: your family.

FAMILY BACKGROUND AND BELIEFS

Most of us are by now aware that messages from our parents or guardians early in life have a potent effect on the way we now see the world. The Kennedy children were required to summarize news highlights from the daily paper each night at dinner. It's not surprising that so many of them turned to politics. Politics is, after all, one of the few things as dismal as having to summarize news highlights before digging into a plate of peas and thank yous. Anyway, if your family often sat around the dinner table discussing the need to stay out of debt, odds are that you took greater care to do just that. And some of you have mothers who loved to talk about market trends and ways to find undervalued companies; that gave you the confidence to know that such things were achievable (and you didn't even have to spend $40,000 per year on a business school degree!).

Conversely, if your family lamented how much their forerunners had lost in market crashes or how brokers had ripped them off or how commercialism was killing the planet, you probably don't have too many positive associations with money. These beliefs can become so ingrained that fundamental logic or the experiences of others hold no sway over you. Well, we're not going to take no for an answer. And hey, we're just words on a page. We've got nowhere else to go. We can wait all day, you know? So, let's give it a shot. In order to become a satisfied investor, you need to identify the negative beliefs you hold about money, reason them all the way through, discuss them with people outside your immediate family, and recognize that we all operate in a commercial world, we all consume to survive. You'll need to apply some of these basic commonsense and mathematical principles to ensure your prosperity.

How about writing down three negative thoughts

about money from either family or friends—or maybe even your own—in your past?

1._____

2._____

3._____

Now take another two minutes and write down the best one-line refutation of each of those negative ideas.

1._____

2._____

3._____

Reread all six. Now, last we checked, this workbook wasn't brought to you by one of those pseudo-religious self-help organizations interested in luring you into a mountain community and mailing your parents for money. So we're not going to propose that you should be forever positive in your thinking about money. We'll be the first ones to laugh at that glazed perpetual optimism. Instead, we're simply going to encourage you to look squarely at your three rebuttals and recognize them for what they are: your best shot at getting started on the right foot. Ebenezer Scrooge remade his own attitude toward money and radically changed his neighborhood and his life in the course of one night! Anyone can.

Now it's time to think about how much risk you can absorb en route to building a financial future that has you riding horses in Himalayan valleys or writing books about Ingmar Bergman or whatever you fancy. To get there without escalating blood pressure, you'll have to manage risk.

RISK TEMPERAMENT

How do you feel about losing money? How much risk can you tolerate without upsetting your en-

tire life? These questions need answering. The responses vary from person to person and mind-set to mind-set. You've got to find the right risk level for yourself—the level where your investments excite you but don't cause any sleepless nights. Worrying about your money will not increase your success. In fact, worrying about anything won't much help. You need to settle into your own comfort level, enabling uninterrupted sleep and lazy Sunday mornings. So, let's determine whether you're Evel Knievel or Homebody Hank.

Risk Tolerance Test

Respond to the questions below with the answer that most accurately reflects your point of view.

1. Which of these three cars would you prefer to drive?

   a. Ferrari
   b. Jeep Cherokee
   c. Volvo

2. You would rather eat

   a. At a new, exotic locale you've never been to before
   b. At your favorite restaurant
   c. Leftovers at home

3. You meet someone at a party who you've heard is a successful broker. He gives you a stock tip. Do you

   a. Call your broker immediately and buy 100 shares?
   b. Ask other people their opinion of this broker and this stock?
   c. Have another piece of sushi?

4. If the speed limit is 65, do you

   a. Drive at a minimum of 75 and turn on your fuzz-buster?
   b. Drive between 65 and 74?
   c. Drive below 65?

5. Your cat gets stuck up a tree. Do you

    a. Climb the tree yourself and carry her down?
    b. Climb a ladder to carry her down?
    c. Call the fire department to carry her down? Poor little Sheba.

6. You are given $1,000 from a rich aunt for your birthday. Do you

    a. Drive to Atlantic City, believing it is your duty to go forth and multiply?
    b. Put the cash in a money market fund and research stocks to invest in?
    c. Put the cash in a lockbox in your basement?

Scoring: Give yourself 10 points for each *a* answer, 5 points for each *b,* and 0 points for each *c.*

Write your score here, followed by the appellation you've earned (listed below):

_____

If you scored over 40 points, you are *Captain Ahab,* willing to take risks to accomplish your goals. Ahoy! You *might* make a whale of a killing in the stock market.

If you scored 16–40, you are *Captain Kirk,* willing to take enterprising risks where no cash has gone before, but only after scrutinizing the pros and cons and calculating which move is the most prudent.

And if you scored 0–15, you are *Captain Kangaroo,* preferring to tend the carrots in the garden while hobnobbing with Mr. Greenjeans. Protecting what you have is your utmost priority.

With the knowledge they will acquire from this workbook, Captain Kangaroos might feel empowered to venture forth and dabble in a little adventure. Captain Kirks will have all the necessary tools to support their methodology. And the Captain Ahabs out there might learn that saving some money and spending some quiet time at home won't cramp their style.

Now that you have some sense of how much risk you can bear, you'll need to figure how much time you have to dedicate to all this. If you have a couple of kids, it can be challenging enough just to remember your purse before vacationing. Many of us spend our waking hours on a tight schedule. Where the heck can we fit in the analysis and consistent operational management of our cash? Read on.

HOW MUCH TIME DO I HAVE?

One of the great features of investing is that the amount of time you commit is strictly up to you. You can have successful investments by spending half an hour each year, month, or day. But you need to know, honestly, what's right for you. If you made it this far, and we see that you have, your appetite for knowledge is commendable. But please, start slowly. You can always devote more time when you begin to measure how much you enjoy this stuff. Set yourself up for success, not failure. Remember always this definition of investing: it is the appreciation of wealth and the preservation of capital. You will miss nothing by taking as much time as you need to learn about this stuff before you charge into the markets. We cannot say the same for the reverse.

How Busy Am I?

Circle the response (true or false) that most applies to you.

1. I wouldn't consider visiting a deserted island without my personal planner.   T F

2. I sometimes read the newspaper while meditating.   T F

3. When things calm down, I do only two things at once.   T F

4. Some weeks I'm too busy to sleep more than a few hours a night.   T F

5. Someone else is in charge of my schedule, and I can't get an appointment with myself.   T   F

6. I haven't spoken to my parents or grandparents in six weeks.   T   F

7. I avoid air travel because on planes I can't use my cellular phone.   T   F

8. On occasion I have forgotten to feed my (pets) (children) (self).   T   F

If you answered *true* to any of these questions, you probably need a nap more than you need to be reading this book. Fold the top corner of this page, give yourself two hours with the shades drawn, and then come back. When you return, you'll be diving back into a book that proposes you need do no more than six hours of work per year to keep your budgets in order, your savings money flowing into investments, and your investments providing healthy, long-term returns—and you won't ever have to meet with a trained salesman to do so. Sweet dreams!

HOW MUCH AM I WILLING TO DO?

So, how much time can you give over to your finances without compromising your already overloaded professional and personal life? The bottom rung on our Foolish ladder has you committing at least six hours per year to tracking your money. That's just thirty minutes every month. From there, you can strengthen your financial position by adding extra hours. Of course, many people give hundreds of hours a month to saving and investing, but unless they're crushing the market's return by dozens of percentage points after all expenses are taken out, they may be wasting a lot of time. First, let's see how much time you think you have for this stuff:

"I can reasonably commit _____ (number of seconds, minutes, hours) to investing each month."

OK, you put it in writing. We'll consider that a blood oath.

With time set aside, let's consider what financial tools you have at your disposal.

WHAT TOOLS DO I HAVE AT MY DISPOSAL?

Where would Delilah be without her scissors, Zorro without his sword, or Rocky without a side of beef? Nothing can be accomplished without the proper tools. The good news is that to excel at saving and investing, you already have much of the necessary equipment no more than an arm's length away.

While it is helpful to have a computer and access to our Fool.com website, it isn't necessary. All the work in this book can be done with paper, pencil, and a calculator. And with a local library, TV, newspapers, and magazines, you can access all the information you need. Don't forget that you have some very valuable personal resources, as well. We can't discount your brain, your experience, your instincts, and your sense of humor—all of which (particularly the last!) are virtual necessities for surviving in the world of investing.

Since you're going to be learning a good deal about business here—the business of your personal finances and the businesses that you invest in—start by asking yourself about some of the shops in your local area. Wonder aloud with us for a second by naming what you consider to be the best and worst businesses in your vicinity.

The best business I know is _____.

The worst business I know is _____.

Now let's go one step further and ask you why you made those calls.

The three reasons that your chosen great business is great are:

1._____

2._____

3._____

The three reasons that your chosen lame business is lame are:

1._____

2._____

3._____

As we work together to improve your financial condition, concentrate your attention increasingly on the qualities of those businesses that you love. You're going to want to apply as many of their principles to your own money management strategies, and heck, you may well want to aggregate enough wealth to be able to run a business just like theirs!

OK, we hope you just realized the number of great tools and examples that lie minutes away from you. How about checking through the following list with us?

The Tools and Examples List

If you have the following, place a big fat **X** on the line next to the entry.

Brain	___
Pad	___
Pencil	___
Sense of humor	___
Investment workbook	X
Calculator	___
Computer	___
Telephone	___
Common sense	___
Curiosity	___
Other people to talk to	___
List of local businesses	___
Champagne	___
Kazoo	___

OK, the tools are at your fingertips and you know what dreams you will invest for. But before we draw the most direct route from point A to point B, it's time to take one large step backward before we plow ahead. Let's consider what experiences you've had as an investor already.

WHAT IS YOUR PAST EXPERIENCE?

Do you feel like the kind of person who never does *anything* right? Or does everything you touch turn to gold? You are probably somewhere between Charlie Brown's classmate Pigpen with his cloud of dust and Midas with the magical fingers. Your past experiences are likely to color the way you approach investing.

The key is to take responsibility for your investments, to recognize your past mistakes or successes, and to move forward, knowing that the results you create are your own. It's a disservice to everyone involved—and an easy one at that—to blame your broker, your uncle Stuart, the chairman of the Federal Reserve, or Congress (OK, you can blame Congress). Everyone makes mistakes. Coca-Cola launched New Coke. Quarterback Kurt Warner took the NFL by storm after toiling for several years in the more obscure Arena League and then NFL Europe. Bob Dylan has been booed off stages before. Mistake and failure make us human; the key is to learn from your errors and to aim not to repeat them. If you're like us, you'll repeat at least a few (perhaps numerous times) just to keep from becoming perfect (how boring). Anyway, accepting that you'll have setbacks as an investor is a solid beginning.

MY DUMBEST INVESTMENT

I once heard a lot of fuss about a stock called Comparator Systems. There was some kind of exciting deal in the works, and the boat was leaving port. What was the deal? I had no idea. What did the company make? I had some vague notions, but never bothered to delve deeply. Yet I bought it. Within days, the company had been found to have no new product at all. The story became a scandal as the company started getting hit with lawsuits, and investigations led to the halting of its trading. I lost everything I put into that one (fortunately, not too much!). My experience has shown me there is no such thing as "missing the boat." You always have plenty of time to learn about each investment. It took a bad approach in a bad company to discover this, but the resulting lesson was a good one.

—Tony Miller, Motley Fool community member

LESSON LEARNED: Don't invest in trains said to be leaving stations for good, or boats hurrying out of ports.

After months of due diligence, I bought into Amgen back in January of 1993. It was more than just a market darling at the time; it was a proven leader in the very promising field of biotechnology. I was familiar with the company. I was familiar with its products and pipeline. A month later, earnings jitters had the stock shedding more than half its market value. Wait! Amgen never goes down! Petrified, I dumped my shares. While I still believed the story was intact I felt that I was better off riding the market's near-term momentum. The stock recovered, of course. And I left behind what would have been a fifteen-bagger had I continued to hold today.

—Rick Aristotle Munarriz, Motley Fool writer

LESSON LEARNED: Don't let stock prices force you out of any holding, if you believe the company behind that stock is still succeeding day after day.

SPENDING AND SAVING

We're assembling a nice profile of you now, dear Fool. (Whatever you do, don't let direct marketers get hold of your workbook!) Now let's take a look at spending and saving habits. Actually, before we even think about how you're allocating funds, let's consider some of the numerical basics. Too many Americans think there's no reason to save money, claiming that it'll just sit there waiting to be spent, that their lives will just stand still waiting for some moolah to jump-start them. Well, think for a second about what patience will do for you and consider what happens to $10,000 if you invest it in various ways.

INVESTMENT OVER A 20-YEAR PERIOD

INVESTMENT VEHICLE	GROWTH RATE	$10,000 BECOMES
Treasury bills	3%	$18,061
Bonds	5%	$26,533
Stock market	10.5%	$73,662

Over a period of decades, the amount of money you have in common stock will absolutely blow away the cash you have sitting in a savings account at your local bank. Over time, a return rate that is twice that of another investment vehicle will grow that amount many times over. That's the magic of compounding. But, of course, you need money to invest money. So your initial challenge is just to save more money than you spend, to set aside as much of those savings for long-term investments in stocks, and to repeat that strategy over and again. To paraphrase an old tune by KC and the Foolshine Band from the golden age of disco:

Save, save, save,
Save, save, save,
Save your booty,
Save your boo-ooty!

And invest it.

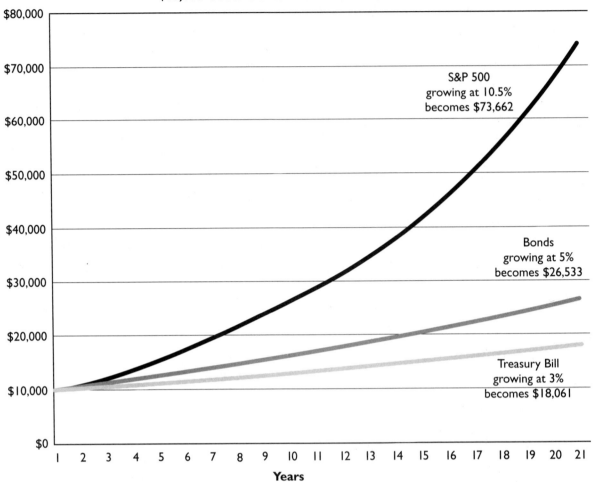

$10,000 COMPOUNDING OVER 20 YEARS

S&P 500
growing at 10.5%
becomes $73,662

Bonds
growing at 5%
becomes $26,533

Treasury Bill
growing at 3%
becomes $18,061

Years

FIVE EXCUSES NOT TO INVEST

Despite its highs and lows, the stock market has proven to be the superior long-term investment vehicle. So it's a shame that so many people aren't investing. Why not? Here are five reasons people sidestep stocks—and five short volleys.

5 COMMON EXCUSES NOT TO INVEST	5 REASONS WHY THEY'RE WRONG
I'll never know enough.	You don't have to be Einstein to be a successful investor.
I don't have enough money.	You can invest almost any amount of money.
I don't know where to start.	You've got this workbook, don't you?
It's for the boys' club on Wall Street.	You've come a long way, Fool.
I don't have enough time.	Sure you do.

SO, WHERE ARE YOU NOW? THE BIG PICTURE!

Fill out this worksheet and see how far you've come already. You can draw many of your answers from previous exercises.

1. If I have many, many years to invest, I'm best off buying

   a. bonds
   b. stocks
   c. Treasury bills

2. My three investment goals are

   a. _____

   b. _____

   c. _____

3. My risk tolerance type is Captain _____

4. Three dreams I would like to make come true through investing are

   a. _____

   b. _____

   c. _____

5. One business I love is _____

6. One business I can't stand is _____

7. The amount of time I am willing to spend investing is _____ hours per month.

8. Tools I can utilize to implement my investing strategy are

   a. _____

   b. _____

   c. _____

   d. _____

9. One investing mistake I will never make is _____

   _____

10. Just as Michael Jordan was consistently great in basketball, there are businesses that are consistently great in their industry.
    True   False

You are now ready to begin tackling financial information. Keep that pencil and mind sharp, borrow an eraser if you must, and let's get ready to rummmmbbbbblllle!

CHAPTER 2

YOU AND YOUR MONEY

HOW MUCH DO YOU HAVE TO INVEST?

Now that you've stopped and considered what kind of Fool you are—per financial perspectives and objectives—it's time to discuss the nuts and bolts of the issue. You may be sitting there thinking, OK, so I know I am a low-risk, conservative, Captain Kangaroo investor who needs to invest in something. Now what?

Whatever mental picture you have put together of what kind of investor you are, you're now ready to move on to the next and crucial point, what you should invest in. Let's get some stock picks out there. Let's start making some money. Right?

Wrong.

Those who are expecting an immediate detailing of different types of investments—like some sorry financial radio advertisement—picked up the wrong book. You'll want the one with that cover photo of a guy pointing at you from inside a pinstriped suit and saddle shoes, promising you, in the book's title, "$1 million in five years!" Good luck over there.

We're not even ready to think about specifics yet. Why not? Because we don't yet know how much you have to invest. Let's spend this chapter figuring

that out and we'll go from there. In fact, based on what we learn, we may even discover that you shouldn't start investing in stocks for a couple of years. Patience will always win the day on Wall Street.

YOUR FINANCIAL PROFILE

Let's get started with a reminder that so few ever receive: *you* control *your* money. Even if you've given it over to someone else to manage, you're ultimately responsible for that decision. We consider it necessary for you to take control of your financial destiny, instead of relying solely and blindly on other people for advice and guidance. We figure you probably agree, since you've purchased this book.

The following quiz is designed to help you figure out whether you're the sort who really does follow the path of your money or the sort who just lets it run willy-nilly out your wallet, into varying accounts, off desperately to cover mortgage payments this month, off to cover minimum payments on three credit cards, helter-skelter, this way and that.

Show Us the Money!

Our list of answers is not exhaustive, so choose the one that most closely fits you.

1. What percentage of your take-home pay goes to pay for your house and/or rent?

   a. 95%
   b. I don't know—I just know it is too much.
   c. No more than 30%

2. How many credit cards do you use on a regular basis?

   a. So many that I have to leave some at home in the drawer.
   b. Ten.
   c. Two or fewer.

3. How many of those credit cards have balances on them that you do not fully pay off each month?

   a. All.
   b. Half.
   c. None.

4. Have you ever gone to pay with a credit card and had the merchant tell you that you are over your limit?

   a. This happens frequently. I just use another card.
   b. It happened frequently when I got out of college— but it hasn't happened in a long time.
   c. Nah, they didn't tell me I was over the limit. They just made me cut up the card right there on the spot.
   d. Never.

5. Do you have a savings account?

   a. No.
   b. Yes, but there is very little money in it.
   c. Yes, and it has a decent amount of money in it.

6. Do you have an IRA account?

   a. No.
   b. Yes, but there is very little money in it.
   c. Yes, and it has a decent amount of money in it.
   d. I don't support radical political organizations.

7. Do you know what percentage of your income goes to debt? In other words, if you added up all your bills for a month, and compared it to your total income—what is your best guess as to what percentage it would be?

   a. 95%
   b. 50%
   c. 25%
   d. I have no idea.
   e. I don't want to know.
   f. Can we stop this now?

8. Do you eat out a lot? How much would you say you spend, as a percentage of your monthly income, on eating out every month?

   a. 40%
   b. 20%
   c. 5%
   d. I have no idea—I just know I hate to cook.

Now you have your answers. Quite possibly, you're not running the tightest ship, and you believe that doing so would make for a lot of headaches and waste a lot of your vacation time. Not so, nay, not so. Read on.

CREATING YOUR FINANCIAL PROFILE

Your financial profile consists of two parts. One part, your balance sheet, looks at your overall financial situation at just one point in time. The other part, your income statement, takes a look at your average monthly income and expenses. Taken together, they give you a good indication of your financial health, as well as provide you with a powerful tool that can help you gain more control of your money.

While some of the exercises below aren't the most fun way to spend a Saturday afternoon, if you have a rainy one, take advantage of it. Completing the exercises is important, in order (perhaps for the first time) to see exactly what your financial situation really looks like. They will also give you a preview of corporate financial statements, which we'll study later on in this book. C'mon, it's not like you have to do this every week or month. Just this one time to start. Maybe you'll find it sufficiently harmless to repeat every three or six months, or every year.

YOUR FINANCIAL PROFILE, PART 1: YOUR BALANCE SHEET

The balance sheet is a snapshot of your financial position at any one point in time. We won't be following salary payments next week or considering your financial position if one of your stocks grows by 30 percent. We're just going to pull the camera out and snap a picture of what things look like today.

HOW MUCH AM I WORTH?

We grant you that figuring out how much you are worth may require a little field trip through those files and those drawers where lie discarded check stubs, loan information, and bank or brokerage statements for the last few years; it may even require a phone call or two. But if you're not going to play along with us, jeez, why are we even trying? (Ah, the tug on the ol' guilt strings . . . works every time.)

ASSETS AND LIABILITIES

Take out your pencil and your calculator. Imagine a sheet of paper with two columns on it. The left column will list your assets and the right side will list debts, or liabilities. We'll proceed item by item and have you figure each amount in turn.

To help you through this process, we have asked Ronald and Sandy if they would be so kind as to let us use their information as an example for you. As they need all the financial help they can get, they quickly agreed. As you calculate your net worth, we'll calculate their net worth. Let's start by listing assets first.

ASSETS

What is an asset?

Here's our definition of the word *asset:* anything that you own that has economic value. In most cases, that's either cash or something that could be converted to cash, like property or IOUs. For our purposes, let's start with your short-term assets.

SHORT-TERM ASSETS

What do these include? Actual cash on hand, any cash in your bank account, certificates of deposit (CDs), as well as any securities (a fancy word for stocks and bonds) that you own. Short-term assets are cash and anything you plan to convert to cash to pay down expenses over the next twelve months.

In the case of Ronald and Sandy, they don't have much cash on hand. However, Sandy does admit she keeps a secret cash stash of around $200 under the mattress. So their cash on hand is $200. Time now for you to write down whatever amount of money you have on hand (maybe under the mattress, in the cookie jar, in your purse, your wallet, or in the glove compartment of the car). A rough estimate to the nearest $100 works fine—no need to count out those penny jars, unless you have a free hour, in which case go right ahead.

CASH ON HAND

You	RONALD & SANDY
_____	$200

Next, write down how much money you have in your bank accounts—both checking and savings. If you have accounts at several banks, include them all. (Of course, this assumes you have a bal-anced checkbook! If you do not have an accurate total of the money in your account, you may want to consider starting there before completing this part of the workbook, or take your best guess for this exercise.) Ronald and Sandy have $2,500 in their one checking account. They don't have money in any other type of bank account, nor do they have any CDs (*certificates of deposit*—rest assured they have amassed quite a collection of compact discs for that Bose home theater system). If you do have CDs, make sure you include these as well. Our goal is to figure out how much you have in each account.

SHORT-TERM ASSETS

	You	RONALD & SANDY
Checking accounts	_____	$2,500
Savings accounts	_____	$0
Certificates of deposit (CDs)	_____	$0

What about securities? If you own stocks, bonds, or mutual funds, get the latest copies of your various account statements and enter the amounts shown as the value of your holdings. As of their last brokerage statement, our happy couple had $3,000 in securities (all mutual funds).

SECURITIES

	You	RONALD & SANDY
Stocks	_____	$0
Bonds	_____	$0
Mutual Funds	_____	$3,000
TOTAL SECURITIES	_____	$3,000

What if you have an IRA, 401(k), 403(b), Keogh, or any other retirement account? Save that for now. That amount goes into your long-term assets.

So, our short-term assets list for Ronald and Sandy looks like this:

SHORT-TERM ASSETS

Cash on hand	$200
Checking accounts	$2,500
Savings accounts/CDs	$0
Securities	$3,000
TOTAL SHORT-TERM ASSETS	$5,700

LONG-TERM ASSETS

The distinction between short-term and long-term assets is that the latter are not readily convertible into cash. Anything in long-term assets, you do not plan to convert to cash over the next twelve months.

Long-term assets are things like houses, automobiles, retirement accounts (such as IRAs, SEP and SIMPLE accounts, Keoghs), valuable collectibles, and jewelry. When you list these items, you need to list them at "fair market value"—not what you paid for them. For example, your three-year-old automobile is probably worth 30–60 percent less than you paid for it.

For our purposes, just make estimates. If you bought your house for $180,000 but you think it's now worth $190,000, list $190,000. Although you may have paid $4,000 for your fancy computer five years ago, you might find it's worth more like $350 today. List $350. How about cars, furniture, or DVDs? You spent $4,000 on your stereo—and you think you could sell it for $3,000 in the next year. You should just value it at $3,000, right? Nope. You have to set a reasonable long-term value on all of your merchandise. Aha! So for all long-term assets, *you must estimate their worth five years from now.*

You can expect the stereo to continue to decline, or depreciate, in value.

You probably already know that buying a sturdy house is much more important than buying a nice car or home entertainment center. Your house will hold or appreciate in value; the other stuff depreciates, in some cases down to zero. You'll want to list those depreciating long-term assets (you know what that means now, right?) at a reasonable value five years from today. In many cases, your depreciating assets are headed to that depressing ultimate value of $0. Here, make your best estimate on what they'll be worth five years hence.

HOW CAN YOU DETERMINE WHAT YOUR HOUSE IS WORTH ON THE OPEN MARKET?

The best way to estimate the value of your house is to make comparisons with similar houses in your neighborhood. You can check on the Internet at sites such as www.housevalues.com or call a Realtor who sells houses in your neighborhood and ask her for an opinion. She'll have access to all the recent sales in your area, along with details on each property. Be careful, of course. If she's a good agent, she'll not only have helped you pinpoint your price range—she might suddenly convince you to sell your house!

Time, then, to start a new section on our balance sheet, labeled "Long-Term Assets." Next to *House* enter the long-term asset value. If your house is worth $125,000, that's the long-term asset value of your house today. In our example, a quick call to a few different real estate brokers familiar with the Washingtons' house and their neighborhood gave us a reliable value estimate of $275,000. And they have other long-term assets (jewelry, cars, and a personal computer) that tote up to $42,000.

LONG-TERM ASSETS

	YOU	RONALD & SANDY
House	_____	$275,000
Other	_____	$42,000

Let's now present the balance sheet for Ronald and Sandy with all of our updated information.

BALANCE SHEET FOR RONALD & SANDY

SHORT-TERM ASSETS

Cash on hand	$200
Bank accounts	$2,500
Brokerage account	$3,000
TOTAL SHORT-TERM ASSETS	$5,700

LONG-TERM ASSETS

House	$275,000
Other	$42,000

We will close with an increasingly common (and good) form of long-term asset now shared by many Americans: *the retirement plan.* That includes individual retirement accounts (IRAs), 401(k) plans, and any number of similar devices with acronyms that scare people away. Below, add in the present value of all your retirement plans. And that's exactly what we'd do for Ronald and Sandy, had they managed to maintain theirs. Alas, when they needed money to pay for that second car (the Manatee Coupe), they cashed in the two IRAs at a horrendous tax penalty. But they had to do it, they told themselves, as there was no credit left on their credit cards and they couldn't get a bank loan. Mercifully, though, Sandy has a 401(k) at work that she managed to fund, which is now worth $5,200.

Here, then, is our completed list of assets for Ronald and Sandy:

BALANCE SHEET FOR RONALD & SANDY (ASSETS)

SHORT-TERM ASSETS

Cash on hand	$200
Bank accounts	$2,500
Brokerage account	$3,000
TOTAL SHORT-TERM ASSETS	$5,700

LONG-TERM ASSETS

House	$275,000
Other	$42,000
IRA/401(k)	$5,200
TOTAL LONG-TERM ASSETS	_____
TOTAL ASSETS	_____

Now, activate that calculator of yours and add up all of Ronald and Sandy's numbers for their total long-term assets and total assets. What did you get? Our calculator returns $322,200 (total long-term assets) and $327,900 (total assets). Jeepers! They're rich!

Right?

Ah, to be is very different from to seem.

Let's take some space out now to allow you to sum up in one place your own list of total assets. (And remember not to get too terribly excited until we've completed the liabilities section, too.)

MY BALANCE SHEET (ASSETS)

Your name: _____

Date: _____

Your astrological sign: _____

(Who knows, it might help to know this.)

SHORT-TERM ASSETS

Cash on hand   _____

Bank account   _____

Savings account   _____

Brokerage account   _____

TOTAL SHORT-TERM ASSETS   _____

LONG-TERM ASSETS

House   _____

Other   _____

Retirement plans   _____

TOTAL LONG-TERM ASSETS   _____

TOTAL ASSETS   _____

You are now done with the first part of the net worth exercise. We hereby declare a brief sabbatical so that you may take time to reward yourself. Be back here in fifteen minutes to start on the next part. Go make a sandwich or something.

LIABILITIES

Your minisabbatical over, your pencil in hand, your mind once again a sharply honed razor, you are now ready to face down some accounting terminology.

The first thing to recognize is that if you're like most of us, you don't own outright all of your assets. Rather, you've borrowed money to pay for some of the things that belong to you. These debts are "liabilities," which will make up the second half of your balance sheet.

We will therefore begin unceremoniously and predictably with the next section.

SHORT-TERM LIABILITIES

Given what has gone before, you may be able to predict some of what constitutes this category. Try, for instance, any bill that you owe immediately and that has no fixed term. Credit cards come to mind! If, like most people, you have at least one card with an unpaid balance on it, that counts as a short-term liability.

It is thoroughly fitting to lead off our investigation of liabilities with America's Most Wanted: credit card debt. For most, this is the greatest portion of their short-term liabilities. In early 2002 the amount of credit card debt per American household exceeded $8,000. Sadly, many are unable ever to rid themselves of these enervating financial burdens—or don't know that they should be trying to.

To begin throwing off the yoke, the first thing you must do is to gather all your credit card statements. Add together the total owed on each into one grand figure, entering that on the line entitled *Credit card debt*. For our example here, we went through the shoe box that Ronald brought to Fool HQ, and after digging around for the better part of an afternoon we determined that Ronald and Sandy owed the sum total of exactly $8,500 on all their credit cards. We hope it doesn't take half a day for you to do the same thing.

Our first line for Ronald and Sandy's short-term liabilities reads like this:

BALANCE SHEET FOR RONALD & SANDY (LIABILITIES)

SHORT-TERM LIABILITIES

Credit card debt $8,500

INSTALLMENT DEBT

Are you paying any other minor debts off on a monthly basis? Dental bills, medical bills, student loans, personal loans, car loans? Perhaps even the IRS? We refer to these as *installment debts.* For all of these, again, we need the total amount owed—not the amount of your monthly payment. For example, if you had a crown repaired and the total bill was $390 and you are paying your dentist $25 a month, we need to know how much you still owe the dentist in total. Make a call to the dental office if for some reason your bill does not reflect the total amount due. Almost all loans generate annual statements that tell you how much principle you still have left. If you haven't kept track of these, then go ahead and call your lender.

Whether or not it's nighttime, it's time for you to put on your sunglasses because Ronald and Sandy have a blinding amount of installment debt. It is our Foolish hope that you'll have only a fraction of the amount they've saddled themselves with.

BALANCE SHEET FOR RONALD & SANDY (LIABILITIES)

SHORT-TERM LIABILITIES

Credit card debt	$8,500	

INSTALLMENT DEBT

Dentist	$5,000	(Sandy's midlife orthodontics)
Medical	$12,300	(Ronald's tummy tuck and chin work)
Home entertainment	$8,000	(big-screen TV with monster dish)
Car loan(s)	$38,400	(two cars)
Graceland Travel	$12,200	(balance from the last European trip)
Cellular Nirvana	$3,200	(balance from cell phone contracts)
Ben's Bathrooms	$11,290	(balance from Jacuzzi and tile work)
TOTAL INSTALLMENT DEBT	$ _____	

Time to tote up all that installment debt. Our own computations suggest the figure is extremely close to $90,390, an immense amount. Throw in Ronald and Sandy's credit card debt, and one's admiration grows for their ability to even be here at the bookstore, eating crumpets and drinking large lattes.

LONG-TERM LIABILITIES

While large corporations often finance their growth through numerous, complicated types of long-term debt, the average household's version typically consists of one major item—a mortgage. Thus, in this section of your balance sheet, you should list the total amount of all mortgages or home equity loans on any and all properties in your possession.

In many cases, this is easier said than done! How do you know how much you owe on your house? Well, if your mortgage didn't come with a payment booklet showing the balance after each payment is made, a quick call to your mortgage lender will get you your current balance. (Those guys are only ever too happy to answer, eh?) It really is that simple—even simpler if you track the information using a good financial software package, like Quicken or Microsoft Money.

Meanwhile, a quick call to Ronald's mortgage company told us they owe around $255,000 on their house. They had paid down the balance on their mortgage at one point, but then took out a home equity loan—Sandy told us it was for the sec-

LONG-TERM DEBT

	RONALD & SANDY	YOU
House (mortgages)	$255,000	_____

ond honeymoon, to Maui. Consequently, they once again have very little equity in their home.

Sound the foghorn! Why? You are *done* with your information gathering. Let's see how our balance sheet looks for Ronald and Sandy so we can calculate their net worth. In the meantime, you do the same with your information.

NET WORTH

OK, dear readers, flip back to the page where we calculated the couple's assets. What was the total?

BALANCE SHEET FOR RONALD & SANDY

ASSETS	
SHORT-TERM ASSETS	
Cash on hand	$200
Bank accounts	$2,500
Brokerage account	$3,000
LONG-TERM ASSETS	
House	$275,000
Other	$42,000
IRA /401(k)	$5,200
TOTAL ASSETS	$327,900

Now, what was the total of their liabilities?

LIABILITIES	
SHORT-TERM LIABILITIES	
Credit card debt	$8,500
Installment debt	$90,390
LONG-TERM LIABILITIES	
House (mortgage)	$255,000
TOTAL LIABILITIES	$353,890

OK, so what's the difference?

NET WORTH

Total assets	$327,900
Total liabilities	$353,890
DIFFERENCE (NET WORTH)	-$25,990

What does this mean? It means that Ronald and Sandy have a negative net worth of $25,990. You may very well have run across a couple like this in your life. On the exterior, they appear to be thriving, but there's no gold behind the glitter. If they continue at this pace in this direction, look out below! Just as huge businesses like Kmart can declare bankruptcy while small local businesses inch forward profitably, so too can seemingly wealthy couples disintegrate while their frugal counterparts can inch ahead.

Now, the fact that Ronald and Sandy owe more than they own isn't good, but it isn't hopeless either. If you find yourself in a similar boat, don't panic. Let's look at *your* net worth now and then think a few of these assumptions through.

So now you know your net worth! But you may be left wondering what this all really means. Keep reading.

THINGS TO LOOK FOR IN YOUR BALANCE SHEET

POSITIVITY VERSUS NEGATIVITY

Is your net worth positive, or negative? If it's positive, we have little to say to you here, other than "Attaboy!" and "Keep up the good work!" Our only suggestion would be that you continue to pay down your highest-rate debt as it comes. You shouldn't own investments that might appreciate at 11 percent per year, if you have outstanding credit card debt charging you interest of 18 percent per year. Start wiping out your highest-rate debt, aiming to be your own Microsoft—loads of cash assets, nonexistent liabilities.

Now, if you fall into group two, with a negative net worth, you need to squint your eyes at the numbers and begin to figure out how you can improve the asset side of the ledger. We're going to have to simultaneously cut spending while also attacking the highest-rate debt. If you have credit cards charging you 18 percent per year, you're going to want to consolidate all of those debts on lower-rate cards. A few phone calls to different card com-

MY BALANCE SHEET

Name _____

Date _____

Favorite sport _____

ASSETS

SHORT-TERM ASSETS

Cash on hand   _____

Checking accounts   _____

Savings accounts/CDs   _____

Brokerage account   _____

(stocks, mutual funds, etc.)

LONG-TERM ASSETS

Car   _____

House   _____

Furnishings, belongings   _____

IRA/401(k)   _____

TOTAL ASSETS   _____

LIABILITIES

SHORT-TERM LIABILITIES

Credit card debt   _____

Installment debt   _____

LONG-TERM LIABILITIES

House (mortgage)   _____

TOTAL LIABILITIES   _____

Total assets   _____

Total liabilities   _____

DIFFERENCE (NET WORTH)   _____

panies—and direct negotiation with your existing card company—should get you down a handful of percentage points. That can be critical to your success.

Let's take a closer look at Ronald and Sandy's debt.

DEBTS, LIABILITIES, AND THE LOSS OF TRANQUILLITY

Take a look at the credit card and installment debt that Ronald and Sandy are trying to pay off. Sandy admits they are barely able to pay the monthly minimums anymore on all their bills. No wonder. Ronald was stunned when we pointed out to him that—if you take the total of their short-term debt and assume that the average interest rate is 18 percent for credit cards and 8 percent for other debt—they'll have to pay approximately $8,760 per year in interest charges just to keep even. And all those payments without paying down any part of the underlying debt!

THE WASHINGTONS' SHORT-TERM LIABILITIES

SHORT-TERM LIABILITIES

Credit card debt	$8,500
Installment debt	$90,390
TOTAL SHORT-TERM LIABILITIES	$98,890

$8,500 × 18% = $1,530
$90,390 × 8% = $7,231
PAYMENTS = $8,761

PAYING DOWN DEBT

We think it is obvious that the Washingtons must reduce their debt levels immediately. If you are sit-

ting there looking at your own level of short-term debt, what does it look like? Are you in the danger zone?

My total short-term liabilities   _____

My average interest rate   _____

Short-term liabilities × average interest rate = annual interest payments.

$_____ × _____ % = $_____

PAYING DOWN HIGHEST-RATE DEBT FIRST

If Ronald and Sandy had a great deal of equity in their house, we would recommend they pay down their short-term debt (which has such high interest rates) by taking out a second mortgage. The two advantages to taking out a second mortgage are

1. The interest rate is usually much lower than credit card interest, and often lower than that of other installment debt.
2. The interest payments will be tax deductible.

Sadly, Ronald and Sandy have already taken out a second mortgage and spent the money. So this option is not available to them.

OTHER INCOME

Even though his business has been facing hard times, Ronald mentioned to us that he expects to receive a substantial bonus for overtime work during the past year. He's expecting that bonus payment in the next sixty days and wonders what he should do with that cash:

- Put in an IRA account and begin investing for the long term?
- Pay down existing long-term liabilities, like that house payment?

- Load up on fuel and try to outrun creditors to the Mexican border?
- Vegas, baby!?!
- Pay down existing short-term liabilities, like credit cards?
- Invest in real estate, since it holds or appreciates in value?
- A little bit of all of the above?

What do you think?

After much clacking of calculators, our laboratory mathematicians have determined that the single best decision the Washingtons can make is to *pay down the highest-interest short-term liabilities, such as credit cards*. The short-term debt carries the highest interest rates, and in the case of the Washingtons, is eating hundreds of dollars each year. Pay down the $8,500 in credit card debts, then when the next cash infusion comes, weigh the consequences of paying down the installment debt (dental loans, car payments, and so forth) against investing the money in a retirement plan.

YOUR FINANCIAL PROFILE, PART 2: YOUR INCOME STATEMENT

Where does my money come from and where does it go?

Now that you've created your personal balance sheet, know what your net worth is, and understand how you can use your stats to assess your financial health from time to time, it's time to figure how much money you make and where it all goes.

To adequately track whence your money came and whither it is bound, the second part of the financial profile will help you create an income statement. Unlike a balance sheet, which lists your assets and liabilities at one particular point in time, an income statement shows the flow of your money. Changes in your income statement will show up eventually in your balance sheet. And if you're thoroughly confused about the difference between the two—read on. We should be able to bewilder you even more.

What help is an income statement? It fires warning flares and sounds ear-splitting alarms if your expenses are disproportionate to your income. It will also show where you can slim down your spending, yielding more money for investment.

KEEP IT SIMPLE

To start out, we suggest you select one recent month for analysis. Here you'll need everything from checkbook stubs to credit card and brokerage statements to ATM receipts. If you're like us, there's a pretty good chance that at least a few ATM slips have disappeared, and that you might have trouble locating a banking statement or two. If that's the case, then make your month in review an upcoming month.

As we study this month, please disregard all extraordinary, one-time costs or gains—like buying a house, losing $420 during your last trip ever to Atlantic City, or collecting back wages from your one-time stint as an elephant rider in the traveling circus. These are unusual benefits or costs that will only serve to skew what's really happening week in and week out with your money. In order to evaluate your *regular* income, let's set them aside.

WHAT INFORMATION WILL YOU NEED TO HAVE ON HAND?

In order to determine your cash flow, you will need to gather together the following information. Get the pencil out and start putting check marks in there. If you've kept all records from a previous month, excellent! Proceed!

OK, let's check the list:

____ All canceled checks and bank statements for the month

____ ATM deposit and withdrawal slips

____ Paycheck stubs

___ Stubs for any other income that you received during the month

___ Brokerage statements, if you have a brokerage account(s)

___ Credit card statements for the month

___ Receipts for all purchases—groceries, movie tickets, bowling, books, magazines, etc.

___ Bills from utilities

___ Monthly health insurance bill*

___ Monthly life insurance bill*

___ Monthly car payment*

___ Monthly mortgage payment*

___ Monthly rent payment*

* Even if you pay for these on a quarterly or yearly basis, you'll need to calculate how much you pay out on a monthly basis. So, if your mortgage costs are $12,000 per year, that's $1,000 per month.

THE MONEY YOU MAKE—HOW MUCH ARE WE TALKING ABOUT HERE?

Use the worksheet that follows to write down in one place all your sources of income.

If you work and are paid a salary, this one's simple. Just collect your paycheck stubs. If you are married, get your spouse's stubs, too. (Yep, we believe in complete financial disclosure between spouses—particularly if you want to avoid the possibility of a few nasty, ugly, and downright awful surprises in the future.)

Now, what do you see when you look at your paycheck stubs? The first line will be your total wages, followed by a list of deductions. For our purposes here, we want you to take the net amount, after all deductions, and put that amount at the top

of the pad. *For those of you who are self-employed or have additional sources of income, just enter (as "salary") the average amount you earn in a month, after you have taken into consideration your tax liabilities.*

OK, we sense that some of you are getting frustrated. The cover says this is an investment workbook, and here we are tracking down receipts from the Dairy Queen (mmmmmm, Blizzards) and looking through shoe boxes for pay stubs. Despair not, for we are doing two things. First, someone wanting to invest must first develop a good idea of how much she can safely invest. Second, believe it or not, you're learning accounting. The worksheets we are doing right now are not too different from the statements you're going to be reading from companies. So yes, we're doing some setup work, but there is an old adage that says, "Measure twice, cut once." We're just doin' some measurin'.

401(K) MONEY

A gold star to you if you already have money deducted automatically from your paycheck for a 401(k) plan, automatic share purchase, or other investment program. However, don't add that money back into your net income amount. Treat it just as if it is an obligation like a debt—it's a debt to yourself for the benefit of your future. You've chosen to pay yourself before your other debts. Since this money is out of sight, it should be out of mind.

MY INCOME

Net monthly salary	_____
Other income	_____
TOTAL	_____

Let's meet up with our old pal Jim. We'll start by taking a look at Jim's paycheck stubs. He's netting $1,290 per paycheck and getting paid twice a month. So Jim is getting paid $2,580 per month.

INCOME

	JIM	YOU
Monthly net salary	$2,580	_____

Now, do you get any other money each month? Do you receive stock dividends or income from other sources? If so, add that in. Jim tells us he receives a share of the monthly payments from the sale his family negotiated of some acreage in Bradford, Pennsylvania. His payments tote up to $125 per month. Time to add another income line, which we'll simply call *Other income.* Add $2,580 and $125 and what do you get? $2,705.

CASH FLOW STATEMENT

	JIM	YOU
Monthly salary	$2,580	_____
Other income	$125	_____
TOTAL MONTHLY NET INCOME	$2,705	_____

Voilà! Our income analysis for Jim is now complete. And so is yours. Hey, this stuff isn't too painful, is it?

THE MONEY YOU SPEND— WHERE THE HECK IS MY STUFF?

OK, we need a nice clean page to start on. So let's start a new worksheet for "Expenses." We want you to list your expenses from most to least essential. Start with your basic necessities. Unlike supermodels, you do have to eat. Unlike the technologists in Silicon Valley, you do have to sleep. Unlike the Rolling Stones, you do need a stable home. Contrary to Howard Hughes's approach, you do need human contact and affection. Let's cover the necessities first.

MONTHLY EXPENSES

Rent/house payment	_____
Utilities	_____
Groceries	_____
Eating out	_____
Car insurance	_____
Health insurance	_____
Renter's/homeowner's insurance	_____
Car payment	_____
Clothes	_____
Other stuff	_____
Installment debt	_____
TOTAL MONTHLY EXPENSES	_____

Now let's review Jim's expenses one by one.

JIM'S EXPENSES

Rent. Jim is paying $550 a month in rent to live in that stylish one-room apartment overlooking McKeesport.

Utilities. How much do you spend on electricity? And gas? And water? And for local and long-distance telephone service? And for cable or satellite

TV? And for that cell phone or pager? When we asked Jim about this, he didn't know off the top of his head. Most people don't. So, we went back and looked at his various canceled checks. It turns out that Jim is spending $95 per month on basic utilities and $70 per month on the telephone bill. He doesn't subscribe to cable and is given a cell phone by UPS for business purposes. So, all told, he's spending $165 per month for utilities.

Food. How much did Jim spend at the Piggly Wiggly last month? And how much at the 7-Eleven, McDonald's, that steak dinner at Lone Star Steakhouse, and the dinner party Jim threw for Alison's family? (Which one was Alison again?)

We're looking over some of Jim's bills now, and wow—the guy likes to eat. But clearly he hates to cook. In Jim's case, there are only two receipts from the grocery store for the entire month. As we spy his food receipts over the past week, it was like a *Who's Who* of fast-food heaven. And we might add, much more expensive than eating at home. Oddly enough, Jim's a pretty trim guy.

OK, so the total damage for food came to a whopping $686 for one month. Whew! As you're toting up your own numbers, if the thought of writing down all your food-related expenses for a whole month intimidates you, then simplify. Do what Jim did. Just keep track of the money you spend on food for one week, then multiply by four.

INCOME STATEMENT (IN PROGRESS)

	JIM	YOU
Total monthly net income	$2,705	_____
EXPENSES		
Rent/mortgage	$550	_____
Utilities	$165	_____
Food/eating out	$686	_____

Insurance. OK, time to warm up those calculators. In our review of the cost of your car insurance, life insurance, home owner's or renter's insurance and health insurance, we're going to need to reduce it down into monthly expenses. Thus, if you pay quarterly, you're going to have to divide those payments by 3. If you pay twice a year, divide by 6. Hey, if you pay once a year, what must you divide by . . . ?

Yep, 12. Good job.

So, here is what Jim pays.

ITEM	EXPENSE PER MONTH
Car insurance	$200 (speeding tickets, ouch!)
Health insurance	$50
Renter's insurance	$10

These are the monthly insurance expenses. Onward!

Transportation. Jim has about two more years before his car is paid off in full. He's paying about $180 per month in payments, on top of which he spends about $50 each month on gas. All told, Jim's spending consistently about $230 a month between gas, regular maintenance, and car loan payments. A horse would be cheaper. Maybe.

Clothing. Jim likes to look good for Alison and the other women he dates. Skimming through some of Jim's past month's receipts, it looks like he's spending anywhere from $150 to $200 a month on clothes. Swank!

Other Expenses. Ah, here we consider expenses that aren't necessary to survival. In Jim's case, these include money for beer, compact discs, computer software, and baseball tickets every once in a while. We averaged out these expenses and they came to around $300 a month.

Installment Debt. Jim has been good about not racking up lots of credit card debt. He does have that heavy tuition loan, though. Duly noted in this column.

So, how does Jim's income statement look now? While we're tallying his, get ready to tally yours.

JIM'S MONTHLY INCOME STATEMENT

Total monthly net income	$2,705
EXPENSES	
Rent	$550
Utilities	$165
Food/eating out	$686
Car insurance	$200
Health insurance	$50
Renter's insurance	$10
Transportation	$230
Clothes	$200
Other stuff	$300
INSTALLMENT DEBT	
Tuition loan	$235
Credit cards	$50
TOTAL MONTHLY EXPENSES	$2,676
TOTAL MONTHLY NET INCOME	$2,705
MONTHLY OVER/UNDER	+ $29

Now it's your turn.

We hope that your over/under is positive. It's not easy to begin investing if you aren't actually making any money.

WHAT DO MY FINANCIAL STATEMENTS TELL ME?

We haven't had you run through these exercises for your health, though they may improve your well-

MY PERSONAL INCOME STATEMENT

INCOME	
Total net income per month	_____
EXPENSES	
Rent/mortgage	_____
Utilities	_____
Telephone	_____
Food/eating out	_____
Car insurance	_____
Health insurance	_____
Renter's/home owner's insurance	_____
Transportation	_____
Clothes	_____
Other stuff	_____
More other stuff	_____
INSTALLMENT DEBT	
Credit cards	_____
Car payment	_____
Other installment payments	_____
TOTAL MONTHLY EXPENSES	_____
TOTAL MONTHLY NET INCOME	_____
MONTHLY OVER/UNDER	_____

being. The point has been twofold. First, we want to be *absolutely sure* that you've got the financial stamina to begin long-term investing. It's vital to remember the trade-off that we mentioned before: the stock market has historically returned 11 percent, but credit card debt usually costs in the neighborhood of 18 percent. It doesn't make sense to begin putting money into one, while continuing to owe the other. If you have any other high-interest debt, too, you need to take care of that before investing. On the other hand, you want to begin investing when you are young, especially in tax-deferred retirement accounts. To make sure that you're making the best choice with your money, run through *The Motley Fool Personal Finance Workbook*.

The second point of the exercise is to introduce you to financial statements, which we'll be talking about at length later in the book. Once every quarter, companies perform the same exercise that you just finished. There you will see lots of jargon that may look foreign and unfamiliar, like "accounts receivable" and "accrued expenses." Don't let the words frighten you. The basic concepts are the same as those in this chapter. Now that you've gone through it for yourself, it will be a lot easier to understand the meaning of accounting terms.

The ground prepared, the foundation laid, let's get started investing!

CHAPTER 3

ARE YOU READY TO START INVESTING?

Now that you've defined some of your financial goals and assessed your financial situation, let's make sure you're ready to do some investing. The single greatest mistake that would-be investors make is to jump into the market too quickly.

That's exactly what Jim did when he threw a couple of thousand dollars down on Trapshooter O'Reilly and the prospects for gold in Vancouver. Heck, how much does Jim—the farming guitarist who drives a UPS truck in Pennsylvania—know about mining operations in Canada? How much do *you* know? We don't know a darned thing about it. This single line will save you more money over your investment career than any other:

"I don't know a darned thing about it, so I'm not going to invest in it."

If you're like most Americans, that means you shouldn't really be investing in anything yet. Why? Because the stock market seems huge, indecipherable, and more dangerous than Tommy Lee Jones in suede. Mishandled, the stock market can smush you, reducing your savings money to nothing and sending you back to the starting line. But learning to invest your money intelligently is less like learning to fly a 747 than to ride a bicycle. Don't let the pro-

fessionals make you think it's so tough that you need them to help you out at great expense! It ain't. Let's start with a short quiz.

Are You Ready?

Have you

____ eliminated your high-interest credit card debt?

____ finished your MBA?

____ stashed away at least $350,000 in your trading account?

____ quit your job so you can trade stocks full time?

____ selected a full-service broker who will tell you what to buy and sell?

____ told your full-service broker just not to lose your money out there?

____ learned about options, futures contracts, and day trading?

___ learned about candlestick charting, the McClellan Oscillator, trend lines?

___ paid $1,200 for expensive software and stock-quoting devices?

___ smiled and had a good laugh just now?

We hope that you checked the first entry and the last, and left the remaining ones blank. We're just kidding about the others, which we consider to be wholly unnecessary (if not harmful). It's unfortunate that so many people don't consider investing in stocks and mutual funds because they figure they'll need a lot of money, a lot of expensive information, and a lot of graduate-level training. Nothing could be further from the truth.

How well you invest will depend on many factors—and none of them have to do with your starting amount of cash or your ability to roll Wall Street jargon off your tongue at hoity-toity cocktail parties. Nope. Your success will rely mostly on the degree to which you understand *your own* circumstances. If you've continued reading this far, you should have a pretty good idea of what your financial goals might be. To get to this page, you should have taken care of all high-interest debt. Have you eliminated your credit card debt? Nice job, bravo! And have you set up at least a loose budgeting system allowing you to sock away some savings each month? Oh, encore, encore! Outstanding. So you've got some cash to invest, you have a regular stream of new money coming in, you haven't a lick of prepayable short-term debt, and you're fired up for your money to start earning you money. Onward to the castle then, Fool!

TIME HORIZON

One of the most important decisions about investing is also the most straightforward: what money should you invest in the stock market and what money shouldn't you invest? Another critical mistake that many greenhorn investors make is treating the stock market like a gambling machine. How so? They invest money hoping to generate winnings over a short period of time. A simple rule of thumb is that *any money you'll need over the next three to five years should not be in stocks or mutual funds.* Over that period of time, the stock market could get beaten about the head and neck like a rag doll. In fact, that happened to a whole lot of investors in the years 2000 to 2002. Be aware that stock values could disintegrate once again in just a few weeks, reducing what you "bet" on the market into half of what you bet in no time.

Those beginning-of-the-millennium investor blues were nothing new, though. Between 1972 and 1974, stock prices fell, on average, 30 percent. One of our nation's greatest companies, Coca-Cola, saw its stock fall by 65 percent. Had you invested money in either the market generally or Coca-Cola specifically, and had you been forced to pull out at the darkest hour, you might have seen your house, car, job, dirt bike, golf clubs, parakeet, and scuba gear repossessed by your creditors. Bet on stocks over the short term and you can bet that you'll get hammered eventually. So . . . what money shouldn't investors be putting in stocks? You tell us.

Money You Should *Not* Invest in Stocks

Below are ten investing scenarios. Number them from 1 (worst) to 10 (best) in terms of the attractiveness of the situation to Foolish investors. For the very worst situation, scratch in the number 1. For the best, scratch in 10. And go from there, people!

Money . . .

a. ___ for your retirement

b. ___ for your two-year-old's college tuition

c. ___ for a mortgage payment in three months

d. ___ to make a down payment on a house in two years

e. ___ from an inheritance with all short-term debts paid down

f. ___ for tuition when you go back to school this fall

g. ___ from a 401(k) account at your last job

h. ___ from a cash advance you can get on your credit card

i. ___ for a top-of-the-line new sports car you plan to buy next year

j. ___ for medical procedures needed in the next eighteen months, which you can pay for in full if stocks do just average over the next year and a half

OK, let's go from worst to best.

First—*h*—that's a disaster. Don't ever buy stocks on cash loans from your credit cards. The cost of those loans are, on average, far more substantial than the typical gains you can expect from stocks. As exciting as the stock market can get, hey, it's just a numerical beast. And the numbers don't justify buying stocks on credit.

Second—*c*—is nearly a disaster. Investing with a three-month time horizon just isn't *investing*. It's trading or gambling. Any gains you get over that short period will be taxed five times over—once by the IRS, twice by your broker in commissions, and twice by market makers who make money off the spread between what a stock can be bought for and what it can be sold for at any point in time. Hey, if you don't know what spreads are, don't worry about that right now. You've taken enough from this short paragraph if you've taken away that you shouldn't buy stocks with a three-month time horizon.

Third—*f*—is potentially catastrophic as well. Why didn't we make it the second worst, given that "this fall" could be just a couple weeks away? Well, we figure if you blow your money in the stock market and have to miss college for a semester, that's a filly's nose better than losing your house! In fact,

given that Bill Gates of Microsoft, Michael Dell of Dell Computer, and Larry Ellison of Oracle—three of our nation's greatest business successes—all dropped out of college, hey, maybe you should gamble that tuition money away! Nah, if you want to skip college, save the money for something other than short-term gaming on the stock market.

Fourth—*j*—is pretty darned bad in its own right. Eighteen months is a good deal longer than the other disasters, but in this case, you're risking your health on the performance of the market. What if stocks fell by 40 percent over that eighteen-month period? You might have to skip the operation altogether. And that might mean the difference between reading and not when you're sixty. Again, the simplest concept here is just that you not invest in stocks unless you have at least thirty-six months to spare.

Fifth—*i*—is only moderately less bad. In this case, the investor has twelve months. That's a good deal better than the mere three months in scenario *c*. But it's also not enough time. The only reason we don't consider this an out-and-out disaster is that, heck, losing a little money in stocks might save the buyer of a flashy sports car some money, all told. We don't think you should spend much on an automobile, given that its value depreciates the moment you drive it off the lot. But here as well, losing money on the stock market isn't the best way to reinforce a separate lesson. Don't fritter money away on unnecessarily snazzy new wheels—and don't gamble that money away over a short-term period on the stock market.

Sixth—*d*—OK, here you have two years and what's at stake is a down payment on an unselected new house. There are enough fluid variables here that investment in stocks might not be a terrible thing. After all, if the market gets hammered, well then, you just rent for another year. Maybe you don't buy that new house for another five years, in a soft market. But if for some reason you need that money in two years, don't put it in mutual funds or stocks.

Seventh—*g*. Now we're finally getting into the good stuff. Transferring a 401(k) plan into, say, a self-directed IRA and then investing it for years or decades is an excellent strategy. Set to!

Eighth—*e*—makes for fine investment money. Wherever that money has come from, we suggest making a modest donation to an organization that champions your benefactor's ideals. Beyond that, with all your short-term debt paid down, we suggest plowing that money into the stock market; and thus we recommend continuing to read to the end of the workbook!

Ninth—*b*. Bravo! Your two-year-old will be eternally grateful at age eighteen, when he buys his first beer on your savings account. With each successive beer, the memory of who to thank will grow dimmer, and you might start hearing from your dear son less than once a month! But initially at least, he'll be thankful. Oh, and we strongly recommend that when the little guy reaches age seven or eight, you start him on his own investment portfolio—buying stocks like Nike, Disney, and Coca-Cola. But we'll speak of that in chapters ahead.

Tenth—*a*. Excellent! You'll be astonished at how much money you can earn via the stock market over one, two, three, and four decades. If you're twenty-two, without debt, and with savings to invest for the rest of your life, take a day off and celebrate. May we suggest bringing food over for all of us at Fool Global Headquarters, in Alexandria, Virginia? May we?

OK, now that we've walked through that, let's cut through some of Wall Street's jargon en route to readying you for a lifetime of investing.

THE JARGON DEMYSTIFIED—POOF!

Let's start with three words that might simultaneously bewilder and bore you: *pretax, posttax,* and *tax-deferred*. These terms are important for a couple of reasons. But let's define them first.

Tax-deferred money is cash typically parked in longer-term savings vehicles like retirement accounts. You don't pay taxes on the earnings in these accounts until you withdraw the money. The government sets up these tax shelters in order to inspire you to save for your future and invest in American corporations. You know our government isn't *all* bad, Fools. Their incentives to invest for your future are on target.

Non-tax-deferred accounts are just what you'd expect them to be. They require you to pay taxes on money you earn from transactions, every year on April 15. If you buy $1,000 of stock at $10 per share and the stock rises to $15 per share and you sell your holding, you just made $500. Woo-hoo! Ah, but then the government swoops in and takes on the order of 30 percent of those winnings—or $150 of your earnings. Youch. That's why we recommend putting as much money as you can afford not to touch for decades right into your retirement account—avoiding the annual tax bite and preserving it as permanent savings.

So what exactly is *pretax* money? It's simply the money that is deducted from your paycheck and dunked into an investment account. You haven't paid income taxes on this money. And if the money goes into your 401(k), 403(b), or 457 retirement savings account, you won't pay taxes on this income until you withdraw money from the account, usually at age fifty-nine. We suggest that you max out the number of dollars that your employer will let you direct into your retirement plan—particularly if they're matching you dollar for dollar.

Posttax money is what most of us put into our savings and checking accounts on payday. You earn a salary, the company deducts to the IRS and other agencies, and what's left is your take-home pay. For obvious reasons, that's called *posttax* money. If you save part of this money each month (which we hope you do), the money goes into your investment or savings account *post tax*. Not as favorable as if it didn't meet up with the IRS until you turned fifty-nine, but then again, you have access to that cash today.

You'll want to have tax considerations swimming somewhere in your head as you begin to invest. But now, let's think about your retirement.

RETIREMENT SAVINGS

Fool, take a second, close your eyes, and begin dreaming with us.

There you are. (Hey, how are you reading this? Your eyes are supposed to be closed!) Yes, there you are. You're sixty-one years old. Your spouse is sitting right alongside you there. You're still in love. Neither of you gave in and married a statue trophy. Nope. And what a relief! Your one true love still has that wacky sense of humor, that same blend of daring and preparation, and still looks great in a swimsuit. There you are, on the deck of the *Fool-E-2*, ringing around the southern tip of Chile en route to Bouvet Island, then Cape Town, South Africa, then toward Malaysia, then Samoa, then Hawaii, then a three-game series between the San Francisco Giants and the Los Angeles Dodgers at Pac Bell Park.

Thank goodness you put that money into an IRA plan when you were twenty-four years old and working as a legal assistant at Procter & Gamble. Sometimes you wonder aloud what life would've been like if you'd started investing even earlier, when you were fifteen years old, or ten years old. But then you click out of it. You don't want to beat yourself up. No, no. Life is pretty fine. The kids are through college. And you and Snookie (those nicknames are too much!) are just a few weeks into your gliding, year-long cruise around the globe. Aaaahhhhhhhhhhhhhhhh. "Yes, a glass of lemonade, a bottle of sunscreen, and we'd like to sign up for the evening French classes. Can we do that through you? Yes? Aha, perfect. Thank you!"

OK, we hate to say this, but, "Snap out of it!" Snap, snap! Clap! "Hey, snap out of it!" Snap. Slap, slap. Wack! Boom! Bif! Ka-pow! "Hey, wake up, Fool!" Smack, smack. Ahh, there you are, welcome back. We're sorry about that . . .

Your retirement accounts can take you nearly out of this world, or right into the center of it, whatever your fancy. They are critical to the last few decades of your life. Social Security might not be around a few decades from now. Given that, you have to get your investments for retirement going as soon as possible. This can't happen until you've eliminated your short-term debt, but it can happen almost instantly after that. It should.

Now, once you start thinking earnestly about investing, you probably remember just why you've avoided the whole matter. Fear, uncertainty, doubt, panic, denial, confusion—pick your favorite noun. How else are you supposed to react to these sorts of critical issues, when our school system literally taught you nothing about your money? Add to that problem that people in the investment community make money by convincing you that they know *much* more about this than you. The whole world seems to be conspiring to keep you ignorant about your moolah. And gigantic corporations spend oodles of their research and development time trying to figure ways to confuse and abuse you.

If that sounds like the paranoid ramblings of a maniac, just look at the next unsolicited credit card mailer you receive. The fine print tells the whole story—the marketing pitch obfuscates the whole story. Go figure. They don't want you to understand what you're doing with your money. Imagine that!

Wall Street is precisely the same; via mutual funds and brokerage firms, it hits unsuspecting investors with a host of hidden fees. Hefty commissions and management fees pouring into Manhattan generally earn investors little more than a mediocrity, and often quite a bit less. It's because of nonsense like that and the fear Americans have about investing that we burn candles late into the night writing workbooks and answering questions online at Fool.com. After all, the best fear killer around is nothing more than learning and knowledge.

WHY SET UP RETIREMENT FUNDS?

IRAs and 401(k) plans have one thing in common: they're both tax-deferred. Any money you earn on your investments in these accounts grows tax-deferred until you withdraw it. Sometimes even the money you put into the account to use for investments grows tax-deferred, if it is pretax money directly from a paycheck. Taking advantage of these accounts can be the difference between a slow sixty-first year on the *Fool-E-2* and a long sixty-first year pouring midnight coffee at a doughnut shop. Over time, your money will accumulate much faster if you aren't pulling taxes out each year, and that money will go right smack in the middle of your daily life, when you retire.

There are many other tax-deferred savings vehicles you can use for retirement, depending on your circumstances. These include Keogh plans and SEP IRAs for the self-employed. The first time you face investment decisions, however, you're likely to be deciding how to invest your IRA or choose from the options in your 401(k) or 403(b) plan. Most 401(k) and 403(b) plans have the choices limited to mutual funds, maybe some company stock, and a guaranteed investment contract or money market fund. That last one provides a set annual return, which, though secure, is generally poor. You're just putting money in the bank there and letting them invest it for their own profit. Given that you have a number of years ahead of you, this is a bad idea. If you have less than three years ahead of you before retirement, though, go for the money market, yes.

Your next option is your company stock plan. This one is relatively easy to grasp, because you already know a lot about the company. You know how strong or weak your company management is; you know how well your products are faring in the marketplace; you know how fierce your competition is; you can easily learn more about your company's financial standing; and you may even know what new products are being developed. We will cover stock valuation in more detail in a later section. You can start just by doing the qualitative work yourself. One way to think creatively about your investments is to consider whether you would invest in the people or organizations around you. Tell us whether you'd buy stock in the following, and why or why not:

INVESTMENT TYPE	YES / NO	ONE REASON YOU WOULD OR WOULD NOT INVEST IN . . .
1. Your company	_____	_____
2. Your brother	_____	_____
3. Your dog	_____	_____
4. Your alma mater	_____	_____
5. Your favorite restaurant	_____	_____
6. Your neighbor	_____	_____
7. Your favorite business	_____	_____

Your final option in retirement plans, and by far the most confusing one, is buying mutual funds. You'll hear of international funds, growth funds, index funds, bond funds, aggressive funds, emerging-market funds, technology funds, REIT funds. If you're not careful, you'll fall over backwards thinking about all the options.

How about taking a minute to jot down the investment options available to you in your 401(k) or 403(b)? The list will serve as a handy reference later, when you want to make sure you've parked your money in the best spot.

My 401(k) or 403(b) Choices

1. _____

2. _____

3. _____

4 _____

LIVING IN AMERICA

One offering that makes very little sense to us is that international fund option. Mind you, we think there are a lot of great foreign markets to invest in—but we also think that many American corporations give you the best way to be involved in those markets. General Electric, Microsoft, Gillette, Coca-Cola . . . these companies and many others have massive amounts of international business.

Don't be lured by the pressure to diversify out of the U.S. stock market.

SO, WHAT *ARE* YOUR CHOICES?

You have more than you think!

The choices you're given for company-driven retirement plans should be clearly outlined for you. Remember that investing for retirement is a long-term thing. If you're going to be invested in this stuff for years and years, do a little bit of research with us first. We think some of the performance figures of the various mutual funds will startle you.

A useful fact that many people don't know about retirement accounts and rollover IRAs—where money has been rolled out from a 401(k) or 403(b) plan and into an IRA account—is that the money invested via those vehicles is not limited to mutual funds. But you wouldn't know that from the sales strategies on Wall Street! In many cases an individual's first introduction to an IRA comes from a bank, a brochure that accompanied a bank statement, or a flyer from a mutual fund company. Let's blow their cover right here. You can open an IRA account at a discount broker and invest in a wide variety of things—from individual stocks like Pepsi and Nike, to mutual funds, to whatever you want. The same is true if, when you leave a company, you roll your 401(k) or 403(b) money into a self-directed IRA in a brokerage account. Those kinds of choices afford you an enormous amount of flexibility. And again, when we take a look at the perfor-

mance of managed mutual funds in the remainder of this book, you'll understand why that *flexibility* is key to your success.

More good news. If you already have IRA accounts opened with mutual fund companies or banks, and you get to the end of this book and realize you should be in stocks, you're not stuck. You can roll this money over, too. If you are unhappy with the returns and want to manage and invest the money yourself, you can do so by opening a brokerage account and asking for the forms you need to roll over existing IRA money into the account. The paperwork involved is painless. And no one's going to call you names or spit on your shoes. Really.

TAX-DEFERRED BROKERAGE ACCOUNTS

Oh, brother, that title looks pretty daunting, eh? Jeez, we're talking about how to open a brokerage account before even teaching you how to invest! Well, it's not that tough. Let's race through it.

Opening a brokerage account is very much like opening a checking or savings account at a bank. You stumble down to a discount broker, fill out the paperwork, and deposit your money there. You can often take care of all the paperwork by mail, without going anywhere in person, if you're lazy and there's a good rerun of *Welcome Back, Kotter* on cable. Some discount brokerages out there will even let you write checks against money in your account, and some have credit cards tied to the accounts. So they can be extremely similar to regular bank accounts.

For the cash you do not invest initially, or that gets doled out to you in dividend payments, you'll probably drop it into a *money market account,* which will earn you small interest on that cash. And when you make investments—say, buying 10 shares of Dell Computer—the brokerage transfers money out of the interest-bearing savings account and into your investment. Remember, Fool, you won't be doing any of this with money you need in the next thirty-six months—right?

OK, now let's review the sweet advantages that come from letting your money grow tax-deferred.

But first, a mild setback. There are limits to the amount of money that you can put into tax-deferred accounts like IRAs and 401(k)s each year. The guv'ment isn't going to let you grow all your money without some licks! For this reason, we recommend that you max out your IRAs and 401(k) plans (if you determine there are good investment options in there). Why? Well, over the past seventy years, even with the recent market downturn, the stock market has grown at an average rate of 11 percent per year. Just take a look at the chart on compounded growth in taxed and tax-deferred accounts.

COMPOUNDED GROWTH

	INVESTED CASH	GROWTH RATE	TAX RATE	40-YEAR RETURNS
Taxed	$15,000	11%	30% a year	$291,554
Tax-deferred	$15,000	11%	30% final	$682,509

It pays to delay your tax payments, when the government encourages it! The same amount of money growing at the same rate as the stock market's average return in a tax-deferred account just blows away the taxed account. Use those IRA credits, Fool.

GETTING STARTED, LOOKING FOR MAGIC

You don't need to be a master stock picker and portfolio management guru to get started. In fact, you don't have to be either to excel at investing. Too many articles on investing have portrayed it as if excellent returns are possible only through magic and witchcraft, obscure calculation, and expensive academic training. Whatever. Investing is as easy as looking around at the products and services you use and love, and just investing in the companies that offer them. There are one or two additional steps you'll want to toss in, but you can learn those in a few hours—the hours it'll take you to get to the end of this book.

Chances are, if you're currently putting money into a retirement account, it's going straight into mutual funds. And there's a better-than-average chance that you don't know much at all about those funds—whether they're managed by superstars or duds, whether they are better than average or worse, whether they're too expensive or not, whether an additional five minutes of research would improve your chances of getting on the *Fool-E-2*. Read on!

BE AMBITIOUS: MEET OR BEAT THE MARKET!

The stock market has grown at an average annual rate of 11 percent. That's a good place to start. Even though the market can collapse, it's enduring returns not only have been positive—they've proved better than any other investment vehicle out there. Better than bonds, better than gold coins, better than your house, better than buying antique cars, better than betting on Spanky at the local dog track.

Stocks beat everything. And for good reason. When you buy shares of stock, you purchase an ownership position in a business that is fighting to grow bigger, more defensible, more rewarding to its management and employees, more profitable. You have hundreds or thousands of people working for you when you become part owner in a public company.

Now, why do you invest in stocks? To get better returns on your money than you can land at the local bank. But what returns are good when you're investing in stocks? Fools use the performance of the entire stock market as their measure. How is the performance of the whole mess of thousands of stocks measured? By the list of companies represented by the Standard & Poor's 500 Index, or the S&P 500. This index lists five hundred leading names in business—from Coca-Cola to Microsoft to General Electric to Ford—and combines their individual performance into an entire group.

The S&P 500 has risen an average 11 percent per year since 1930. Our Foolish aim is to beat that. We'll talk more about this, but would it surprise you to hear that, historically, about 80 percent of all mutual funds have *under*performed that average return from the S&P 500 over any ten-year period? Yep, it's true. Uh-oh, look out . . . it's time for a pop quiz!

Pop Quiz!

True or false?

There is no one perfect investment method. Different tools for different Fools. ____

You can invest in individual stocks through an IRA account. ____

Tax-deferred investments can save you lots of money over long periods. ____

Investing in multinational companies like Gillette or McDonald's can get you all the international diversification you need. ____

Professional investors want you to be confused so that they can charge you big bucks to manage your money for you. ____

Garbanzo beans are sometimes called chickpeas. ____

Your seven-year-old should be investing some of her allowance in companies she loves. ____

Buying shares of an unknown mining company that might hit it big is a bad idea. ____

Most mutual funds lose to the stock market's average return each year. ____

The answer to all of these is *true*. Please pass your papers to the front of the class. Take a brief recess period and when you return, we'll talk about how much time each year it'll take you to invest your money.

(Jeez, shouldn't this stuff be taught in schools?)

HOW MUCH TIME YOU WANT TO SPEND

Time is on your side. No, the vacuum cleaner salesman doesn't want you to believe this. Most stockbrokers don't want you championing patience. Hmm, nope, your insurance salesman doesn't want you to reread the contracts over and again to be certain that you understand why this may not be the best deal for you. Nope. Salesmen want you to rush. Every time you act hastily and buy, buy, buy, they get to take a slice of commissions. We're sorry Hartford, Connecticut (home of insurance in America), but with the Internet, Americans are going to keep getting a whole lot smarter about their insurance policies.

So patience, dear reader, is the strongest suit in your hand. Patience left, patience right, patience off-tackle—these are the best plays in your investment handbook. The single most important decision you can make about your money (hey, we know we've listed, like, ten things under this heading now)—the single greatest thing you can do is just to take your time. Investing is for the long haul. You will end up making most of your money ten years from now, and more than that twenty years from now, and a slew more thirty years from now. So start out slowly, and don't worry so much about what happens day to day: it's year-to-year and decade-to-decade that requires your focus. Be methodical. And don't worry about how much you have to invest now—if you're starting with $35, hoo-hah! Let's get cracking.

Finally, don't even think about timing the market—trying to figure out if *now* is the best time, or if maybe you oughtn't wait until the stock market crashes before buying. There are plenty of opportunities for folks with money to invest for five years, ten, twenty, or more. The longer your time horizon, the less important is the timing of your entries and exits. And, the amount of time you spend each year on investing needn't ever rise above fifteen hours. Perhaps, though, you'll come to view the market as a great learning adventure, home to every business imaginable, making every product imaginable—from Windsurfers to Rollerblades, from gas exploration to wildlife preservation, from cheap red wine to the finest lobster on the planet. The stock market will teach you history, art, geography, biology, philosophy, mathematics, psychology; you'll learn about new technologies and new ideas, and you'll stumble across the same old miserable greed and deceit that has run through human history.

After that rousing appeal, we'll give you another chance to fill in how many hours you can spend learning more about saving, public business, and the stock market:

I can comfortably commit _____ hours per month to learn more about all this.

You can still manage your money Foolishly if you crossed out *hours* and filled in five *minutes* per month, as long as you commit to the notion that time is on your side, that you're not going to let anyone rush you—not salesmen, not advisers, not brokers, not whatever they're calling themselves now. You aren't going to be rushed. You're going to take as much time as need be to learn this stuff, and by so doing you will increase the chance that you're going

to either meet or beat the stock market's average return during your lifetime.

You are. Now stand up wherever you are and shout, "I am! Yes, I am!" OK, now sit down and cover your face with your right hand. You shouldn't have done that. That was embarrassing! Cover this book up; we don't want to be associated with your antics! Why didn't you tell us that you were in a public place?

OK, we now know for sure how much time you're going to put into this. Let's be absolutely sure we know how much money you have to invest.

HOW MUCH MONEY DO YOU HAVE TO INVEST?

Earlier in this workbook, you took a good long look at your current financial picture. Take a second and return to your *personal balance sheet* and copy your net worth in here:

$ _____

You've got a positive number there, right? Good.

Now let's go back to your *personal income statement*. What was your monthly net income for the month? Write that amount here:

$ _____

Another positive number? Good! Now you're on a roll.

OK, that net income—hey, how much of this money do you want to invest? We think you should be putting away at least 10 percent of your salary each year for reducing debt or investing in stocks. Is that reasonable? Hey, how much do you think you can afford to invest this upcoming month? Write that in here:

$ _____

All right! That's just one month. Now multiply that by twelve and let's see how much moolah you're planning to put away for your future over the next year. Write that in here:

$ _____ × 12 = $ _____

Outstanding. Your aim over the next twelve months is to meet or beat that amount. Our bet is that you can add fully another 5–10 percent to that amount without cramping your style. Make a go of it, and let's meet back here in a year to see how you did.

WHAT CAN YOU DO WITH WHAT YOU HAVE?

OK, so you've got that money, but what the heck can you do with it? Maybe you wrote in $67.50 above. Or maybe it took you a minute or two to write down a number with loads of zeroes after it. Whatever your situation, that money is going to open up unbelievable opportunities for you in the decades ahead. Let's figure some intelligent ways to get it invested.

If You've Got $3,000 or Less. If you have less than $3,000 saved, does that mean you can't buy stocks? Well, no. At the same time, you probably shouldn't run out and plunk all of it into the stock market, because more likely than not you will need some of that money in the short term.

A viable option for you is to buy stock directly from a company, bypassing all brokerage fees. Many large companies have programs for this, known as DRIPs (dividend reinvestment plans). Just call your favorite company directly (you can find contact numbers for any public company at our Fool.com website) and then methodically add new money to that investment every week, month, or quarter. You can add in as little as $10 into most DRIPs, so you can keep socking savings away at every turn. Probably right now you're thinking, Yeah, but it doesn't really add up. *Oh, yeah?* Let's say that your DRIP company grew at a rate of 13 percent per year over the next sixty years. Further, let's assume that you add $10 every week to that

investment for the next sixty years. You tell us—how much pretax money will you have in sixty years?

a. $46,247
b. $124,170
c. $246,453
d. $781,190
e. $1.4 million
f. $5.6 million

It's going to surprise you, but the answer is *f.* Just adding $10 per week into the DRIP of a company growing a strong 13 percent per year will put $5.6 million in your pocket in six decades. If six decades sounds too far off for you, hey, consider that we were talking about only $520 of savings per year. Certainly you can do better than that, eh?

OK, so what if you invested $40 per week—equivalent to $2,080 in savings per year—into the same company for thirty years? You tell us, Fool, how much pretax dough do you have?

a. $159
b. $12,401
c. $149,357
d. $610,322
e. $3.1 million
f. $12.8 million

Aha, we caught you on this one, didn't we? The answer is *d.* And the astonishing lesson taken from these numbers is that what matters most is *how much time* you have to invest, not how much money you have. Certainly both are important, but the Fool saving $2,000 per year is going to end up making less after thirty years than the Fool saving $520 over sixty years. And so, the lesson here is: start early and invest often. If your children aren't learning how to invest, they should be. It can be loads of fun.

If You've Got $3,000–$5,000. If you have between $3,000 and $5,000, oh, the temptation is to get out there and buy mutual funds. The problem is that over 80 percent of those funds are managed by people who lose to the market.

Picture a well-dressed young man in a dark blue suit, peach yellow shirt, and red tie, with neatly cut hair, polished shoes, and bloodshot eyes. It's about 5 P.M. on Friday night and he's wandering through the Upper East Side of Manhattan, looking for 551 Park Avenue, apartment 3X. But he's having trouble finding Park, for heaven's sake. He has an open bottle of whiskey in his left hand, and whoa there! Holy cow, he's weaving through oncoming traffic. A bus driver is jeering at him now. Get up on the edge of your seat, Fool. He's just tripped over a lamppost. Now there's an elderly woman helping him. He's up again. OK, there he goes. He's trailing slowly away, around the corner, and now he's out of sight.

If you buy mutual funds, there's a pretty good chance a young fellow like that is managing *your* money! We don't mean to mock revelry. We aren't suggesting that youths shouldn't spend some of their time bowing to Bacchus. And we're certainly not going to suggest that young men and women who drink whiskey on occasion can't properly manage money. Hooey! Ahh, but what we do notice is that many mutual fund managers are living a rather high life these days, while *still* underperforming the average! And how can this be possible? Because Americans are only now just learning how to measure investment performance after the deduction of all apparent and hidden fees.

We'll talk more about mutual funds in the next chapter, but fill in the blank with us here. What is the percentage of all mutual funds that underperform the market's average returns?

_____ percent

Yep, you got it.

OK, so what should you do with more than $3,000 to invest? We have two suggestions, and their explanation is coming up in the chapter ahead. One of them is an S&P 500 Index fund, a mutual fund that simply buys all five hundred stocks in the Standard & Poor's 500, thus duplicating the market's return. And because of this, the index needn't pay a manager (it's mostly managed by computers), you needn't shell out much in fees, and you can expect to beat 80 percent of all the funds on the market. There are other funds matching other broad indices of the market, such as a total stock market index fund, which invests in the six thousand or so companies that make up the total domestic stock market. That's also a great choice.

Our second suggestion is that you move your money into stocks. Three thousand dollars is plenty of money to begin buying ownership slices of public companies; but here, you're very much going to need to worry about commissions costs.

What do commissions have to do with anything?

Well, it doesn't make much sense to buy $250 worth of stock and pay $25 to make the trade. You just paid 10 percent of your total investment right off the top—essentially eliminating the positive returns that an entire year would give you in stocks. And when you sell out, even if you've doubled your money, you'll pay another $25, or 5 percent, leaving. And then to finish it all up, whoa there, you'll pay 20 percent in taxes on your gains. So you tell us, Fool, how much did you make when you put $250 into a stock that doubled?

a. $415
b. $305
c. $160
d. $112

The answer is *c*. You made $160. You paid $50 to your broker and $50 to the IRS. And while that may seem fine, on average you're going to double your money in stocks every six years. So that was six years of work for $160. Not worth it.

Nope, you'll want to keep entry commissions below 2 percent of your investment at all times. This means if your discount broker charges you $25 per trade, you should invest no less than $1,250 in any single transaction. How much money can you invest in a single transaction if your broker charges you the following? We're really going after you on the numbers here. Good luck out there.

	FEE	MAXIMUM PERCENTAGE OF INVESTMENT	MINIMUM INVESTMENT
Discount broker A	$10	2%	_____
Discount broker B	$35	2%	_____
Full-service broker C	$120	2%	_____
Full-service broker D	$225	2%	_____

OK, so we're giving you the answers right here. We hope you're not sneaking a look! (Oh, by the way, all you have to do is multiply the fee by 50, since 2% × 50 = 100%.)

A: $500

B: $1,750

C: $6,000

D: $11,250

You see what happens when you take your money to an expensive full-service broker who justifies high commissions by impressing you with gold cuff links and fancy mumbo jumbo? That kind of appearance doesn't come cheap. To keep commissions under 2 percent, you'll have to have twelve times more money per transaction at a full-service broker (D) than at a deep-discount broker (A). Whatever your fancy, you'll want to keep your transaction costs below 2 percent, always.

What If You Have More Than $5,000 to Invest? Read on. We believe you should consider investing this money directly into stocks, and we aim to show you a handful of approaches that won't take much time, won't run up commissions costs, and won't keep you up at night.

As you progress through this guide, keep consid-ering how much time you want to spend managing your investments. The Foolish investment principles you'll learn—valuing a company's stock, evaluating a company's prospects, calculating returns, reading financial statements, and so forth—are useful for helping you make decisions about your IRA and 401(k) and 403(b) plans, not just when you're buy-ing individual stocks.

We've covered a lot of ground. Congratulations for staying awake this long. A lot of the hard work is behind you—a lot of the fun lies ahead. By now, you have a good handle on where you are, what your goals are, and how to make some basic decisions about investments. You know to be pa-tient, ask a lot of questions, keep the costs of in-vesting to a minimum, and get as much moolah into your tax-deferred retirement accounts as you can. If you don't start doing so now, you're going to be the only one on your block that doesn't spend the summer on Pluto in 2050. Don't fall be-hind!

Finally, before proceeding, think how much you've learned already. Did you know how to read a balance sheet or income statement—let alone build your own—before you started? You're thriving, Fool. Now let's get back out there and nail a couple of more gymnastic jumps, or sink a couple of more fifty-foot putts, or blast through another 3k. You're into the good stuff. We're going to start investing for profit in the decades ahead, starting on the *next* page.

CHAPTER 4

HOW DO I START INVESTING?

Ahh, good, you're still reading. You've fought through all that budgeting, you've sucked the air out of your short-term-debt balloon, you've been saving money from your salary each month, and you're ready to make a go of investing. The answer just has to be mutual funds, right? They're run by professionals who know the market through and through; perhaps they even manipulate share prices by revving up and down their own holdings; and they work for enormous companies with whom everyone has their money. Fool, you don't want to be the only one with a motley umbrella among a crowd of jet-black umbrellas, do you?

Yes   No

We're not going to answer that question until the end of the chapter. But let's immerse ourselves in a few lessons about mutual funds, for starters. If you're investing right now, you probably have some, if not all, of your money in funds. How are they doing?

MUTUAL FUNDS

Did you write down *less than twenty minutes a year* for the time you're willing to spend investing? Prob-

ably not—since it's already taken you a few tediously long days to get this far in our Foolish workbook. Believe it or not, many Americans out there want to and do spend less than a half hour each year thinking about their financial future. The money comes in and, *plink*, it goes out in the form of heavy spending or, *plink*, it gets deposited into a savings account or, *plink*, it gets dropped into mutual funds.

Beginning to invest with mutual funds is like exploring the wide world by watching Discovery Channel documentaries and reading *National Geographic*. In other words, they're a great way to get started. You wouldn't want to end up alone in the Amazon rain forest in blue jeans, a T-shirt, running shoes, and a Fool ball cap. Much better is watching professionals from the comfort of your bed, with chips on your stomach, as they navigate the Amazon River, taking all the right precautions. When you invest in mutual funds, you buy into the idea that the fund managers have a few decades more experience than you, know which strategy is safe and which fraught with peril, and how to grow your money consistently in the years ahead.

What exactly is a mutual fund, you ask?

A mutual fund is a pool of money contributed by investors, often across the globe. The fund is managed by a bevy of researchers, mathematicians, marketers, and stock-picking gurus, and it buys stocks, bonds, gold, wheat, even real estate, depending on the strategy outlined in the fund's prospectus. The most common sort of mutual fund is a *diversified* one, which is invested in dozens or hundreds of holdings with no single holding exceeding 5 percent of the fund's total assets. A diversified mutual fund with $500 million in total cash under management, with no single holding exceeding 5 percent of the total fund, has as its maximum possible position how much money invested?

a. $10 million
b. $25 million
c. $50 million
d. $75 million

Nice job, just wanted to keep you on your toes. Five percent of $500 million is $25 million. OK, now there are other kinds of mutual funds out there that don't buy from everywhere in the general U.S. market. These more narrowly focused funds include sector funds, international funds, balanced funds, growth and income funds, bond funds, asset allocation funds, money market funds, index funds, hedge funds, socially responsible funds—funds, funds everywhere! If you don't know what all of those mean right off the bat, don't worry. The truth is you don't have to know the lingo to succeed at investing. But with almost nine thousand mutual funds from which to choose, you'll have to narrow the field considerably to have any sense of what you're doing.

You need a filter. You've hired the Fool. Let's start by studying mutual fund fees and then we'll review their performance. Only after analyzing these, the simplest vehicles for investing, should anyone dive into an ocean of common stocks with all the smartness and daring of Jacques Cousteau.

Fees? Yes, fees. You have to pay these fund managers for their effort. But how much?

FEES

Remember those pesky brokerage commissions we were considering in the last section? Remember how we proposed that you should keep them under 2 percent per trade? Well, managing costs when buying mutual funds is just as important. The investor is never entirely rid of transaction costs, even when buying or selling in a mutual fund or buying or selling wares at an auction. Some of these fees are purposefully hidden from your sight—it's a nasty world out there—and some of them sit out like a babe in the noonday sun. Let's review the most common fees: *loads*, *expense fees*, and *12b-1 fees*.

LOADS

In the mutual fund industry, the word *loads* is simply a euphemism for the word *charges*. A loaded fund is one that charges you for the professional management of that fund. A typical load fee is between 2 and 6 percent of your initial investment, though they go by a few different names.

Many mutual funds charge you front-end loads, taking a percentage of the money you initially invest. Perhaps you've invested in a mutual fund with a front-end load of 3 percent. That means that for every $1,000 you invest, you pay $30. If you put in $100,000, you just paid $3,000 in sales fees. Hey, how about if you invest $3,554,134 in that fund . . . what would be your front-end load payment to the managers of the fund?

a. $10,135
b. $4,845
c. $106,624
d. $182,549

The answer is *c*. You'd pay over $106,000 to the fund manager before he has even lifted a finger to grow your investment! For the wealthiest Fools out there, look out. Percentage fees are your bane. Even though mutual funds will somewhat mechanically divide out their managed money into various positions, the fund shareholder with $3.5 million invested will spend a heckuva lot more on management than the average investor. If you're enormously wealthy, invested in mutual funds, and reading this book, we may just have alerted you to a problem. You shouldn't be paying hundreds of thousands of dollars in sales fees.

OK, so there's the front-end load; they hit you upside the head when you enter the fund. Appropriately, there are also *back-end loads,* where they give you a swift kick in the arse for leaving the fund. The back-end loads are a little sneakier, designed as they are to keep you in the fund, even if the going ain't good. Numerically, though, a back-end load of 2 percent and a front-end load of 2 percent amount to the same thing, the same total payment coming and going.

OK, there's only one more of these beasts left. Read on.

Less favorable than either front- or back-end loaded funds are those with *annual loads.* Rather than a one-time charge against your assets at the start or end, the annual-loaded fund levies a fee once each year. Let's imagine that you're going to invest $5,000 into a mutual fund and hold it for five years. And let's assume the fund will grow at 10 percent per year. Which fee structure ought most appeal to you? This one's tough. Our recommendation is that you either take some time before answering, or cheat and read ahead.

    a. Front- or back-end load of 4 percent
    b. Annual load of 1 percent

Which is the more favorable scenario? (*Jeopardy!* music please, Alex.) OK, calculators out. Tap, tap, tap. Tap, tap, tap, tap. Times that. Click, click, click. Times that. Tap, tap, tap. (Hey, we're actually doing the work here!) Tap, click, punch! Bing!

It turns out the front- or back-loaded fee, though apparently higher, is more favorable. They are one-time charges against your assets. The annual load, though 75 percent lower, is hitting you each of those five years. The difference over very long periods of time will prove substantial.

Arrrrgggh! All those charges! Well, rest easy, a bunch of people realized pretty early on that loaded funds were getting too much money and not offering enough value in return. So what did they do? They created no-load mutual funds, which do noth-ing more than charge very minimal administrative expense fees each year. Much better, right? Not necessarily.

EXPENSE RATIOS

Every mutual fund out there charges an annual administrative fee called an *expense ratio.* This money is used to run the fund, paying for salaries, trading costs, and research materials. These fees average between 0.5 percent and 2.5 percent per year, although some are significantly lower or higher. Unfortunately—though it's entirely to be expected—the differences between no-load funds charging expense ratios and loaded funds charging back, front, or annual fees are blurring.

When buying either a no-load or a load fund, you should pay particular attention to the expense ratio. Sometimes a fund with a load and a low expense ratio can cost less over time than a no-load fund with high expense fees. What you'll need is a calculator at every turn, and nothing more than a few hours a year applying basic, grade school mathematical equations. Either that or you need to keep reading and learn why you shouldn't be buying almost any mutual funds!

12B-1 FEES

Oops, we have one fee left, and it's a fee that the Securities and Exchange Commission (SEC), charged with regulating the stock market, should've exed out from the start. It's the dreaded 12b-1 fee, and in many cases it's hidden from view. You'd have to read the seventy-eight-page legalistic fund prospectus to find buried therein some mention of a 1 percent annual 12b-1 fee.

What are 12b-1 fees? These fees are used strictly to support advertisements and marketing campaigns for your mutual fund. They put your management team on financial television, or sit them between beer ads during the Super Bowl, or lay them down between the pages of your favorite magazine. Yep, you've probably seen a lot of ads for mutual funds in magazines. Those are paid for by the mutual fund's shareholders, via 12b-1 fees. A typical 12b-1 fee can hover near 0.5 percent per year, though some of them can ride as high as 1 percent per annum. The comical thing about 12b-1 fees is that they eat into shareholder monies without providing *any direct benefit* to the shareholders. Some funds that are closed to new investors—and therefore have absolutely no business advertising their existence to nonfundholders—*still* charge 12b-1 fees. Interesting concept, that one.

Pop Quiz!

Circle which is better in each case.

a. Front-end load	1.25%	or	3.75%?
b. Back-end load	5.75%	or	0%?
c. Expense ratio	0.5%	or	1.5%?
d. 12b-1 fee	0.21%	or	0.66%?

Answers: a. 1.25% b. 0% c. 0.5% d. 0.21%

THE TURNOVER RATE

One final important statistic that speaks to the cost of your mutual fund is its turnover rate. The word *turnover* here refers to the fund's trading activity. The more a fund is selling positions, the more it will be paying in brokerage costs—and the higher will be your tax payments at year end! So, you want a low turnover rate. A turnover rate of 0 percent means that nothing was sold. A rate of 100 percent means that, on average, the entire holdings of the fund were turned over—sold—during the year. A turnover rate of 50 percent means half the shares, on average, were traded during the year, or that the average holding period for a stock in the fund was two years. The turnover rate for the average mutual fund is now upwards of 80 percent—meaning big tax payments for fund shareholders.

PERFORMANCE AND MANAGEMENT

So, we've slogged through all the various fees, and your head is hanging a bit. All this stuff about Foolish investing ain't what your next-door neighbor said it would be. Here we are, dealing with petty mathematics and walking through charges as if we were price shopping down at Wal-Mart. This may surprise you—but we hate this stuff as much as you do. Writing about mutual fund fees is about as much fun as eating a stale peanut butter and liver sandwich. It's nearly as bad as suffering that modernist literature seminar in college, while our friends were out learning to rock climb or deep-sea dive, or running softball leagues for profit, or producing inexpensive short films with their friends. Mutual fund fee chatter is deadly boring, but it must be endured before we can get to our main dish, common stocks. Why? Because so many Americans are wasting substantial amounts of their hard-earned money and investment power buying mutual funds.

How so?

Get this. Over the past fifteen years, over 80 percent of all managed funds and all equity funds have underperformed the stock market's average return. Yeah, yeah, you've read that here already. But we have to keep writing it because it just baffles us. Why are trillions of dollars being poured into a mold that is cracked? Why are so many Americans so easily persuaded that these fund managers actually know what they're doing with all that money?

The reason so much money is going into mutual funds is, of course, that they're extremely easy to invest in, they give at least a false sense of stability and expertise, and everyone else is doing it. Never mind that betting on them to beat the market is like betting on the twenty-to-one horse every day and every race at Pimlico. Never mind that expecting them to be more than average is like expecting the sun to stop rising altogether. They're popular because they're popular.

We have a feeling all that is going to change, and soon. In fact, it already is. The change started a few years ago. Read on and you'll see.

MAKING SENSE OF RETURNS

Let's take a look at a somewhat fictional mutual fund, the Well-Dressed Wise Man Fund. You've probably seen these guys advertising, well, everywhere. They ran that promotional spot during the Sunday night Movie of the Week, proposing that you let trained pilots drive your financial airplane. They've run similar ads in financial magazines and the *Wall Street Journal,* and they always follow them along with their performance report.

The tag line goes something like this: "If you want strong growth and security, you'll get wise with the Wise Man." Then, *ka-chung,* their numbers appear on the screen.

THE WELL-DRESSED WISE MAN FUND

(ANNUAL RATE OF RETURN)	
1-year rate of return	+ 13.1%
3-year rate of return	+ 9.2%
5-year rate of return	+ 8.3%

Ka-chung! The screen goes black, then you get the next set of numbers from the Wise Man, focused on total performance over the one-, three-, and five-year periods.

THE WELL-DRESSED WISE MAN FUND

(TOTAL RETURN)	
1-year total return	+ 13.1%
3-year total return	+ 30.2%
5-year total return	+ 49.0%

Jeez, what do all those numbers mean? The first set of numbers are simply the average growth per year of the mutual fund's investments. Had you put

$1,000 in one year ago, it would have climbed 13.1 percent. Had you invested that money three years ago, it would have grown 9.2 percent per year, or a total for all three years of 30.2 percent. And had you invested your thousand bucks with them five years ago, it would have grown 8.3 percent per annum, for total growth of 49 percent. Your $1,000 investment would tote up to pretax money of $1,490 after five years. Was that clear? If not, just read back over the paragraph; there are a bunch of numbers, but the underlying concept is simple.

OK, so the money has grown a total of 49 percent over the past five years and now the Wise Man Fund is running all over the nation telling people about it. With them, they say reassuringly, you steadily make great money. Be Wise, dress well, invest with them. Because so many mutual funds do and say things just like this, the world must suffer Fools a little longer. What's flawed in their presentation? The numbers are plain enough; the mistake is in the promotion. You see, even though that mutual fund gained ground, consider with us now the performance of the overall stock market during that period.

THE S&P 500 INDEX

(ANNUAL RATE OF RETURN)	
1-year rate of return	+ 14.0%
3-year rate of return	+ 10.9%
5-year rate of return	+ 10.6%

THE WELL-DRESSED WISE MAN FUND

(ANNUAL RATE OF RETURN)	
1-year rate of return	+ 13.1%
3-year rate of return	+ 9.2%
5-year rate of return	+ 8.3%

Holy cow, look at those numbers. The performance of the total stock market, as reflected by the S&P 500 Index, has sped right past the Well-Dressed Wise Man Fund over the last year, the last three years, and the last five years. Blammo. Let's take a look at the total return comparisons and then work up some Foolish conclusions.

THE S&P 500 INDEX

(TOTAL RETURN)

1-year total return	+ 14.0%
3-year total return	+ 36.4%
5-year total return	+ 65.5%

THE WELL-DRESSED WISE MAN FUND

(TOTAL RETURN)

1-year total return	+ 13.1%
3-year total return	+ 30.2%
5-year total return	+ 49.0%

Holy cow, those are some significant differences. Your $10,000 invested in the Wise Man Fund over five years would grow to $14,900. In the meantime, the same money invested in the overall market—if such a thing could be done—would grow to $16,550. And if those rates play out over the next fifty years, the differences between the two funds will run into the hundreds and hundreds of thousands of dollars. To prove that point, we'll actually run some numbers.

The difference between the five-year performance of the two is a bit over 30 percent per year (65.5 ÷ 49 = 1.336, or 33.6%). Let's pull back the numbers to the market's *historical rate of return*, 11 percent per year. Just short of 30 percent beneath that is 8.5 percent; we'll use that as the average yearly return for the Well-Dressed Wise Man Fund. Now, invest your $10,000 in both, and here are the differences:

	MONEY INVESTED	ANNUAL RATE OF RETURN	NUMBER OF YEARS	ENDING PORTFOLIO VALUE
Wise Man Fund	$10,000	8.5%	50	$590,863
S&P 500	$10,000	11.0%	50	$1,845,648

What's the difference between the closing values?

$1,845,648 − $590,863 = _____

You got it. The difference is $1,254,785. The market underperformance of the Wise Man Fund cost its investors over $1.25 million during the five-decade period. Can you believe they *celebrated* that very same performance on every media platform?! Well, you should believe it. When you consider that 80 percent of the managed funds out there today underperform the market every single year—and further, when you consider that most Americans don't know how to measure fund fees and perfor-

mance—then you'll know that the great majority of mutual fund advertisements out there celebrate market underperformance! Incredible. Can you imagine the same at a football game? "We lost! Hooray!"

Right about now, you're probably asking yourself if there's a way to just buy the whole darned stock market, or to buy all those five hundred stocks on the S&P Index and avoid all the hassles of investing in submediocre mutual funds. Aha! Let your eyes move down to the next two words. They are the most important two words an individual investor may ever hear. Well, besides "You're rich!"

INDEX FUNDS

An index fund is a mutual fund that buys and holds the same stocks that are in a particular index. The most common one is an S&P 500 Index fund, which holds all five hundred stocks in the Standard & Poor's 500 in the same proportion; but others, called *total market index funds,* have gained in popularity as well. The S&P 500 Index funds' performance essentially mirrors that of the S&P 500—that index that according to Lipper Services beats out 80 percent of all actively managed mutual funds each year. The most prominent S&P Index fund is the Vanguard 500 Index Fund. It's a fund that the Fool has championed for eight years now; it's been the fastest-growing large mutual fund on the market; and it presents investors with no loads and no hidden fees. Vanguard also offers the Total Stock Market Index Fund, which contains a piece of every public company trading in the United States on one of the three major indices (the New York Stock Exchange, the American Stock Exchange, or the Nasdaq).

You are right to now ask, "Okay, Fools, which are the five hundred stocks on the S&P Index?" We won't bore you with all five hundred, but here's a brief sampling.

What Companies Are in the S&P 500 Index?

Read the clues below to identify some of the companies that can be found on the S&P 500 Index.

_____ Atlanta-based giant soft-drink business.

_____ They brought Snap, Crackle, and Pop to the cereal business.

_____ They make more razors than anyone.

_____ You may know them as Ma Bell.

_____ This car company makes the ever-popular Lincoln Town Car.

_____ Featuring $1 meals and a big guy in a clown suit.

_____ The conglomerate that brings you *The West Wing.*

OK, this time we're going to wait a paragraph before listing the answers.

Let's chat a little more about the S&P 500 Index while we're waiting for those answers to come through. The purpose of this list of five hundred companies is to provide a benchmark, or measuring stick, for the performance of the entire group of ten-thousand-some-odd public companies in America. The index is considerably more popular in the investing community than is the Dow Jones Industrial Average, since the latter factors in only the stock prices of thirty giant corporations. Increasingly, money managers, financial publications, and private investors are using the S&P 500 to measure performance.

OK, so what companies are on the S&P?

The answers to the clues above are Coca-Cola, Kellogg, Gillette, AT&T, Ford, McDonald's, and (if you said NBC, we gotcha!) General Electric. The index also includes technology companies like Microsoft, Intel, Dell, Compaq, and Oracle. For the most part, the five hundred companies are cash-rich, massive American companies with experienced management, long operating histories, and business around the globe. Basically, this is the list of the A students in the class of American business. And much like A students, these folks tend to rack up good grades over and again.

By investing in an index fund, you literally guarantee yourself the market's average performance. If only the rest of the mutual fund industry could do the same.

WHAT'S SO GREAT ABOUT INDEX FUNDS?

Let's list a few of the things you get when you buy index funds:

- Participation in America's robust corporate growth
- Ownership of hundreds of the best companies in the world
- Investment returns that will mirror the index's growth rate

- No load fees and no sneakily hidden expenses
- A very low turnover rate and, thus, minimal tax consequences
- Instant diversification into hundreds of companies operating around the globe
- Zero research or opportunity costs
- Long-term growth on your savings while you learn more about investing
- You get to laugh at mutual fund ads when you see them.

MANAGED FUNDS VERSUS INDEX FUNDS

Right about now you're probably saying, "Hey, well, I know how capitalism works. I bet those index funds cost a lot more money than the managed funds."

Fools, is that good thinking?___Or bad thinking___?

Hey, it's good thinking. That logic should work. After all, in an open-air, free market, quality should rise to the top. The best should cost a little more than the really good stuff, which should cost a little more than the OK stuff, which should be priced higher than the pretty bad stuff, which should cost a bit more than the stuff best described as "pre-garbage." And that continuum should play out from one industry to the next in a capitalist system. Right? Yah?

Actually, no. Marketing is an essential component, when freedom of speech is as protected as it should be. The managed mutual funds have every right to be as promotional as Don King, as aggressive in their sales as insurance dealers, as empty as an 'N Sync tune, as glitzy as a Hollywood flop, as lovable as Elmo, tickled. They are not duty bound to represent their performance clearly, in ways that everyone can determine whether buying their fund is sensible or idiotic. Nope. They can market as aggressively and misleadingly as that credit card company that hasn't stopped knocking down trees across the planet for its unsolicited promotional mailings. Mathematics isn't their trade—pure sales is.

So, no, the index fund is not more expensive than managed funds. Ironically, the absolute reverse is true. Because index funds don't much *need* managers—they just methodically buy and hold the same stocks—they don't charge loads. (At least, Vanguard does not. Many fund managers have seen the demand for index funds and have offered their own versions. Some charge significantly higher loads and fees than others. If you see an index fund with a load, run. Run fast.) Because Vanguard keeps its marketing effort down to a dull, barely audible roar, there are no 12b-1 fees. And finally, because their staff is relatively small, their expense ratios are minimal. The total expense for buying the Vanguard 500 Index Fund is 0.18 percent. Compare that to the 2–5 percent charges in front-end, back-end, or annual-load funds. Compare it also to the hidden 12b-1 fees that many no-load fund investors pay in order for these mutual funds to promote themselves to new investors. Finally, compare that to the expense ratios of other load and no-load mutual funds and you'll find that 0.18 percent is dramatically lower. To beat 80 percent of the mutual funds on the market and to charge a mere 0.18 percent relative to the considerably higher fees of the competition, the Vanguard fund is the mutual fund industry's worst nightmare.

WHY DO MANAGED FUNDS LOSE?

Why do managed funds perform so poorly? Are they really managed by blockheads? Or are there factors beyond managerial control that are hurting their returns?

Because so much money has been pouring into mutual funds, the managers must diversify in dozens of new holdings on a regular basis. This diversification forces many portfolios into an almost-index-fund appearance. Ah, but then you add the various expenses, and their performance compares badly. Mutual funds cannot, by federal regulatory charter, let one holding make up more than 5 percent of their money. Right there, funds have to diversify into at least twenty different companies. Beyond that, the pressures from the marketing department, from the legal department, and from stodgy management teams have most equity funds spinning their diversification out of control. They buy huge numbers of companies, attempt just to stay close to the market's returns, and recognize that through positive promotions they can convince nonnumerical American investors to buy, buy, buy! In essence, they minimize the risks, power up the marketing, and collect fees all the way to the bank.

Although many funds stress a long-term outlook, the marketplace of major shareholders (banks, pension funds, and the like) holds them rigorously to short-term standards. For this reason, mutual funds often trade positions wildly in an attempt to keep up with the market this quarter, this month, next week, tomorrow, this afternoon, right now! That short-term mentality makes bettors out of folks who should be investing money; it drives up management expenses, since brokerage fees and large trading staffs cost money; and it jacks up the end taxes that shareholders must pay come April 15.

It ain't _____. (Fill in the blank . . . we recommend "pretty.")

CONCLUDING POINTS ON MUTUAL FUNDS

Fools, we highly recommend that you drop by our Fool School at www.Fool.com/school and check out our coverage of the mutual fund industry. The results, no doubt, will continue to astonish. From high fees to hidden fees, from heavy promotions to marked underperformance, the mutual fund industry in its present incarnation ain't gonna survive much longer.

We close this chapter with two short recommendations.

One, if you're being sold a mutual fund by bankers, brokers, insurance salesmen, best friends, or brothers, always ask questions about the fund's performance relative to the S&P 500 over the past five years—after all fees have been extracted. Second, hey, it was painful for us to spend so much time on an investing vehicle that consistently underperforms. Head for us into the world of Warren Buffett and Anne Scheiber (don't know who Anne is? we'll tell you shortly), the world of common stocks and business ownership. The index fund is a great starting point for curious investors and a great ending point for those of you who have no interest in learning more about business or no more than thirty minutes per year to invest.

Oh, and we started the chapter asking you how you felt about taking the road less traveled, and not buying the mutual funds that the rest of America is. We framed it this way:

Fool, you don't want to be the only one with a motley umbrella among a crowd of jet-black umbrellas, do you?

Yes   No

Your answer actually should be formed as a circle somewhere just to the right of "yes." There's nothing wrong with joining the crowd into an investment vehicle that makes sense. Over the past several years, Vanguard's 500 Index Fund has been attracting all the black umbrellas its way. If you want to ride that wave as well, we Fools think that makes plenty of sense.

But don't swear off the motley, or patchwork, umbrella. Common stock is just around the corner, and our belief is that you can do much better than the "just average" that the index fund offers. Onward!

YOUR RETIREMENT PLAN

Remember that index funds are a great choice for tax-deferred retirement accounts like 401(k)s, 403(b)s, and IRAs. If your employer doesn't offer index funds in their plan, ask the retirement plan folks there to include index funds. And you can be on your way to whooping the market.

CHAPTER 5

HOW DO I START LOOKING FOR INDIVIDUAL STOCKS?

You have your index fund portfolio, and maybe you're asking yourself, Why should I do any more work than that? I've got my investments. I'm done with all this.

If you are thinking that, that's outstanding. Go get 'em! We are perfectly happy that we have done our job well if an investor gets to the point of buying an index fund (Foolishly selected, of course) and says, "This is all I want to do. This is what I am comfortable with." Keep adding more savings every month, and immerse yourself in other things. Strangely enough, though, no matter where you spend your time, once you've discovered the joy of ownership, you won't be able to stop noticing the public companies that swarm around you.

Are you a mountain climber? A high school Spanish teacher? An army lieutenant? A squash player? A medieval historian? A book reader? A stevedore? Public companies that work in these areas are all around you, and understanding them—whether you choose to invest in them—is essential to understanding the world around you. And if you give them your attention as an investor, you can wend into a world where your savings grow and into a life where you have better control of your des-

tiny. But, you say, you don't know a thing about public companies and picking stocks? You're no expert? Well, surprise! You have an inside track on stocks in a way that the so-called experts don't—and never can.

> Stop listening to professionals! Twenty years in this business convinces me that any normal person using the customary three percent of the brain can pick stocks just as well, if not better, than the average Wall Street expert.
> —former Fidelity Magellan fund manager Peter Lynch, *One Up on Wall Street*

Looking for great individual stocks to research and invest in is no more difficult than studying the companies that provide great products or services in your life. Wall Street professionals forty stories up in Manhattan may get overpaid to do just this, using a variety of tools, but then in contests against a chimpanzee armed with a finger (and some stock symbols to point at), the pros often lose. The *Wall Street Journal* runs a regular contest that demonstrates this, pitting expert stock pickers against stocks chosen randomly via the dart and a board, and the dartboard often wins. These experts at big investment firms may also lose in competition with you.

We're going to start—and pretty much end—by simply opening your eyes to the businesses in your immediate vicinity. Have you stumbled across a store with long lines? A bank with better checking deals? A manufacturer placing lots of Help Wanted ads? Each of these points to a company worthy of investigation. Before we get right down to company analysis, though, for a moment consider with us some of the past century's great individual investors.

Some Great Investors

Who's gone before you into the wide world of investing? Match these investors with their descriptions below.

a. Henry Taub
b. Cornelius Vanderbilt
c. Anne Scheiber
d. Peter Lynch
e. Sir John Templeton
f. Warren Buffett
g. George Soros

1. ___ Cities Service Inc. was his first investment, at age eleven. By thirty-eight, he would have investment holdings worth more than $100 million. He's now Coca-Cola's largest shareholder and provides the ultimate example of the advantages to long-term investing.

2. ___ At twenty-two, this man started a payroll-processing company that would merge and acquire dozens of companies. His business, ADP, is now the largest payroll processor in America, worth over $1 billion when he retired, in the mid-eighties.

3. ___ As a child he worked on ferries around New York City, then gained control of the ferry lines, got into shipping, and wound up a rail-road magnate with fortune enough to found a university and create an American dynasty.

4. ___ Hungarian-born immigrant and billionaire financier, his mathematical mastery of the world's currency markets built his wealth. In 1993, he made $1 billion in one day, by shorting the British pound. He now donates hundreds of millions of dollars annually to charity.

5. ___ An investment in Flying Tiger Airlines put this investor through grad school. Since then he's been preaching that investors *buy only companies that they know* and suggesting that the boys' club on Wall Street is overrated. He's largely considered the greatest mutual fund manager that ever lived.

6. ___ This former IRS employee invested an initial $5,000 in stocks in the 1940s. When she died, fifty-one years later, her portfolio had grown to $22 million.

7. ___ This financier managed the world's most successful international fund by looking for neglected, undervalued stocks. His interest in religion led him to establish sizable grants for advances in religious thought.

Answers: 1. Warren Buffett *(f)* started investing when he was eleven years old. 2. Henry Taub *(a)*, at twenty-two, started a payroll-processing company. 3. Cornelius Vanderbilt *(b)* wound up a railroad magnate after riding ferries as a child. 4. George Soros *(g)* donates hundreds of millions of dollars annually to charity. 5. Peter Lynch *(d)* flew Tiger Airlines to get through grad school. 6. Anne Scheiber *(c)* grew savings from an average salary into $22 million in fifty-one years. 7. Sir John Templeton *(e)* provides huge prizes for advances in religious thought.

What these people achieved is remarkable, but not inimitable. Their successes were not made of magic, but of method. The first challenge you'll have as an investor is simply to keep your eyes open to what's going on around you.

WHY BOTHER WITH INDIVIDUAL STOCKS?

You're still reading, so we have to ask you why you're interested in following individual public companies and directly investing in them. Just by reading on, you're making a commitment to learning more—and we're curious as to why.

Your Reasons for Following Individual Companies and Possibly Investing in Them

___ I want to earn even better returns than an index fund can give me.

___ I love the game of investing—using logic to build the best portfolio I can.

___ I enjoy working with numbers.

___ I want to learn more about my company's stock.

___ My financial adviser said I'm not smart enough to understand the market. Hooey!

___ I know that I'm a Fool.

___ Because I have many years to invest, I'm willing to add some short-term volatility.

___ I want to retire early from my job at the plant/office/school/store/farm.

___ I'd like to learn more about how corporations work.

___ I paid for this book, and darn it, I'm going to read it through to the end.

___ This will build common ground between me and my father/mother/sister/brother.

___ I'm eleven years old, and Buffett's got nothing on me.

___ I'm an environmentalist who wants to understand how business affects the planet.

___ I can see a dozen ways the world can be improved, but I'll need cash to fund them.

___ I've already raised nine children, written a best-selling book (sold the movie rights, too), and learned cooking from the master chefs in Europe. I'm bored and ready for something new to master.

Scoring:

0–1 points: Turn back. Don't pass Go. Don't collect $2,000 (was once $200, before inflation). We think that the index fund idea is a terrific one, and maybe that's where you'd be most comfortable!

2–5 points: Very good, you may get something more out of public company ownership! Index funds might remain very attractive to you.

6–10 points: You're going to love investigating and buying individual companies!

11–14 points: Ewwww, did you just drool on the page? Relax, we'll cover all the stuff you'll want to know!

15 points: Holy cow, you raised nine children?!

Keep in mind that identifying the stocks you're interested in doesn't mean you have to buy them now, if ever. Identify them, research them, and then watch them for a while—maybe even for a few years—to see how your ideas play out. During that time, you can easily learn how to read financial statements and value entire companies. Once you get it down, you'll be able to glide through company reports in short order and nail down a fair value for the entire business. And you'll actually enjoy the process.

Don't be impatient. There will always be great new businesses around the bend. Even if you miss a few great opportunities while learning—and you will—you're going to win in the end.

SO, WHERE DO I FIND STOCKS?

Stocks are everywhere around you, but where should you begin? Well, in the middle, of course. You're sitting smack dab in the center of a portfolio right now. You are wearing stocks. You brushed your teeth with stocks this morning (you did brush your teeth, right?). Your house is built with stocks. And the gooey junk food that you're craving this very moment is, most likely, a stock. The simple fact of the matter is that every American consumer is doing stock analysis every time he or she *buys anything, uses anything,* or *goes anywhere.* Whenever you make a consumer choice, you're making a value judgment about some company somewhere.

If you don't believe us, let's all go get a snack.

FRIDGE PICKS

Since you want proof, hop up off the sofa and head over to the fridge with your workbook in hand. Read this sentence: *Close your eyes, open the fridge door, and grab the first item in front of you.* OK, now do it! Really. Close your eyes and grab the first item you can in the fridge.

Open your eyes now. Are you there?

What did you get (or spill)? A carton of milk? A tub of butter? A jar of juice? A box of strawberries? (You know, you should really keep those in the crisper.) If your product has a label, write the company's name right here: _____. If you picked up leftovers, you'll have to default to Rubbermaid, made by Newell Rubbermaid, Inc., or try again. And if you picked up something furry and blue and you don't know how long it's been in your refrigerator, the industry of waste disposal is interesting, very possibly rewarding to investors, and a necessity for your daily life.

OK, let's look at your specific pick.

Your Fridge Pick: What You Already Know

That company name you wrote on the line above is very probably a stock, too. Now, what do you know about the company? Let's find out.

So, why did that product find its way to your refrigerator?

_____

What do you like about it?

_____

Is it more, or less, expensive than other brands?

_____

What else does the company make?

_____

Who else do you think would buy things made by this company?

_____

Do you remember reading or hearing any news about the company?

_____

Where is this company located?

_____

Let's say, for example, that you picked out a jar of pickles—Heinz pickles. While you were chomping away or wishing you'd opened the freezer and grabbed that Sara Lee ice cream pie, you might have noted the following:

Why did that product wind up in your refrigerator? They're the only kind of pickle I can stand.

What do you like about it?
Seems fresher than the generic, store-brand pickle.

Is it more, or less, expensive than other brands?
About the same price as other major brands.

What else does the company make?
Heinz, they're the ketchup people. They probably make a lot of stuff.

Who else do you think would buy things made by this company?
Probably almost everyone. I don't know people who wouldn't, unless they stick to the generics or are just plain weird.

Do you remember reading or hearing any news about the company?
I read something about them in the Sunday business section last month.

Where is this company located?
Lookie there on the label, they're located in Pittsburgh. I'm just a couple of hours north of them.

Already you're well on your way to researching a great company. You don't think so? Well, between January 1, 1981, and January 1, 2001, H. J. Heinz Company saw its stock rise at an annual rate of 19.2 percent, with dividends reinvested. Had you invested $6,000 in Heinz in 1981, you would have suffered a couple of market crashes, but now your investment would be worth $200,000.

We'll revisit the fridge pick momentarily, but right now let's keep hunting for stocks in your vicinity.

NOT ON WALL STREET—ON *YOUR* STREET

When you walk or drive around your neighborhood, what companies do you notice? None? OK, next time keep your eyes open.

Has a big bank taken over the little bank on the corner? Has some clothing chain opened a popular store near you? Is there a gas station that somehow compels you to go to it? Do you dash down to the same ice cream shop every hot summer day? Is there a new conglomerate hiring in your neighborhood? Do you live near a McDonald's or a Wendy's?

Once you've located a few interesting local businesses, you can gather a good deal of information just by asking the salespeople one question: "How's business?" Or just stand there and watch things for a few minutes. You can learn a lot from ten minutes of observation. How many people are going in and out of the building? Are they buying stuff? Do you feel like buying stuff? Does this whole thing look like a fad, or like the future?

Noticing these things and just very casually researching them is a great way to discover potentially excellent investments. Had you asked your computer salesperson in 1994 whether her toughest competition was the guy down the street or that computer mail order outfit Dell Computers, blammo, you might have made one of the great investments of the 1990s. Had you asked the cashier at shopping mall furniture dealer Bombay Company in 1996 how business was, whoa, you'd have learned that business was not at all good. Your initial casual research will turn up winners *and* losers. Taking what you've found in your fridge and around your neighborhood and preparing to do more research on it— *very* Foolish of you.

Let's not end things with just one or two, though . . .

FIELD TRIP!

Go get your coat, sweater, umbrella, or tube of sunscreen, and hold on to your workbook. It's time for a tour of your neighborhood or a trip downtown for an hour or two. Those of you living on Panther Pond in Raymond, Maine, a good distance from any businesses, you'll have to buzz over to town in your Humvee. While you're there, jot down any companies that arouse your interest. In the remaining pages of this workbook, we'll be digging in for a more thorough researching of these companies. Let's find ten businesses.

Ten Companies in My Neighborhood

1. _____

2. _____

3. _____

4. _____

5. _____

6. _____

7. _____

8. _____

9. _____

10. _____

Hey, we're just getting started. We still have two *more* spots where you can look for potential investments. And some of you thought you knew nothing about companies to invest in!

IN THE PAPERS AND ON TELEVISION

Newspapers and television programs are other great places to get investment ideas. Just pay attention to the trends or developments that surface. Follow the advertisements as well. And think about the effect they'll have on consumers in America.

Perhaps a *Seattle Times* news story says that scientists have discovered the gene for blindness. If that interests you, you might want to e-mail or call the business editor and ask the name of the company that funded that research. Investing in medical research can be a huge boon for you, if you know the industry well.

Flip your television set on, and whoa there, the screen fills up with buff guys and gals in red bathing suits, playing volleyball after a long day of lifeguarding. If you can stand it, tune in to the rest of the show and just casually keep your eyes open for any products that roll through. Television shows like *Baywatch,* for better or worse, drive public opinion among their demographic reach. There are investment possibilities there. You just have to use your imagination a bit to figure what the show communicates to people.

One more channel flip and the grinning game show host Wink Martindale is pitching prizes at America. Home entertainment centers, automobiles, vacation packages, even a meat smoker! And all of those products are from companies that you could partially own. You could also invest in the company that syndicates Wink's program.

Occasionally resist channel surfing and keep your eyes on the advertisements. When Intel began its enormously successful "Intel Inside" advertising campaign, the ads showcased one of the nation's premier businesses. When Nike embarrassed exclusive country clubs with its world-beating Tiger Woods campaign, there lay one of the great investments of the 1990s. And when Coca-Cola and Pepsi dueled it out in a taste test in the 1980s, there were another two extraordinary companies in which you could become a part owner.

Finally, the owners and distributors of all those programs and stories often make for great investments as well. Newspaper companies like the Washington Post Company, film and television companies like Disney, and radio syndicators like Westwood One—these have made for phenomenal investments as well. And you run across them week after week.

Let's name a few, then, shall we?

Being Your Own Media Mogul

Five companies whose products are on, or are, the tube:

1. _____

2. _____

3. _____

4. _____

5. _____

Five advertisers on the tube:

1. _____

2. _____

3. _____

4. _____

5. _____

Five companies from newspapers or radio:

1. _____

2. _____

3. _____

4. _____

5. _____

CREDIT CARD PURCHASES

The final place we'll look for potential investments is among credit card purchases. By consuming, you're already investing in dozens of companies every week. You're just trading your present or future savings for a product. When you buy a piece of the company instead of just the product, you'll be

trading your cash for the possibility of monetary reward in the years ahead. It makes sense when investing to always consider first the companies you buy from directly. Let's do so. Grab your credit card bill from the last month or months and list ten companies that you bought stuff from.

Ten Companies You Bought Stuff from on Your Credit Card

1. _____

2. _____

3. _____

4. _____

5. _____

6. _____

7. _____

8. _____

9. _____

10. _____

Bonus company! The bank that issued your credit card:

_____

YOU HAVE GREAT IDEAS, BUT WHAT DO YOU DO WITH THEM?

GATHERING BASIC INFORMATION

You've named about forty companies in this chapter, everything from Campbell Soup Company to *The Oprah Winfrey Show* (distributed by a public company, King World Productions). All forty of these companies may be excellent investments. Or maybe only twenty are. Or maybe only five. To winnow them down to a group of potential investments, though, you must first find out which of those companies are publicly traded. Let's work through this second step.

Wait! Second step? Well, what was the first step? It was so painless that you didn't even notice. Remember when you closed your eyes, opened the refrigerator door, and grabbed something? You wrote down a few notes about it. Right there, what you did—in industry parlance—is a bit of "fundamental research." For a few minutes, you studied the goodness and purpose (or lack thereof) of a product. Often it doesn't take much longer than that to determine whether something is successful or flawed, a potentially great investment or a dud.

But you'll need to know which of these companies that you've noted are publicly traded—ownable by average folks like all of us. Because we don't know what you grabbed out of the refrigerator, we've picked Heinz as an example. What if you had picked Thelma's Rutabaga Tarts, a slightly less global enterprise than Heinz? How do you know if Thelma's is a stock you can buy? How do you find out?

The easiest way is simply to call the company and ask. Read the label of the item you picked. If the label doesn't have the phone number or a website listed, it most surely will have an address, which'll lead you to an area code. Call information to get the phone number. Heinz, our label says, is in Pittsburgh. That's area code 412. Guess what we just did? We *just called Heinz on the phone* and asked:

- Are you guys a public company? (They are.)
- What is your stock symbol? (HNZ.)
- Which exchange does your stock trade on? (The New York Stock Exchange.)
- What's your address? (H. J. Heinz Company, 600 Grant Street, Pittsburgh, PA 15219. Telephone: 412-456-5700.)
- Hey, so how's business? (As they should, they said it was great.)

At the end of your call, say, "Cool, thanks." Just like that. It's critical that you say, "Cool, thanks," at the end just so that you are, in fact, cool yourself.

FINDING OUT IF A COMPANY IS PUBLICLY TRADED

Step 1: Get the company's address and phone number off its product label.

Company: _____

Address: _____

Phone Number: _____

Step 2: Call the company or search for it on the Internet and get a few answers.

Is it a public company: Yes ___   No ___

Then, if yes, find out what the stock symbol is: _____

Then find out what exchange it trades on:
_____

Finally, if the company you've called is publicly traded, ask them to send you some investment information. In a few weeks, you'll receive an investor's packet. In the chapters ahead, we'll be helping you dig through it all.

GET A SENSE OF THE BIG PICTURE

Our next step is to figure out the size of the companies you selected. As you can imagine, the larger the company that you invest in, the lower, often, the risk. General Electric's business, valued at more than $300 billion, is so fundamental to the world's economy that the likelihood of its crumbling is slim. Conversely, Checkers Drive-In Restaurants, Inc., whose business is valued at $120 million, could go under in the years ahead. At one point its stock fell from $16 per share to less than $1 per share, which forced it to have a one-for-twelve reverse split to stay listed on the Nasdaq. By doing a reverse split, the number of outstanding shares was reduced and the share price increased proportionately. Big companies are more secure in their position and usually make for safer investments. However, not always— we all remember Enron, don't we? Of course, smaller companies—though more volatile (more likely to have significant swings in their business and their stock price)—can provide superior investment returns, since they can have much more room to grow. Whichever you fancy, we suggest that you consider investing in a selection of both. You'll want to know how big or small your companies are.

Let's consider a few examples.

Checkers Drive-In Restaurants has 10 million shares of ownership and its stock is trading at about $12 per share. You guessed it: the number of shares multiplied by the price per share gives you the total value of the company. In this case, that's 10 million shares times $12 per share, for a $120 million company. Or as experienced investors are wont to say, Checkers has a *market capitalization* of $120 million.

How about *H. J. Heinz Company*?

Heinz has 350 million shares of ownership outstanding, and its stock is trading at about $42 per share. Whoa, brother, time to get the calculator out: 350 million shares times $42 per share equals a total company value of $14.7 billion. Just for the heck of it, consider how much larger Heinz is than Checkers Drive-In Restaurants. Divide $14.7 billion by $120 million and you'll see that the ketchup maker is about 122 times larger than the restaurateur.

Now let's look at the *Coca-Cola Company*. Coke has 2.5 billion shares of ownership outstanding, and its stock as of this writing is trading at about $50 per share. That values the company at $125 billion, which makes its market capitalization a little less than nine times bigger than that of H. J. Heinz and more than a thousand times bigger than that of Checkers Drive-In Restaurants.

MARKET CAPITALIZATION

Try calculating the total value of the following public companies. Each share of stock is trading at a particular price, and each public company has a set number of shares outstanding.

COMPANY	SHARES OUTSTANDING	PRICE PER SHARE	MARKET CAPITALIZATION
Sears Roebuck	325 million	$38	_____
Microsoft	5.4 billion	$60	_____
Polo Ralph Lauren	98 million	$22	_____
Johnson & Johnson	3.1 billion	$60	_____
eBay	275 million	$55	_____
Vans, Inc.	18 million	$13	_____
Starbucks	381 million	$17	_____
Lone Star Steakhouse	24 million	$12	_____
Tootsie Roll	50 million	$38	_____

MARKET CAPITALIZATION *(continued)*

Answers (arranged from smallest to largest market value):

COMPANY	MARKET CAPITALIZATION
Vans, Inc.	$234 million
Lone Star Steakhouse	$288 million
Tootsie Roll	$1.9 billion
Polo Ralph Lauren	$2.2 billion
Starbucks	$6.5 billion
Sears Roebuck	$12.4 billion
eBay	$15.1 billion
Johnson & Johnson	$186 billion
Microsoft	$324 billion

STOCK MARKETS AND SIZE

The three major markets that American stocks trade on (from largest to smallest) are the New York Stock Exchange, the Nasdaq Stock Market, and the American Stock Exchange. These three differ in the minimum requirements they impose on the companies they list. For example, under one requirement, the minimum market capitalization for a stock to start to trade on the Nasdaq Stock Market is $75 million. If the market capitalization dips below $50 million, the stock may be delisted. Or, under a second option, companies may have no required minimum capitalization as long as they have $6 million in assets and $1 million in pretax income. For the New York Stock Exchange, the minimum market capitalization is $100 million. For the American Stock Exchange, it is $3 million. Here are the exchanges of the companies mentioned just above:

Vans, Inc.	Nasdaq
Lone Star Steakhouse	Nasdaq
Tootsie Roll	New York Stock Exchange
Polo Ralph Lauren	New York Stock Exchange
Starbucks	Nasdaq
Sears Roebuck	New York Stock Exchange
eBay	Nasdaq
Johnson & Johnson	New York Stock Exchange
Microsoft	Nasdaq

CAPITALIZATION TAXONOMY

In addition to the precise dollar capitalization (or "cap"), investors use a basic taxonomy for classifying companies by size. Here are the classifications:

Micro-cap	below $250 million
Small-cap	$250 million to $1 billion
Mid-cap	$1 billion to $5 billion
Large-cap	over $5 billion

Based on these criteria, which of the companies whose values you calculated are

Micro-caps: ____________________

Small-caps: ____________________

Mid-caps: ____________________

Large-caps: ____________________

LARGE-CAP STOCKS

Large-cap stocks, also known as *blue-chips,* are well-known, huge companies that typically have business in many different corners of the world. As we noted, these are considered safer investments than smaller companies. They pose less risk of company failure—but less chance of enormous intermediate-term gain as well.

It's not that large-cap stocks can't beat the market. The best companies certainly do. It's just that given their size and reach, these necessarily have less potential for fast growth than do smaller companies. In exchange for that reduced growth potential, you'll often get a regular dividend from a large-cap stock. All told, great money can be made investing in large-cap companies.

Large Caps That Are (Probably) a Part of Your Daily Life

The company that made the oldest, most reliable major appliance in your house:

_____

The company that refined and sold the gasoline you put in your car:

_____

The company that made your car:

_____

The company that sells you long-distance phone service:

_____

The company that refined and boxed your breakfast cereal:

_____

MID-CAP STOCKS

We don't have to go into much detail here. Mid-caps fall right between large and small. You'll often get speedier growth than with a giant, but usually without the dividend. And you'll typically get slower

growth than with the small-cap company, but without the heartburn.

SMALL-CAP STOCKS

These are companies that don't have oodles of money invested in them yet, and often ones still in an embryonic business phase. In two years, they could be wiped out. In ten years, they could be a large-cap with operations around the world and a brand name that your entire family knows.

With small-caps, investors are hoping to find good growth potential. Such companies might be small, established firms with a long record of success, or they could be newborns that just started selling their stock to the public and have been in business for only three years. Investors are also looking for companies whose stock prices don't tell the whole story. One of the tenets of our philosophy is that the smaller the company, the less likely it is that major investment firms are following it yet. And the fewer the number of firms that are following it, the more likely the company might be dramatically over- or undervalued.

The market on which you'll find most small-caps, and most high-growth companies, is the Nasdaq. Most of these companies need to pump profits back into their business and rely on a mathematical and enterprising management team to not miss a beat. You find few small-caps that pay dividends to shareholders, and you won't find many that let you rest easy at night. But find the right one or two or three and they can fuel your entire portfolio.

MICRO-CAP STOCKS

Beware to any investor who travels into this universe. These very small companies too often have short operating histories, fragile business models, and glorious stories about how they plan to conquer the world. The odds against publicly traded micro-cap companies are huge. Historically, too many of them have collapsed under poor management or have been blown out of the water by competition—or both—for us to recommend that you spend much time or money here. This isn't to say that people haven't made money investing in the mites, just that you'd better know an awful lot about the business and probably ought to know management personally before putting your hard-earned money into one of these companies.

THREE REASONS TO INVEST IN SMALL-CAPS

Small-cap stocks can be risky, but being able to identify, research, and evaluate them successfully is delightful. Why? There are a number of reasons, but the biggest one is that doing so lets you beat the Wise to the punch. If you get in before they do, and if you've bought a great company, when they start investing their gazillions of dollars in it, blammo, your holdings can increase dramatically. Let's walk through three specific reasons to consider some small-cap investing in your portfolio.

1. Due to the size of most mutual funds, the way they are set up, and some federal regulations, fund managers have a hard time establishing any kind of meaningful position in small-caps.

The first hurdle is their size—most funds are just too darn big to be able to take advantage of small-caps. They can't start investing in these companies until they've grown larger. Why? In order to buy a position large enough to make a difference to their fund's overall performance, they'd have to pick up sometimes 10 or 20 percent of the entire small-cap company's stock. Before they can do that, though, they have to file with the SEC. By doing so, they tip their hand to the market; buyers swarm and begin buying at a greatly inflated price.

Another factor that handcuffs many mutual fund managers when it comes to small-caps is their own prospectus. One of the things a fund has to put in its mission statement is its investment approach. And in an attempt to sell their funds as "safe" vehicles, they insert clauses about minimum market capitalization of stocks in the portfolio. If they were to buy a stock that didn't fit their stated investment objec-

tives, they could be held liable, even if the stock rises!

That the big boys can't play these small-cap reindeer games is a great asset to the individual investor, who has the ability to spot promising companies and get in before the institutions do. That institutions cannot compete with individuals for smaller companies creates numerous opportunities. Individuals are in the enviable position of being able to sell to large institutions at significantly higher prices, once the company has grown. Of course, not all small-cap companies grow!

2. Another reason to buy small-caps is management. Lots of small-caps are owned by their managers—men and women who wake up every morning and worry about the overall value of the enterprise. Since most of their potential for wealth is tied to their own shares, you can bet that they'll be working very hard to increase the value of the stock.

3. Probably the best reason to buy small-cap growth companies is that they grow—sometimes very quickly. America, more than any country on the planet, embraces start-up entrepreneurialism, recognizing that more jobs are created by small companies than any other group. And a small company's rapidly multiplying earnings often translate into quick growth in share price.

This isn't any great revelation of ours. Investors like Peter Lynch have encouraged small investors to scour the nation for small companies, buy them if their prospects look good and their management is sound, and hold them for profit. We'll be learning how to value these and other companies later in the book.

AND NOW, FOUR REASONS *NOT* TO INVEST IN SMALL-CAPS

Small-caps certainly aren't for everyone. In a single day, you might see your stock rise or fall 15 percent without a lick of news, with no explanation for the move.

1. Small-caps aren't for the novice investor. To buy intelligently from this group, you have to know your way around an income statement and a balance sheet, as well as be thoroughly familiar with the industry that the company is a part of. Cut your teeth on some large- and mid-cap issues first. Follow some of your small-cap ideas on paper for a year or two before plunging in with your rupees.

2. Small-caps should only be part of a larger whole, part of a well-balanced diet. Just like sugared cereals, they can be fun, they can give you a little extra kick, but too much of either is not a good thing. Eat from this bowl of Fruity Pebbles in moderation. Indeed, moderation in all things.

3. Time is another dissuading factor—or rather, the lack of it is. Finding good small-caps can involve a lot of work and takes even more attention after you've made your purchase. If you don't have the time, energy, or inclination to keep up with the news on your portfolio, you're better off in an index fund.

4. The last reason to stay away from small-cap growth stocks may be your natural aversion to risk. How did you rate yourself back in "What Kind of Investor Am I?" Remember that Risk Tolerance Test? Go back to it now and remind yourself—were you Captain Kangaroo, Captain Kirk, or Captain Ahab? If the mere thought of a single-day 5 percent drop for your entire savings account gives you an ulcer, save your stomach! Small-caps aren't the only way to beat the market.

Everyone has his or her own risk tolerance, and you should never make any investment that makes you feel uncomfortable. Money in an index fund will get you respectable returns and keep you off the acid blockers that advertise during the nightly news. That approach also gives you time to learn how to invest without leaving your money just sitting in a cash account at the bank.

All of those warnings noted, once you have some experience under your belt (even if it's only on paper), and if you aren't averse to volatility and know thoroughly the companies you plan to invest in, small-cap growth stocks can make a wonderful addition to your portfolio.

It's time for recess, students! We suggest the following exercise to keep you out of trouble during the break, and in the future.

THE MOTLEY SMALL-CAP FOOL LIB

Title: _____ Small-Cap Adventure _____ _____ decided one day to invest in _____ small-
   [your name]   [your name]   [adverb]   [adjective]

cap stocks. Without reading or _____ing much about them, he/she just plunked all his/her _____ money
                                        [verb]   [adjective]

into three companies: Allied _____ Conglomerators, _____ _____ Corporation, and International
                                        [noun]   [adjective]   [noun]

_____ Transmogrifier. _____ didn't keep track of these _____ investments, though, and didn't no-
   [noun]   [your name]   [your name]

tice when _____ of the companies fell on _____ times and plummeted. _____ learned
                  [number between 1 and 3]   [adjective]   [your name]

some _____ lessons from this experience. Now, _____ has become a lot more attentive, researching and
         [adjective]   [your name]

_____ing stocks before buying, and following them afterward. This has paid off in a _____ way, as
   [verb]   [adjective]

_____'s investments are now doing well and the whole portfolio is something to _____ at.
   [your name]   [verb]

BEYOND FUNDAMENTALS: THOUGHTS ON INDUSTRIES

As you begin to move out into individual stocks and away from the effortless approach of the index fund, you're going to have to learn more and more about entire industries. It won't be enough to buy a company without valuing the shares of its stock. Factors that may affect the price of one stock will likely affect the price of the stock of related companies. You see, companies are in many ways like teenagers—they tend to hang out in packs and act a lot like one another. In the case of companies, this is because investors often treat one like another, even if sometimes they have to stretch a little to find similarities.

One excellent example of this is the so-called technology industry, a motley collection of mostly computer- and Internet-related businesses. Although computer games and semiconductor components as true industries face largely different challenges, big-money little-research investors like to lump them together as "technology stocks" when they are considering their prospects.

Understanding individual companies in their larger industry context is an important step in making sense of the numbers and figuring out why the price of the stock is changing. And with that, let's push on into the next chapter and—you guessed it—a look at some of the numbers.

Don't fret, don't pout. It's painless, we tell you, painless.

CHAPTER 6

HOW DO I READ ALL THOSE NUMBERS?

Where did our love for numbers go? As kids, we thrived on hopscotch. We raced through "One potato, two potato." We fanatically followed baseball statistics. We were at one with digits as we kept score on sandlots and sang travel songs about beer on the wall and ways to leave your lover. Yet, older now, we somehow believe that math is for accountants and engineers and tollbooth operators and high school baseball coaches who also teach math. We dread balancing checkbooks; we snarl at the thought of setting a budget. We've become financial lightweights. Julia Child could box us around the ring and gnaw on our ears, with her quarter cups of egg whites and her four teaspoons of vanilla extract. Beyond the numerical elements of time and date, many of us consider ourselves numerically challenged.

Enough!

It's time to learn again the love of numbers, to rediscover the joys of the simple art of calculation. Let us show you how to dig into a company's balance sheet with pencil, calculator, and, yes, your ego. This stuff is not prohibitively complicated. The business concepts and the mathematics are pretty simple.

So, dispatch your dread. Let's crack open a company's annual financial report with zeal. Let's go beyond the glossy pictures, where we often learn no more than how wide a smile the CEO can stretch over her mahogany desk. Instead, we'll embrace the colorless and drab financial tables. Yes, bring your childhood zest, pack a light snack if you must, put on your high school football or ice hockey helmet, keep your chin up and a wide stance. We're going in.

THE BALANCE SHEET

Do you remember the personal balance sheet you created for yourself a few chapters back? We used the balance sheet to assess how your financial situation is looking right now, assessing things like your short-term debts, your cash position and how much of your savings you had invested. Flip back to Chapter 2 and spend two minutes looking through your notes.

Pretty straightforward, right? Well, public companies present a very similar balance sheet (along with a few other documents we'll discuss soon) to the public every three months. Every thirteen weeks, every U.S.-based public company must tell the world about the state of its finances. Financial reporting requirements are stricter in the United States than anywhere else—and the level of accountability driven by those requirements has resulted in greater efficiency and superior performance in America.

The balance sheets that companies present, much the same as the one you did, show assets (reflecting what the business *owns*) and liabilities (representing what it *owes*). Think of them as a snapshot photo of a company's underlying financial situation, with everything reflected, from cash to heavy equipment, from office desks to business travel costs. Let's take a closer look at these two main components of the balance sheet: assets and liabilities.

WHAT EXACTLY ARE ASSETS AND LIABILITIES?

Assets can be everything from cash in the bank to unsold products to that three-legged desk propped up by a pair of phone books. Assets cast such a wide net that, on the balance sheet, they are broken out into two groups: "current assets" and "fixed assets."

Current assets are those that can be turned into cash quickly, like money in a savings account. Businesses that list items under current assets expect to translate all of that stuff into cash over the next twelve months. What could that stuff be?

1. Cash itself, and investments in Treasury bills, bonds, and stocks.
2. Bills that a business expects to collect in the next twelve months, called "accounts receivable."
3. Inventory in all stages, from raw materials to finished products waiting to be delivered to stores for sale.
4. Company-owned office buildings slated for sale in the next ten years.

Whoa there! Number 4 is bogus. Office buildings are not current assets. Take your pencil and draw a line right through the middle of number 4. Give yourself three blue stars if you spotted the error yourself.

Among long-term assets, called *fixed assets,* sit the bulkier items like machinery, land, and equipment. Since these items can't be quickly translated into cash, they ain't "current." As you will see in the subsequent chapters of the workbook, we particularly like companies with few heavy assets, since they usually represent large investments that had to be made to run the business. Our preference is toward lighter, more agile businesses, for which smaller up-front investments had to be made. But we'll get to all that in due time. It's important here only that you understand the distinction between current assets (oncoming cash) and fixed assets (stuff that probably isn't getting turned into cash anytime soon).

Then what are liabilities?

Just flip-flop everything. Like assets, liabilities can be either current or fixed—though, in name, they are classified as either "short-term" or "long-term" liabilities. *Short-term liabilities* are debts that the company must pay within the year. For example, if it licenses products from other companies, it has to pay those suppliers. All short-term bills that the company hasn't gotten around to paying yet are listed under accounts payable. Do you remember the current-asset equivalent of "accounts payable"?

CURRENT ASSETS	SHORT-TERM LIABILITIES
Accounts_____able	Accounts_____able

Routine, yep. On the liability side, you have bills that you have to pay over the next year *(payables)*. On the asset side, you have payments owed to you that will be collected over the next year *(receivables)*.

Elsewhere in the short-term-liability category, you have regular lease payments and short-term bank loans. And over in the long-term debt group, the heavy stuff, you have all the money that the company has borrowed and must pay down in the years ahead. Nothing listed under long-term debt is due in the next twelve months.

So, to sew up the introduction to the balance sheet, you have assets, current and fixed, listed on the left side of the page. And you have liabilities, short- and long-term, listed on the right side of the page. Anyone with questions, raise your hand. Any questions? No? Good. Now, let's see how well you understand it.

Balance Sheet Taxonomy

Circle each item's asset or liability class.

1. Cash

   a. current assets
   b. current liabilities
   c. fixed assets
   d. long-term liabilities

2. Accounts payable

   a. current assets
   b. current liabilities
   c. fixed assets
   d. long-term liabilities

3. Finished products

   a. current assets
   b. current liabilities
   c. fixed assets
   d. long-term liabilities

4. A big orange crane

   a. current assets
   b. current liabilities
   c. fixed assets
   d. long-term liabilities

5. Outstanding bills to be collected by guys with tire irons in the next three months

   a. current assets
   b. current liabilities
   c. fixed assets
   d. long-term liabilities

6. $15 million owed to Bank of New York over ten years

   a. current assets
   b. current liabilities
   c. fixed assets
   d. long-term liabilities

7. Credit card bills that the company owes

   a. current assets
   b. current liabilities
   c. fixed assets
   d. long-term liabilities

And the answers are . . . 1. *a* 2. *b* 3. *a* 4. *c* 5. *a* 6. *d* 7. *b*

You nailed them all, right? And to think that, not that long ago, you may never have thought you could read financial statements!

SCRUTINIZING THE BALANCE SHEET

We are going to concentrate on two ways to analyze balance sheets:

1. comparing the entries this year against those last year
2. studying the relationship between assets and liabilities

We're betting that you already know exactly why we'd do both, but here's a brief explanation. First, we'll compare this year to last year in order to draw conclusions about how the company is changing. Are they borrowing a lot more money this year than last? If so, is this because they're in trouble, or because they see oncoming opportunities that will demand some cash? Are finished-product inventories going through the roof this year? If so, does this mean that the company is not selling its products effectively, or that it is building up inventory in preparation for high demand in the coming quarter? How much more (or less) cash does the company have today than twelve months back? Comparing the financials from one year to the next is critical to understanding the present state of business.

Second, we'll consider the relationship between assets and liabilities so as to grasp how well the company is managing its money. Is it collecting its bills promptly? Is it holding more cash than long-term debt? How "heavy" is the overall business—that is, when you compare fixed assets and long-term debt to current assets, does the company have to spend heavily on assets to keep itself going, perhaps even taking on more debt and draining cash and investments from current assets?

To show how fundamental this is to investing and how simple it is to grasp, let's take the balance sheet from our now legendary (well, to us at least), still mythical company Messages Inc.—the tasty little manufacturer of edible messages slipped into fortune cookies and the like, which we featured in *The Motley Fool Investment Guide*. On the following sheet, you'll notice that next to each class of asset and liability, we offer three columns. The first represents operations in 2002; the second, operations in 2001; and the third, the growth between the two, represented as a percentage. We'll consider first the assets half of the balance sheet, and then the liabilities. Check it out.

(*Note:* When dollar amounts are given "in thousands," just add three zeros to ascertain the proper figure. For example, "24,000" stands for "24,000,000" —because 24,000 × 1,000 = 24,000,000.)

MESSAGES INC. BALANCE SHEET
YEAR 2002 COMPARED TO 2001

(IN THOUSANDS)

ASSETS	2002	2001	CHANGE
CURRENT ASSETS			
Cash and equivalents	24,000	20,000	20%
Accounts receivable	34,000	14,000	143%
Inventory	20,000	10,000	100%
Prepaid expenses	1,500	1,000	50%
TOTAL CURRENT ASSETS	79,500	45,000	77%
FIXED ASSETS			
Property, plant, and equipment, net	10,800	5,200	108%
TOTAL ASSETS	90,300	50,200	80%

Let's break in right here and review a couple of interesting points.

1. Cash and equivalents (those being largely money market funds) have increased by 20 percent over the past year. So, the company has added bucks, either from more sales, or more borrowing, or another sale of stock to the public. Cash is up; that is probably a plus.

2. Accounts receivable has risen 143 percent since 2001. Receivables represent money from sales that the company has already counted as revenue but that it has not yet collected from the debtor. Receiv-

ables generally track sales growth (though, ideally, you want receivables to rise more slowly than sales), so if the growth in sales was close to 143 percent, the situation at Messages is probably OK. When a company has receivables rising dramatically faster than sales, it *may* mean that it is announcing significant amounts of revenue but is having a hard time getting customers to pay for goods sold. The phrase for this situation is "Uh-ohhh!" Investors want receivables to be held in check, indicating that buyers of the company's products hunger so much for them that they're willing to pay up front, or at least soon thereafter. Consider Messages' accounts receivable in terms of total assets. Divide the $34 million in receivables by the $90.3 million in total assets, and you'll see that over 37 percent of the company's assets are bills they've yet to collect. Maybe, in order to sell their product, they had to promise to collect only six months after its delivery, and only if the customer was keenly satisfied. This is a weak position. If accounts receivable are rising faster than sales, this may be a disaster in the making.

3. Inventory is up 100 percent, from $10 million to $20 million. Whoa there! We're going to have to dig deeper into Messages' strategy here. Like accounts receivable, inventory growth should be compared to sales growth. If sales are slow and inventory represents finished products that have been sitting around for a while, Messages might well be in big trouble. If, however, the growth reflects the company's investment in the development of new products that they expect customers to greet with great demand, then we weight its importance differently. As with accounts receivable, rising inventory is either a neutral or a very bad sign.

We'll let you in on a secret right now: Messages' sales growth is 94 percent. What can you conclude from that? If you said that the assets side of the balance sheet doesn't sparkle as we'd like it to, you're right. Sales growth has been slower than the rise in both receivables and inventory. That is generally not good.

You'll notice that, with the exception of cash, we generally do not want the things that our company owns—its assets—to rise dramatically. A ton of inventory may very well be a bad thing. But, let's hold on to our "wait and see" attitude and continue over to the statement of liabilities.

MESSAGES INC. BALANCE SHEET
YEAR 2002 COMPARED TO 2001

(IN THOUSANDS)			
LIABILITIES	2002	2001	CHANGE
CURRENT LIABILITIES			
Short-term debt	0	0	0%
Accounts payable	6,500	3,200	103%
Accrued expenses	18,000	10,000	80%
TOTAL CURRENT LIABILITIES	24,500	13,200	86%
Long-term debt	0	0	0%
TOTAL LIABILITIES	24,500	13,200	86%
SHAREHOLDER EQUITY	65,800	37,000	78%

What have we found here?

1. Messages Inc. has no short-term debt, meaning that it doesn't have to pay money back to lenders in the next twelve months. It's not surprising that it doesn't have short-term debt, since it doesn't have long-term debt, or money that it owes to lenders after the coming year. Messages is blessedly debt-free, which is a nice way to be.

2. Accounts payable has risen by 103%, to $6.5 million. The company owes its business partners over $6.5 million now. At first blush, this looks like a bad thing. Ah, but there is a twist here. Payables carry low interest charges. In other words, holding off these payments allows the company to use that money for its own gain before paying it to creditors. For this reason, we treat the rise in payables as a good thing and the rise in receivables as a bad thing. Please stop for a few moments to ponder this. Put the pencil and book down and think about the relationship between payables and receivables. One last reminder—if there are no interest charges on either, then for aggressive cash management wouldn't you want to get all money owed to you up front and delay paying all your debts as long as possible? It makes sense.

3. Whoa, accrued expenses up 80 percent! We dropped a note to Dale Wettlaufer, one of our good friends, and asked him for a definition of accrued expenses that might explain this change in the fortunes of Messages Inc. Here's what he came up with:

> Accrued expenses are expenses that the company has racked up (on the income statement) but has not yet paid out in cash. Here are two examples of what might be going on with your company: One, the balance sheet is released to the public on June 30, reflecting all costs, but the salary checks don't actually go out until July 1. Because the payments haven't been made yet, they are listed as "accrued expenses." Another possibility: Messages Inc. knows that insurance bills are coming down the pike in mid-July for cost of coverage during the June period. The costs have been incurred, but the payments haven't been made yet. Given this, they're listed as accrued expenses.
>
> Hey, do I get to go on *Oprah*?

Thanks, Dale. So, knowing that there may be an innocuous explanation for this 80 percent rise in accrued expenses, how should we interpret it? We'll call it a neutral. It may indicate that the company has added a bunch of new employees; it may tell us that it's toying around with payment periods; it may suggest nothing more than the timing of the report. We can't draw any good conclusions now, but we will keep our eye on accrued expenses in future quarters to see if a pattern emerges.

No final judgment can be made on how sound a company is simply by looking at its balance sheet. That said, with inventories and receivables climbing, there are some warning lights and sirens firing off. In the quarter ahead, we would hope to see Messages Inc. collecting its receivables, demanding more receipts up front, and more aggressively managing its inventories. In the end, none of these may be possible—the company may just have products that don't much sell anymore. If that's the case and we own the stock, we'll consider selling it. We'll have to keep our eyes on Messages Inc.

Let's take a look at three more items on the balance sheet, and then be done with it for now.

WORKING CAPITAL

The first new item is working capital, which is an expression of how much liquid assets the company has to build its business, fund its growth, and produce shareholder value. "Liquid assets"? That's simply another phrase for "current assets," those which will (we hope) be converted into cash over the next twelve months. If a company has ample positive working capital, it is considered to be in good shape, with cash enough to pay for growth. So let's take a gander at Messages Inc.'s working capital in the year 2002. You do the math. Just turn back a few pages and look on the balance sheet for total current assets and total current liabilities.

WORKING CAPITAL FOR MESSAGES INC., 2002

> (NOTE: WORKING CAPITAL =
> CURRENT ASSETS LESS CURRENT LIABILITIES)
>
> Current assets _____
>
> Current liabilities _____
>
> WORKING CAPITAL _____

No peeking. OK, now take a look at the answer.

WORKING CAPITAL FOR MESSAGES INC., 2002

Current assets	$79,500,000
Current liabilities	$24,500,000
WORKING CAPITAL	$55,000,000

That working capital amount by itself doesn't tell you very much. A company could have $3.5 trillion in current assets and $3.499945 trillion in current liabilities, and it, too, would have $55,000,000 in working capital. That does not mean that the situations are the same. We need a way to establish the relative level of current assets to liabilities. Hey, how 'bout we divide one by the other?

And so the *current ratio* was born. The current ratio provides an investor with a basic test of short-term liquidity, since it simply takes the current as-

sets and divides them by the current liabilities. Ideally, this figure will fall somewhere above 2 to 1 for the typical American industrial company, tending toward higher ratios for small-caps. What the current ratio tells you is how nimbly a company may be able to act to take advantage of an unforeseen circumstance.

In reality, of course, even a high ratio may not help in times of trouble. Taken on its own, the current ratio doesn't actually tell you much about a company's liquidity, because it depends on the company's ability to convert its current assets into cash. That's not always easy. If, for example, Messages' TastiScrolls were found to cause mild increases in the libidos of laboratory rats, one might think that Messages would be far better prepared to deal with this potential crisis with a current ratio of 5 than with a ratio of 1. In the wake of the FDA investigation, however, Messages is going to have to write off all its current inventory. What's more, some of its customers might decide that they aren't going to pay the money they owe Messages, since they can't sell their TastiScrolls either. Messages' inventory and accounts receivable balances won't add up to a pile of glucose in this situation.

For what it's worth, let's calculate Messages' current ratio for 2002 and 2001.

	2002	2001
Current assets	79,500	45,000
divided by Current liabilities	24,500	13,200
equals CURRENT RATIO	3.2	3.4

Messages' current ratio for 2002 was 3.2, which is certainly acceptable. Note that this is down from the previous year's mark of 3.4.

You can apply the current ratio to any annual report you look at, though we've never let it make or break an investment decision for us. We like to see the ratio remain even or trend slightly higher, but you won't find us getting emotional on the subject. Still, a survey of the current ratio can be a useful way to discover potential new investment ideas among financially healthy mid-caps. Just look at the company's snapshot in the Quotes & Data section of Fool.com or flip through the *S&P Stock Guide*, going down the current assets and current liabilities columns (conveniently located next to each other in that august publication).

A second ratio, very similar to the current ratio, is the *quick ratio*. The quick ratio is more cash-centric (to coin an abominable-looking term); it is simply the current assets minus inventories, divided by the current liabilities. It gives you an even better read on how prepared a company might be to encounter unforeseen difficulties or opportunities, or just to meet current short-term debt obligations, so you want to see as high a number as possible.

	2002	2001
Current assets	79,500	45,000
minus Inventory	20,000	10,000
divided by Current liabilities	24,500	13,200
equals QUICK RATIO	2.4	2.7

Messages' quick ratio declined from a powerful 2.7 in 2001 to a still-impressive 2.4 in 2002. Does this drop bode ill for the company's liquidity? Not really. Messages' current assets include $24 million in cash on hand. As of this moment, Messages Inc. could pay off all but $500,000 of its current liabilities with existing cash. In other words, the company is in fine financial shape for the upcoming year.

That said, in studying *working capital*, don't blind yourself to the dramatic rise in receivables and inventories. Those assets may not be as liquid as you think. What if no one will pay cash for the inventories? And what if the receivables cannot be collected? These things happen, and they prevent companies from converting current assets into cash. Even though the company appears to be strong for the year ahead, the best of all current assets by a long shot is simply *cash*. For example, on the balance sheet of one of the greatest businesses founded in the late twentieth century, Microsoft, you will find that most of its current assets—sometimes as much as 80 percent—are in the form of *cash*. For Messages, cash makes up only 30 percent of current assets. Not everyone is Microsoft! But Messages Inc.'s assets line isn't as definitively liquid as we'd like.

THE FOOLISH FLOW RATIO

The Foolish flow ratio is designed to stack noncash current assets against current liabilities, in order to measure how well a company is managing the dollar bills that flow through its business. Allow us to introduce the ratio first and then provide a more comprehensive explanation.

To calculate the Foolish flow ratio, simply *(a)* subtract the cash from current assets, then *(b)* divide that figure by current liabilities minus short-term debt. In the case of Messages Inc., you'll get something that looks like this:

(current assets − cash) ÷ (current liabilities − short-term debt)

($79.5 million − $24 million) ÷ ($24.5 million − $0)

$55.5 million ÷ $24.5 million = 2.27

So, Messages Inc.'s flow ratio is 2.27. Now, pause for a second and tell us whether a company would ideally have a high or low flow ratio relative to its competitors. Tick tock, tick tock. Fill in your answer and explanation here:

_____

_____

_____

Interesting! Here's our answer. Ideally, a company's flow ratio is low. Once cash is removed from current assets, we're dealing almost exclusively with accounts receivable and inventories. In the very best businesses, these items are held in check. Inventories should never run high, because they should be constantly rolling out the door. Receivables should be kept as low as possible, because the company should require up-front payments for its products and services.

So we certainly want the numerator of the equation (current assets minus cash) to be held low.

What about the denominator (current liabilities minus short-term debt)? Rising payables indicate one of two things: either the company cannot meet its short-term bills and is headed for bankruptcy, or the company is so strong that its suppliers are willing to give it time before requiring payment. You can be sure that companies in the latter category use their advantageous position to hang on to every dollar they can. Again, think of every unpaid bill as a short-term, low-interest or interest-free loan. If a company has plenty of cash to pay down current liabilities but doesn't, it's probably managing its money *very* well. Those are the companies that we're looking for.

To close out the flow ratio, then, ideally we like to see this baby sit low. The very best companies have

1. Plenty of cash
2. Noncash current assets dropping (inventories and receivables are kept low)
3. Rising current liabilities (unpaid bills for which cash is on hand)

PRACTICE FLOW RATIOS

	CASH	CURRENT ASSETS	CURRENT ASSETS MINUS CASH	CURRENT LIABILITIES	FLOW RATIO
Microsoft	$9.1 billion	$10.2 billion	$1.1 billion	$3.5 billion	0.31
Coca-Cola	$2.2 billion	$6.3 billion	$4.1 billion	$7.3 billion	0.56
Bombay Company	$2.0 million	$123 million	$121 million	$24 million	5.04
Starbucks	$213 million	$328 million	$115 million	$111 million	1.04
Hershey Foods	$77.3 million	$1.0 billion	$923 million	$841 million	a. _____
Staples Inc.	$106 million	$1.2 billion	b. _____	$603 million	c. _____
Dole Food	$26 million	$1.2 billion	d. _____	$656 million	e. _____
Borders Books	$43.2 million	$964 million	$921 million	$817 million	f. _____
Ivax Pharmaceutical	$75 million	$690 million	$615 million	$217 million	g. _____
Pfizer	$1.9 billion	$6.9 billion	$5.0 billion	$5.8 billion	h. _____

Answers: a. 1.10 b. $1.1 billion c. 1.82 d. $1.2 billion e. 1.83 f. 1.13 g. 2.83 h. 0.86

Final question: The Foolish flow ratio is only one of many, many different checks to run on your company. Keeping that in mind, *which are the six most attractive companies, by flow ratio, in the previous table?* Please write them in order from greatest to sixth-greatest:

1._____

2._____

3._____

4._____

5._____

6._____

Did you write: Microsoft (1), Coca-Cola (2), Pfizer (3), Starbucks (4), Hershey (5), and Borders (6)? Good, you're right!

SHAREHOLDERS' EQUITY

If you've taken the time by now to call up one of your favorite companies to get its financial statements, you may be looking over a real live balance sheet as we speak. Good! If so, you'll notice there's actually a final section of the balance sheet that we haven't yet mentioned. It's listed on the side with liabilities, though it's a horse of a different color: "shareholders' equity."

$$\text{Shareholders' equity} = \text{assets} - \text{liabilities}$$

Shareholders' equity is simply total assets minus total liabilities. It is the owners' piece of the business's assets, after it pays off the debt (long-term and short-term) and other bills that it owes in the form of liabilities. Think of equity in a house; it is the value of the house (the asset) minus the mort-gage still owed on it (the liability). When the house is sold, the debt is paid and the rest of the proceeds belongs to the owners.

We spend little time looking at shareholders' equity, since it is a bit of a fiction. The value of a business isn't really the sum of its assets. It may be more or less than its assets, depending on the company's ability to generate cash in the future. Equity is useful, however, to determine how *leveraged* a company is. The debt-to-equity ratio—which we'll describe soon—gives you a rough idea of how much equity is left in the company compared to debt. Should a company want or need to borrow money, it's helpful to have lots of equity and little debt; creditors like this.

But since we generally avoid investing in businesses that make many appeals to creditors, we'll gracefully end this section here. In fact, before you knew it, we began and completed the balance sheet section, like *that. (Snap!)* OK, to the income statement. Forward, march!

THE INCOME STATEMENT

Four times a year, public companies step out into the spotlight on Wall Street and announce their three-month financial performance. In an instant, Wall Street begins sorting through the numbers, calculating ratios, and divining new valuations for the entire business. Quarterly earnings reports are like baseball scorecards or medical statistics. Laid out on the page, they can tell us about resiliency or disintegration, a healthy consistency or erratic performance. And a surprise in profits, on the upside or downside, can send stocks moving as Wall Street revises its expectations.

We presented the balance sheet first because we consider its importance to be underrated by investment researchers. You see, the investing community concentrates most of its attention on the income statement. It is here that you'll find how much chocolate Hershey sold, how much it cost Hershey to manufacture and package that chocolate, how much it cost the company to distribute and promote that chocolate, and—ever important—how much money from selling that chocolate was supposedly left over after all the bills were paid.

Before these figures are announced, Wall Street's analysts and experts have already made predictions about what sales and earnings for the three-month period should be (we'll discuss this later). So, when these figures actually do get announced, investors race to compare the sales and earnings results to Wall Street's predictions for the quarter. The longer-term investor, who beats the market more often than the trader, usually takes a good while to think before making any assumptions about the quarterly report. Needless to say, while wild trading activity can ensue after an announcement, the most money can be made assessing the strength and viability of the business in the years ahead, rather than just in

the next quarter. Not to add too much complicating stuff right now, but there's another reason that it is important that you not rush to respond to those "earnings reports." One thing that is usually glossed over is whether the earnings are on a reported or a pro forma basis. Wait, don't run away! No more Latin, we promise! "Pro forma" is a fancy way of saying "without bad stuff," and can sometimes be deceptive. Just a fair warning so you don't hyperventilate the next time a company you own makes its earnings report.

There's your preface to the income statement. Now let's scrutinize the statement for Messages Inc. and break up the parts. Sneak a peek, use it as an eye chart if it is completely unclear, and let's meet back at the bottom to make sense of the scribble.

MESSAGES INC. STATEMENT OF INCOME

(IN THOUSANDS)	2002	2001	CHANGE
INCOME			
Revenue	97,000	50,000	94%
less Cost of sales (goods)	46,500	21,000	121%
GROSS PROFIT	50,500	29,000	74%
OPERATING EXPENSES			
Selling/general/administrative	27,500	12,000	129%
Research/development	4,500	6,000	(25%)*
TOTAL OPERATING EXPENSES	32,000	18,000	78%
INCOME FROM OPERATIONS	18,500	11,000	68%
Interest income	1,080	1,000	8%
Income before taxes	19,580	12,000	63%
less Income taxes	6,700	4,100	63%
NET INCOME	12,880	7,900	63%
Earnings per share	$1.07	$0.79	35%
Basic shares outstanding	12,000	10,000	20%
Diluted shares outstanding	12,000	10,000	20%

*The parentheses indicate a negative number, i.e., a *decrease* of 25%.

There we are. Now let's talk about it!

REVENUE AND COST OF SALES

We start with *Revenue,* or sales, which is, as one might expect, the total dollar value of all products and services sold over the course of the year. Those numbers appear as the first line on the statement, which explains why an increase in revenue is often referred to as "top-line growth." Messages fared well this quarter. Sales almost doubled, ramping up to $97 million from $50 million the year before. If the word "almost" is too vague, let's whip out our calculators and be blunt. If we divide the current year's sales of $97 million by the $50 million in sales the year before, we see that sales this year were 194 percent of those last year, which means sales grew by 94 percent. On average, a mature business may see its sales increase by 5–15 percent per year. Because Messages Inc. is a relatively small and new operation with a titillating product, its revenue growth has naturally been more rapid. But 94 percent growth over last year looks strong. People clearly want more messages!

There is more to the story than sales, however. What if the company is selling those messages for very little money—perhaps not enough money to cover the cost of manufacturing them? Consider this workbook, for a second. If Simon & Schuster charged a mere 25 cents for it, it might sell 15 million of them. S&S would also happen to lose millions of dollars in the process. So, while sales can rise dramatically, you'll next have to study how well the company is keeping expenses under control.

Among the costs of running a business, companies pay money for raw materials and the manufacturing labor to assemble them, and these items fall under the category of *Cost of sales.* Now, one might expect, with sales of tasty fortune cookie messages on the rise, that costs would also be significantly higher, since making twice as many messages requires twice as many ingredients, like glucose, gum, and red dye #5. Yep, not surprisingly, the cost of sales did rise, from $21 million last year to $46.5 million this year. Tap, tap, tap on the calculator, and you'll see that costs were 221 percent of last year's, meaning they rose 121 percent—notably higher than sales growth of 94 percent. So, while the company may still be making money (and we'll see that it is), the rate of its profitability has declined as sales have risen substantially. Hey, there are a few somersaults of mathematical logic there. Are you with us? It's not too tough.

Now let's look at some ways to assess the company's profitability.

GROSS PROFIT AND GROSS MARGIN

MESSAGES INC. GROSS PROFIT

(IN THOUSANDS)	2002	2001	CHANGE
INCOME			
Revenue	97,000	50,000	94%
less Cost of sales (goods)	46,500	21,000	121%
GROSS PROFIT	50,500	29,000	74%
GROSS MARGIN	52%	58%	

Gross profit is the cash left after the cost of sales has been subtracted from revenue. First, look at 2001. Of $50 million in sales, the company garnered gross profits of $29 million. And thus, the company had what is called a *gross margin* of 58 percent. Can you guess what gross margin is? Yep, simply the percentage in gross profits relative to sales ($29 million ÷ $50 million = 58%). In our experience, any company with a gross margin above 50 percent is running an extremely inexpensive, or light, business. That was the case for Messages in 2001. How about 2002?

In 2002, the company drove gross profits higher, to $50.5 million on sales of $97 million. The rise in gross profits was substantial, up 74 percent. Many investors would wildly celebrate this climb. Ahh, but you'll note that gross margin actually *fell*. So, while sales and earnings rose, the level of profitability actually went the other way. Why did that happen? Maybe competition has prompted the company to cut prices. Maybe the only way that Messages can grow rapidly is by buying more expensive machinery and materials, thus driving higher its cost of doing business. Whatever the reason, the investing community may get jittery, even if the result was more gross profit for the company. You'll definitely want to study the gross margin of any company you consider for investment.

Before we go on to operating expenses, do you understand the relationships between sales, cost of sales, gross profit, and gross margin? It can tangle you up the first time through, but the concepts are pretty simple.

OPERATING EXPENSES AND OPERATING MARGIN

MESSAGES INC. STATEMENT OF INCOME

(IN THOUSANDS)	2002	2001	CHANGE
INCOME			
Revenue	97,000	50,000	94%
less Cost of sales (goods)	46,500	21,000	121%
GROSS PROFIT	50,500	29,000	74%
OPERATING EXPENSES			
Selling/general/administrative	27,500	12,000	129%
Research/development	4,500	6,000	(25%)
TOTAL OPERATING EXPENSES	32,000	18,000	78%
INCOME FROM OPERATIONS	18,500	11,000	68%

We'll start with the top entry in operating expenses, *Selling, general, and administrative expenses,* or *SG&A.* Even before defining that, we can't help but notice that it has exploded skyward in 2002—up 129 percent, to $27.5 million for the year. Scary, eh? Well, it might be, if you knew what the heck SG&A expenses are. So let's find out.

Selling, general, and administrative expenses include things like salary expenses—paying for software programmers, the overpaid management, and the underappreciated cleaning crew (say it with us now: "Yay, cleaning crew!"). It also includes the incidental costs of running a business. The huge expenses for the company's accountants and lawyers would fall into this category, as well as the expenses for keeping the lights on and the water flowing at Messages' headquarters. The costs associated with keeping the company's salespeople on the road looking for new opportunities fall under SG&A as well. These expenses don't involve the material product being sold itself, but arise from much of the business surrounding the product.

Drop down a line now to the *Research and development* costs. These are the expenses that fund Messages' scientists working overtime in two New Mexico laboratories to develop the next great medium for message distribution. Will it be Messages' chewing gum, melting on your tongue, not your fingers? Has Messages set up a high-tech system for the delivery of notes between bar patrons? Or is Messages developing encryption decoders for the CIA? Whatever the mission, these are all research and development (R&D) costs to the company.

Hey, it looks like we have some financial relief for Messages here. They successfully cut R&D costs by 25 percent. The company only had to pay out $4.5 million for research this year. Ahh, but is that really good? Not necessarily. Problems will arise if Messages resides in an ever-changing industry where new products in the pipeline are crucial to enduring success. Take the pharmaceutical industry. Drug makers can't sit still just because they created a concoction that successfully treats stomach acid. They must plow profits back into R&D to go in search of the *new* wonder drug. In Messages' case, by shortchanging their research and development efforts, the company successfully trimmed short-term costs but may have compromised its future. Falling R&D expenses are generally not something investors love.

OK, now add up SG&A and R&D (gotta love the acronyms!—by the way, what *does* "OK" stand for?) and you'll come up with the *Total operating*

expenses of the business. About now, if you haven't before, you should begin realizing how difficult it is to run a successful business, even in America. Even as sales rise dramatically, the material cost of those sales, the marketing and promotional expenses, and the ongoing expense of R&D can narrow profits down to not more than a razor's edge. And we haven't even gotten to taxes yet!

Now study the line dedicated to *Income from operations*. From operations last year, Messages made $11 million. In 2002, the company boosted operational profits to $18.5 million. But we can't hoohaah and celebrate yet, right? We have to calculate "operating margin." While gross margin represents money remaining after merely the cost of the product (or "cost of sales") is removed, operating margin shows the profitability after all of the daily expenses of running the business (SG&A) and expanding for the future (R&D) are subtracted as well. You calculate the operating margins by dividing income from operations (shown on the income statement) by total revenue. Perhaps read that again, slowly, and then use what you've just learned and calculate Messages' 2001 and 2002 operating margins!

CALCULATE OPERATING MARGINS

	2002	2001
Revenue	97,000	50,000
Income from operations	18,500	11,000
OPERATING MARGIN	____%	____%

Answers: 2002, 19.1%   2001, 22.0%

To repeat: Earlier we subtracted the cost of sales from revenue to obtain gross income, and divided that by revenue to get gross margin. Now we have subtracted the operating expenses as well to get operating income, and divided that by revenue to get operating margin. It's a mouthful, but not difficult.

There's only a little more before we get to the end of the income statement. Most companies also enjoy a dollop of income from interest on the company's cash sitting in the bank. (If the company has sizable debt, it will owe more interest than it collects, so this line will be *Interest expense* rather than *Interest income*.) For the years 2001 and 2002, Messages took in $1 million and $1.08 million, respectively, in interest income; thus, the final total for *Income before taxes* was $12 million in 2001 and $19.58 million in 2002. Now, close your eyes. Now open them. Poof! Who's that elderly gentleman in a white top hat, garbed in red and blue, and decked in stars? It's Uncle Sam, and he's here to collect income taxes!

INTEREST AND TAXES	2002	2001	CHANGE
Interest income	1,080	1,000	8%
Income before taxes	19,580	12,000	63%
less Income taxes	6,700	4,100	63%
NET INCOME	12,880	7,900	63%

The tax man takes his 34 percent cut, and Messages is left with profits, or *Net income,* of about $12.9 million in 2002, an increase of 63 percent over the previous year. Because earnings sit at the bottom of the income statement, after all costs have been removed, it's often referred to as "the bottom line." Stand up where you are and say it with us to be cool: "Messages Inc. had $12.9 million on the bottom line in 2002. Fire!" Got a few stares, eh? Sweet!

PROFIT MARGIN

You've mastered the gross margin, you've conquered operating margin, and now your fans want to see if you can figure what Messages' "profit margin" (also known as "net margin") is. We'll set you up helpfully, once again.

	2002	2001
Revenue	97,000	50,000
Net income	12,880	7,900
PROFIT MARGIN	___%	___%

Yes, simply divide net income by sales, and you've calculated the net margin. In 2001, Messages had net margin of 15.8 percent. In 2002, the company showed net margin of 13.3 percent. Just as we noted above, even as the company is selling more and more product, the level of final, bottom-line profitability on each sale is falling. The investing community much prefers to see rising margins. It usually indicates that the company is *(a)* selling its products at a higher price relative to cost (gross margin); *(b)* reducing operating costs as a percentage of sales (operating margin); *(c)* managing debt or cash better; or *(d)* some combination of the three. In general, it is a positive development. Investors love to see rising profit margins. Keep your eyes fixed on them.

EARNINGS PER SHARE

Think we're done with the income statement?

Almost, but not yet. Now we have to figure out *Earnings per share.* If you hold ten shares of Messages Inc., you'd like to know how much profit is backing each one of your shares. This is particularly important because in most quarters, the total number of shares that are publicly owned (a.k.a. shares outstanding) changes. Some companies use their cash to buy back shares in the marketplace and retire them, thus increasing the value of those shares that remain. Most companies, conversely, release more and more shares with time. They dole out employee and executive options, use shares to acquire smaller companies, or sell more shares to the public in a secondary offering. Thus, you'll need to keep your eye not just on the total profits but, most important, on the profits per share. Let's check in with Messages.

MESSAGES INC. STATEMENT OF INCOME

(IN THOUSANDS)

	2002	2001	CHANGE
NET INCOME	12,880	7,900	63%
Earnings per share	$1.07*	$0.79	35%
Basic shares outstanding	12,000	10,000	20%
Diluted shares outstanding	12,000	10,000	20%

* Net income and shares outstanding are in millions, while earnings per share is always an absolute dollar amount. Dividing net income by the shares outstanding gives you the earnings per share.

Huh? Messages has given us two sets of shares outstanding here—basic and diluted. It's OK, that's standard, and the difference between them is pretty straightforward. *Basic shares outstanding* is simply the number of shares of common stock the company has issued. They may have issued them in a variety of ways—direct sale to the public, options given to employees that have been exercised, convertible bonds that have converted, and so forth—but the bottom line is that these are the shares that are currently outstanding. *Diluted shares outstanding,* on the other hand, represents the basic shares outstanding plus any *potential* shares out there. This can include employee stock options that are "in the money" (that's the slick Street term for options with a purchase price lower than the current market price), convertible bonds still outstanding, and warrants the company has issued. We don't need to get into how it's all calculated; you get the general idea.

Which number do you want to use when calculating earnings per share? Typically, analysts and media folks will use the *diluted share* count. We prefer it because it gives us a better idea of how much our share of ownership may be diluted under current contracts. In Messages' case, however, it doesn't matter, since the two numbers are the same. Over the course of the year, Messages issued 2 million more shares. As we'll soon see on the cash flow statement, these shares came from a sale of shares to

the public, which is known as a *secondary public offering* for companies that are already public (that is, have already had their *initial public offering*).

Because of those additional shares, the company's profit increase of 63 percent became, for shareholders, an increase of only 35 percent—when measured in earnings per share. (Though the company pie was much bigger this year, a few more people got a slice of it.) To calculate earnings per share, remember, you just divide the total amount of bottom-line earnings (net income) by the total number of shares outstanding. Voilà, the company had $1.07 of earnings per share (EPS) this year, versus $0.79 in EPS last year. Now you'll know what investors are talking about when they say, "Hey, Apple Computer missed estimates by 10 cents." They didn't miss Wall Street's expectations by a mere dime, no! They missed them by 10 cents *per share.* And were that to happen to Apple, with its 350 million shares outstanding, it would translate into underperforming estimates by $0.10 × 350 million = $35 million. That dime sounds a lot more important now, doesn't it?

There you have Messages Inc.'s income statement for 2002. While the company reported sales growth of 94 percent, a good deal of that growth was lost on new expenses. Company profits increased only 63 percent, and the bottom-line EPS growth was just 35 percent. Rising expenses dragged down what might otherwise have been stratospheric gains, and a 20 percent jump in shares outstanding was a black eye for shareholders.

Quiz: The Income Statement

OK, let's see how good you are. Can you nail all seven of these questions?

1. If Messages were to report revenue of $126 million in the year 2003, versus the $97 million in 2002, how much would sales have risen?

   a. 15%
   b. 30%
   c. 43%
   d. 130%
   e. Who cares? All I know is this is more money than I have.

2. If cost of sales was $65 million in 2003, given $126 million in revenue, what would the gross profit be?

   a. $61 million
   b. $32 million
   c. $191 million
   d. $19 million
   e. 48.41289%

3. In that case, gross margin for 2003 would be

   a. 61%
   b. 58%
   c. 48%
   d. 52%
   e. You figure it out. You wrote this confusing book.

4. Selling, general, and administrative expenses for 2003 came in at $33 million, a 20 percent increase over the $27.5 million the year before. From question number 1's sales figures in 2003, SG&A expenses relative to those in 2002 were

   a. lower
   b. higher as a percentage of total sales
   c. lower as a percentage of total sales
   d. none of the above
   e. all of the above

5. Remember that in the year 2003, Messages announced sales of $126 million. Let's say earnings for the year were $14 million. What's the company's net margin?

   a. 10.2%
   b. 4.9%
   c. 9.4%
   d. 11.1%
   e. I hate this quiz and I'm burning your darn book.

6. Given your answer to question 5, do you think Wall Street will be happy with Messages' performance in the year 2003?

   a. Very much so, yes.
   b. Nope, it doesn't look good.
   c. You haven't given me enough info.
   d. I skipped the section on profit margin.
   e. I already burned your book.

7. Messages' net income came to $14 million in the year 2003. If this great American business had 12.5 million shares outstanding, EPS would then be

   a. $1.05
   b. $1.12
   c. $1.17
   d. $0.89
   e. My answer cannot be heard over the roar of the flames.

The answers to these problems: 1. *b* 2. *a* 3. *c* 4. *c* 5. *d* or *e* 6. *b* or *c* 7. *b*

In all seriousness, if you got any of these seven questions wrong, you should return to the beginning of this section on income statements. It's only a few pages, and getting it right might prove for you a difference between investing in a company with $17.4 million in net income and investing in another company with minus $17.4 million in net income (also known as "net *losses*"). And compounded over the rest of your life, the gains you can expect if you understand the income statement—and the balance sheet—can be dramatic.

Don't exhaust yourself trying to figure every single last thing out about a company. But, yes, you should get all seven of the above questions right before proceeding.

And once you've done so . . . onward! To the statement of cash flows.

STATEMENT OF CASH FLOWS

You have a firm grasp of the balance sheet; you've tackled an income statement; and now, to put it all together, we bring . . . the statement of cash flows. Cash flow, huh? What we'll be measuring here is the directional flow of cash into and out of Messages' business. We're tempted to play a trick on you and say something like, "This stuff is easy! You'll have it down in no time." The truth is that the cash flow statement is a tricky beast, but it is very important. Too many investors never look at it.

Take your first glance at Messages' statement of cash flows. Chances are you're going to be confused as heck. But we'll untangle it after the full presentation. Without further ado, voilà!

MESSAGES INC. STATEMENT OF CASH FLOWS

(IN THOUSANDS) CASH FLOW	2002	2001	CHANGE
CASH FLOW FROM OPERATING ACTIVITIES			
Net income	12,880	7,900	63%
ADJUSTMENTS TO RECONCILE NET INCOME TO NET CASH			
Depreciation	1,200	800	50%
EFFECTS OF CHANGE IN OPERATING ASSETS AND LIABILITIES			
Accounts receivable	(20,000)	(5,000)	300%
Inventory	(10,000)	(4,000)	150%
Accounts payable	3,300	2,000	65%
Accrued expenses	8,000	4,000	100%
NET CASH provided by (used in) operating activities	(4,620)	5,700	n/a
CASH FLOW FROM INVESTING ACTIVITIES			
Purchases of property, plant, and equipment	(3,000)	(1,500)	100%
Purchase of investments	(10,000)	(8,000)	20%
Sale of investments	12,500	5,000	150%
NET CASH provided by (used in) investing activities	(500)	(4,500)	n/a
CASH FLOWS FROM FINANCING ACTIVITIES			
Proceeds from debt	0	0	0%
Payments of debt	0	0	0%
Proceeds from sale of stock	11,620	0	n/a
NET CASH provided by (used in) financing activities	11,620	0	n/a
NET CHANGE IN CASH	6,500	1,200	442%

While it won't fetch much at the art gallery, it is certainly worth a look to see how much money came in, and how much came out, over the course of the past year. Earnings and cash flow are not the same thing. A company can report a loss in their income statement yet still have accumulated a positive net difference in cash from doing business. On the other hand, a company can report a gain but end up losing cash, or getting it from a source outside its business. We need to walk carefully through each section of the statement.

CASH FLOW FROM OPERATING ACTIVITIES

This is a key part of the cash flow statement. It outlines exactly how much cash the business brought in through operations. In many ways, this is what being in business is all about. It's not about borrowing money, it's not about selling property; it's about making cash money from what you are doing. It's surprising how many businesses don't. Let's see how it works.

NET INCOME

The first item on this shortened statement of cash flows is *Net income*. For those with a photographic memory, or if you're simply smart enough to thumb back to the previous "Income Statement" section and find the net income figure for 2002, you will see that they are both indeed the same $12.88 million figure. If only the whole statement were that easy to grasp. Mind bender oncoming. Do not operate heavy equipment while trying to think through the remainder of this section.

DEPRECIATION—WHAT'S THAT?

Below the restatement of $12.88 million in net income, you see the item *Depreciation* under the line *Adjustments* blah blah blah. It's listed as $1.2 million. *Depreciation* is the key word there, and gener-

ally you know that it means a sinking, or declining, in value. So why is $1.2 million *added* here? Well, because cash does not actually leave the company's coffers when depreciation is recorded.

Messages Inc. has accounted for the declining value of all of its equipment—much as you might recognize the declining value of your sharp new sports car. Those "expenses," however—which you'll often find in a line item on the income statement and subtracted from the *Property, plant, and equipment* item on the balance sheet—aren't real *cash* losses; they're *value* losses. The company already paid for that equipment, the cash is already gone, so the depreciating value isn't a cash loss today. The mission of the balance sheet is to track the *value* of the company's assets. The mission of the cash flow statement is to track the *cash* going in and out of the register. Thus, we need to add back in the $1.2 million in equipment value that was recognized as depreciating on the balance sheet.

You are with us, yes? OK, good. On to the next loop-de-loop on the roller coaster.

ACCOUNTS RECEIVABLE ON THE CASH FLOW STATEMENT

Do you remember, back on the balance sheet, how accounts receivable *rose* by $20 million in 2002? If not, well, they did. And do you remember how we claimed that, even though they're listed as current assets, with the company expecting to collect the cash in the year ahead, nevertheless we took rising receivables as a sign of weakness? Here comes further explanation of that.

On the cash flow statement, we're tracking the dollars in the here and now. We're studying the present flows of cash. Messages reported that *Accounts receivable* in 2002 were $34 million, $20 million higher than in 2001. (To avoid double counting, the cash flow statement concerns itself only with the difference since the last reporting period.) Because Messages doesn't yet have that additional $20 million, we have to subtract it from its net income. That's going to hurt. Why? Well, you see what's happened here, don't you? The company announced sales of $97 million and earnings of $12.88 million. But in those sales and earnings, there are millions in cash that the company has yet to collect. If that seems like a good thing, remember that Messages has already announced to the world that they have all those sales and earnings. Collecting the money is just a formality to Wall Street; to the company, it may be a challenge—if there are products returned, refunds, or insolvent business partners. So that additional $20 million in receivables in 2002 is going to significantly damage the present state of cash flows. Rises in accounts receivable are not a good thing. Messages' business is starting to look even wobblier.

INVENTORY

Receivables were bad enough, but we're not yet done subtracting.

In 2002, the company showed inventory growth of $10 million, to $20 million total. And you guessed it: though that inventory is listed as a current asset—since the company plans to sell it as finished product in the year ahead—it isn't yet cash. The cash flow statement, then, deducts that $10 million out of net income. And if you're thinking that's just too cruel to handle, remember that in a number of industries, businesses are unable to sell their inventory at various times. They have to dismantle it and sell it as scrap—even if that! So, the list of inventories as an asset on the balance sheet can be as misleading as the accounts receivable figures.

Because it ain't cash yet, inventories get subtracted out as well.

ACCOUNTS PAYABLE AND ACCRUED EXPENSES

Ahh, after all those subtractions, it's time for an addition or two. Let's sweeten up the statement by reflecting the monies that the company has saved by not yet paying all of its bills. *Accounts payable* of $3.3 million and *Accrued expenses* of $8 million are both liabilities that have yet to turn into an *outflow* of cash.

You grasp that concept, yes? The cash river flows both ways. We stick net income at the top; add back depreciation; pull out all the current assets that aren't cash; add back all the current liabilities that haven't been paid—and we end up with an understanding of flow of cash through operations. Is this company really making money? Or is it announcing earnings in the form of receivables, or riding heavy inventories—factors that aren't shown on the income statement? In the case of Messages, we'll soon see!

FINAL TALLIES

The end result of all our tallying falls down on the line *Net cash provided by (used in) operating activities*. This reveals whether the company wound up with more or less cash from their business operations over the course of the year. Uh-oh, in Messages' case, the results—a negative amount, as the parentheses indicate—weren't inspiring.

	2002	2001	CHANGE
NET CASH provided by (used in) operating activities	(4,620)	5,700	n/a

The company is consuming more cash than it is taking in. In 2001, cash flows were positive, by $5.7 million. But in 2002, they got loose with their receivables, let inventories spiral up, and ended up with negative cash flow of $4.62 million.

This should send flags and flares in the air and sound sirens. Negative operating cash flow is not necessarily the end of the world. At times, companies want to increase inventory. For example, a retail company has to increase its product count before Christmas. It doesn't want to sell out of Elmo dolls, so it mass-produces them. And when the balance sheet for that quarter arrives, the company may show a tremendous rise in inventory, but it isn't problematic. This is where your knowledge of the business comes into play. Not all of this stuff is quantitative.

All of that said, more often than not, rising receivables and inventory are signs of a problem, and you'll want to avoid companies (particularly unproven companies) with negative cash flows from operating activities.

OTHER SECTIONS ON THE CASH FLOW STATEMENT

The cash flow statement doesn't end with operating activities. The two sections remaining on a cash flow statement represent investing and financing activities. We'll take a quick look at them now.

CASH FLOWS FROM INVESTING ACTIVITIES

This section contains the company's investments in and sale of securities, joint business ventures, and capital equipment. We'll focus here on the concept of *free cash flow,* which represents cash left over after a company has met its basic obligations. Free cash flow is what's left over after all the necessary business expenses are funded—operations and purchases of plant, property, and equipment (a.k.a. capital expenditures). It is the money available to repurchase shares, pay down debt, or offer dividends. In some sense, it's the amount of money that the company gives back to you, its owner, in one form or another. A major part of valuation work involves estimating a company's sustainable cash flow, so this simple number is a good starting point for a valuation framework.

The basic formula for calculating free cash flow is

Free cash flow =
cash from operations − capital expenditures

MESSAGES' CASH FLOWS FROM INVESTING ACTIVITIES

(IN THOUSANDS)	2002	2001	CHANGE
Purchases of property, plant, and equipment	(3,000)	(1,500)	100%
Purchase of investments	(10,000)	(8,000)	20%
Sale of investments	12,500	5,000	150%
NET CASH provided by (used in) investing activities	(500)	(4,500)	n/a

Look back at the cash flow statement and plug in the numbers to figure out free cash flow. How much spare cash does Messages' business produce?

_____ (cash from operations) −

_____ (capital expenditures) = _____

As we saw, Messages used $4.62 million for operations. It also spent $3 million on additions to property, plant, and equipment. Two negatives equal . . . a bigger negative! Messages' free cash flow is negative $7.62 million. Yikes! For a company that announced $12.88 million in net income, that's not very good—in fact, it's a full $20.5 million worse.

One last note on this section. There are different definitions for free cash flow, many of which produce different results. There isn't agreement on this matter. One analyst may use a different measure of FCF than another. On this score, we can't give you a definite answer. Financial analysis isn't easy. Even the simple definition provided above often requires adjustments, which we can't cover in this space, and people argue a great deal about what those adjustments should be. Remember that your education on security analysis is an ongoing venture. Be ready and willing to grow past this simplistic level of analysis.

In fact, we face a puzzler right now. If Messages' free cash flow was negative, how is it that the company has more cash now than it did a year ago? Shouldn't it have a cash balance some $7.6 million *lower* than the previous year? Read on!

CASH FLOWS FROM FINANCING ACTIVITIES

Included under the financing section is money that flows between the company, creditors, and shareholders. If a company sells stock, it raises cash. If a company repurchases stock, it decreases cash. The same is true of debt. If a company issues debt, its cash balance rises. If a company retires debt—meaning it pays money back—cash falls. All of these activities, as well as the payment of dividends, are listed in the financing section.

If a company produces negative cash flow from operations and negative cash from investing activities, either it's getting financed by creditors and shareholders or it's going out of business. After reviewing the cash flow statement, you should know the sources of a company's funding.

MESSAGES' CASH FLOWS FROM FINANCING ACTIVITIES

(IN THOUSANDS)	2002	2001	CHANGE
Proceeds from debt	0	0	0%
Payments of debt	0	0	0%
Proceeds from sale of stock	11,620	0	n/a
NET CASH provided by (used in) financing activities	11,620	0	n/a

We already know that Messages has no debt—we found that out on its balance sheet. The cash flow statement gives confirmation. So where did the money come from? Remember the increased share count we saw on the income statement—12 million shares, as opposed to 10 million in 2001? It looks like some of that stock was sold to the public to raise money: $11.62 million, to be exact.

Let's review. Free cash flow was minus $7.62 million, but the cash balance at the company increased by $4 million. It looks like the company funded its activity with the sale of stock. That's not always a bad thing. When a company is starting up, it often needs to raise some cash through selling shares of itself. That's why companies go public in the first place. It's a valid source of funding, but it's not a *sustainable* source. Eventually, companies have to make money through operations. Messages was there in 2001, but it seems to have slipped in 2002. The result is that current owners saw the value of their shares diluted—not a pleasant experience.

WRAPPING UP CASH FLOW

In many ways, generally accepted accounting principles (the rules under which companies present their financial statements) are convoluted and byzantine. Sometimes they can be downright misleading. Your company may sell something and count it as revenue on the income statement, but not actually get paid for months. Assets can pile up on the balance sheet but have no actual asset value whatsoever. There are work-arounds and devices all over the income statement and balance sheet.

The cash flow statement, on the other hand, is subject to little manipulation. It records actually how much cash went in and came out, and the net result is right there, on the bottom line. Sure, there may be a few adjustments you'll want to make under some circumstances, but the cash flow statement shows you a much more definitive picture of a company's operational, investing, and financing activities than the other two financial statements. It's our favorite.

It's Time for a Parting Quiz!

OK, let's see how well you know your stuff.

1. Net income from the statement of cash flows will match net income from the income statement.

   a. True
   b. False.

2. On the cash flow statement, depreciation is subtracted from net income.

   a. True
   b. False

3. Accounts receivable and inventory items in the cash flow statement are taken from the income statement.

   a. True
   b. False

4. A negative amount (reflected by parentheses) on the operative activities line shows that a company spent more money to run their business than they made from it.

   a. True
   b. False

5. You can get a general idea of a company's ability to generate cash for shareholders by subtracting capital expenditures from operating cash flow.

   a. True
   b. False

Your answers? 1. *a* 2. *b* 3. *b* 4. *a* 5. *a*
To clarify 2 and 3: Depreciation is actually added back to cash (2). And the accounts receivable and inventory numbers are drawn from the balance sheet, not the income statement (3).

OK, so this wasn't as painful as expected, was it? We've just successfully covered the balance sheet, income statement, and statement of cash flows. If you're a common Fool, there's a pretty good chance you had no idea what payables were when you started, or why inventory growth at a business can be a bad thing, or how to calculate earnings per share, or whether a company with positive earnings on the income statement was actually making money over on the statement of cash flows.

Now, we don't expect all of this to have formally settled in, finally congealed, and be irremovable from your head, barring surgery or a bad skiing accident. For many of you, this is just the beginning, and you really should take an hour or two to go back over this chapter to be absolutely certain you grasped it all. From here, you're going to want to get your hands on the financial statements of some companies out there. How about Starbucks, Nike, AOL Time Warner, Intel, and Harley-Davidson? It might be interesting to see how they're doing, eh? Just grab their phone number from their website, give their investor relations department a call, have them send you an investor's packet, and sort through the statements. Better yet, look for the link on their webpage marked "Investor Relations" and find their financials directly online! We recommend printing off a copy rather than marking up your computer screen with calculations. What you'll find will startle you. Not all businesses are rock solid. Some are greatly mismanaged. Yes, some of the very products and services you use are from companies managed by folks who may end up destroying the business. Of course, for most others, studying them, following them, and investing in them will prove a greatly profitable venture for you in the years ahead.

Now, get your hands on your calculator, take a few deep breaths, run a lap around the block, call your uncle and brag to him how much you know, fix a large glass of lemonade, take another couple of deep breaths, make sure you're still holding that calculator, and get ready for the next section. 'Cause when you turn the page, we're going to start learning how to value entire businesses and determine which companies will make great investments and which won't. Remember, had your family invested $3,000 into Coca-Cola in 1919, when it went public, and then followed the company's financial reports and rightly held on to the stock throughout, their stock would be valued above $300 million— after paying down all taxes. Wow.

You'll want to learn how to value companies. You'll want to find the next Coca-Colas and Microsofts. And who knows, the next ones may be Coca-Cola and Microsoft. Let's see!

CHAPTER 7

NOW, WHAT DO I WANT TO SEE IN THOSE NUMBERS?

It's good to see you're still with us. In fact, you're even having a little fun, aren't you? C'mon now, admit it! Learning to invest can be an enjoyable pastime for those inclined toward it. It is not a mystery that has to be left to the professionals. On the contrary, the fact is that the majority of mutual funds and money managers lose to the market each year, while charging considerably more on par than the index fund. The index fund is all you need to be a successful investor. You can simply pour money into it regularly and be secure that, in twenty years, you will have beaten other investment vehicles and more investing professionals. Why go any further?

Yet you kept reading and scribbling. You want to take your knowledge of investing to the next level. You can do it; successful investing relies primarily on the proper understanding of basic mathematics and basic principles of business. You want to learn about business. You want to learn how to value individual stocks. You want to determine whether or not to buy more of the stock of your employer. You want to own the greatest companies on the planet, hold them for decades, and turn a couple of thousand bucks into a couple of million bucks by the time you retire, or your kids retire, or their kids. To

get there, you need only add 6 + 17 successfully (23). You need only multiply 12 × 2.6 (31.2). You need only divide 178 by 14 (12.7). Mostly, you'll just need to keep your eyes and mind open. The future of your financial situation rests more on these abilities than on working triple overtime next month or inheriting a whole mess of money from your great-uncle Cornelius. So, let's ask again: is it time for you to step beyond the index fund and start investing in individual stocks? Let's see.

THREE QUICK QUIZZES

Quiz #1: Why Invest in Individual Stocks?

a. Because I might make a lot of money in the next year.
b. Because there's no other alternative. I have to be in stocks.
c. Because if I'm methodical, I may beat the index funds that beat the majority of managed funds.

Your answer here is c. Chances are you won't make much money at all in your first year of investing. You'll still be learning, and you'll probably make plenty of mistakes. And there certainly are other alternatives to common stock. Index funds are a great way to begin investing. Nope, we believe the right answer is that, with method and resolve, private investors can manage to outperform the market over the long term.

Quiz #2: Why Analyze Individual Companies?

a. To understand how business works and to locate the best investment options.

b. Because I have to; I'm paying $40,000 per year to get this freakin' MBA.

c. I don't have to; I can make enough money just buying hot stocks and selling them a month later, using my stock chart analysis and watching the phases of the moon.

We hope you said a. We're making these too easy. We obviously don't think you need an MBA to be introduced to business, and we think it's a very bad idea to apply to investing the mystical art called "technical analysis"—studying the movement of the stock price with charts rather than understanding the merits of the business for the long term.

Quiz #3: Pick Your Preferred Lifestyle

a. Spending thirty minutes per year investing in an index fund, smiling at all the hullabaloo over managed mutual funds, and going on with life.

b. Spending a few hours a week researching companies, starting an investment club with your entire family or a close group of friends, and trying to beat the market's return.

c. Spending all your spare time poring over research reports, reading trade magazines, and studying the art of security analysis.

As you probably guessed, there's no "right" answer to this one. It's just a matter of personal choice. Let's continue on as we try to determine the level of involvement in investing that will make your life happier.

CAN YOU REALLY BEAT THE PROS?

Is it really possible for an individual investor to outperform the Wall Street professionals, who manage billions of dollars? We'll answer this one: *yes.* They may have teams of researchers; they may buy up reams of business information; they may even have the power to dramatically affect (read: manipulate) pricing in the marketplace over any short period of time, but despite all this, the big mutual fund families and brokerage houses ain't ten-ton gorillas and you ain't their banana.

Bigger isn't better in investing. If you were managing a $500 million mutual fund, you'd probably have a lot of anxious shareholders holding you accountable every week. And you'd have a host of SEC guidelines to abide by—which would dictate that you couldn't invest in just five great companies (like General Electric, Microsoft, Coca-Cola, Merck, and Intel). No, you'd have to buy dozens of companies, and you'd probably feel compelled to buy hundreds of companies. If you were willing to trade frenetically and generate huge commissions in Manhattan, big Wall Street firms would reward you. But would that necessarily be beneficial to your investors? Their management fees would rise; their taxes would rise; and their overall return would most likely go down! This is precisely the reason that most managed mutual funds underperform the market each year.

Believe it or not, when it comes to beating the market, the big institutional investor is at a substantial disadvantage to the small private investor, both because of how they are compensated *and* for the logistical nightmares they face in trying to manage such large sums of money. We've said that again, but you probably don't yet believe it. Do you?

Yes   No

OK, well, we'll try to provide more evidence in the pages ahead.

WHAT YOU WANT TO SEE ON A BALANCE SHEET

If you're committed to finding great companies and investing in them, it's time for us to state clearly what you should actively seek out on financial statements. We've talked about inventories and receivables. We've championed those businesses that avoid debilitating levels of long-term debt. Here now is what you should hope to find when you're studying the report of a company that you're considering for investment. (This will also effectively serve as a review of the terms and numbers introduced in the last chapter.)

Once again, we're going to call on the help of our fictitious friends at Messages Inc. to aid us in our explanation. Below is the company's balance sheet.

MESSAGES INC. BALANCE SHEET—YEAR 2002 COMPARED TO 2001

(IN THOUSANDS) ASSETS	2002	2001	CHANGE
CURRENT ASSETS			
Cash and equivalents	24,000	20,000	20%
Accounts receivable	34,000	14,000	143%
Inventory	20,000	10,000	100%
Prepaid expenses	1,500	1,000	50%
TOTAL CURRENT ASSETS	79,500	45,000	77%
FIXED ASSETS			
Property, plant, and equipment, net	10,800	5,200	108%
TOTAL ASSETS	90,300	50,200	80%
LIABILITIES			
CURRENT LIABILITIES			
Short-term debt	0	0	0%
Accounts payable	6,500	3,200	103%
Accrued expenses	18,000	10,000	80%
TOTAL CURRENT LIABILITIES	24,500	13,200	86%
Long-term debt	0	0	0%
TOTAL LIABILITIES	24,500	13,200	86%
SHAREHOLDER EQUITY	65,800	37,000	78%

Here are some of the things you should be looking for . . .

1. LOTS OF CASH

Cash-rich companies don't have trouble funding growth, paying down debts, and doing whatever the heck it is they need to build the business. Increasing cash and equivalents is good. Messages has $24 million in cash, up from $20 million a year ago.

2. A LOW FLOW RATIO

Here, as you learned earlier, you simply subtract cash from current assets, then divide that figure by current liabilities. You'll prefer the flow to be below 1.25, which would indicate that the company is aggressively managing its cash flows. Inventories are down, receivables are down, and payables are up. This is a perfect mix when a company has loads of cash and no long-term debt. Why? Because it indicates that while the company could (1) afford to pay bills today and (2) doesn't have to worry about rising receivables, they are in enough of a position of power to hold off their payments and collect all dues up front.

Messages has current assets of $79.5 million and $24 million in cash. So subtract the latter from the former, to arrive at $55.5 million. Messages has $24.5 million in current liabilities. Divide the $55.5 million in noncash assets by the $24.5 million of liabilities, and you'll arrive at a flow ratio of 2.26. We consider this high. Another red light whirs on the balance sheet. It must be noted here, however, that larger companies generally have lower flow ratios due to their ability to negotiate from strength. Thus, don't penalize your favorite dynamically growing small-cap too much for a higher Foolish flow ratio.

3. MANAGEABLE DEBT AND A REASONABLE DEBT-TO-EQUITY RATIO

Investors have very different attitudes toward debt. Some shun it, choosing to not invest in companies with any or much debt. This is fine and can result in highly satisfactory investment performance results. But debt shouldn't be viewed as completely evil. Used properly and in moderation, it can help a company achieve greater results than if no debt is taken on.

Think about our own lives. Yes, there are some kinds of debt that you should avoid. Credit card debt, for example, can be extremely hard to dig out from, especially when you're paying 18 percent per year. But without mortgage debt, very few people would own their own homes. Without student loans, competition would be stiff for burger-flipping jobs. Without car loans, buses would be crowded. When managed responsibly, debt can be a good thing.

Debt can be good for companies, too. Imagine a firm that has a reliable stream of earnings. Let's say that it raises $100 million by issuing some corporate bonds that pay 8 percent interest. If the company knows that it earns about 12 percent on the money it invests in its business, then the arrangement should be a very lucrative one.

Note, though, that the more debt you take on, the greater your interest expense will be. And this can eat into your profit margins. At a certain point, a company can have too much debt for its own good. Another feature of debt (or "leverage") is that it magnifies gains and losses (just as buying stock on margin means that your gains or losses will be magnified). Debt, like anything, is best taken in moderation.

To finance their operations, companies need sources of capital. Some companies can survive and grow simply on the earnings they generate. Others issue bonds, borrow from banks, issue stock, or sell a chunk of the company to a few significant investors. The combined ways that a company finances its operations is called its "capital structure." If you take the time to evaluate a company's debt, it could be worth your while. Properly managed debt can enhance a company's value.

CALCULATING THE DEBT-TO-EQUITY RATIO

Without further ado, here's our friend the *debt-to-equity ratio*. Note that you'll want to use *average* numbers. This is because numbers from the balance sheet reflect a moment in time. You want your ratio to cover a period of time, such as a fiscal year or quarter, rather than just a moment.

To calculate average long-term debt, take long-term debt from the beginning of the period you're considering and also from the end of the period, and average them (adding them and dividing by two). Do the same to calculate average shareholder equity. (If you're working with an annual report, you can use the numbers for the most recent fiscal year and the previous fiscal year.) After that, you can calculate the debt-to-equity ratio for Messages.

$$\text{Average long-term debt} = (0 + 0) \div 2 = 0$$

$$\text{Average shareholder equity} = (37{,}000 + 65{,}800) \div 2 = 51{,}400$$

$$\text{Average long-term debt} \div$$
$$\text{average shareholder equity} =$$
$$\text{debt-to-equity ratio } 0 \div 51{,}400 = 0$$

The exercise was a bit unnecessary, since we knew all along that Messages has no long-term debt. It was kind of fun to run through it, though, wasn't it? What, are we the only geeks here?

When you calculate debt-to-equity ratios for your companies, remember that there really isn't a right or wrong number. You just want to make sure that the company has some assets on which to leverage its debt. To that end, look for low numbers, ideally. A debt-to-equity ratio of 0.05 isn't necessarily better than one of 0.15, but 0.65 is probably more appealing than 1.15. You should also evaluate the quality of the debt and what

it's being used for. If you see debt levels spiking upward, make sure you research why. Certainly, long-term debt can be *used* intelligently. But in our experience, the companies in the very strongest position are those that don't need to borrow to fund the development of their business. We prefer those companies with a great deal more cash than long-term debt.

Are any of our balance sheet guidelines hard-and-fast rules? Nope. We can imagine reasonable explanations for each. As we mentioned earlier, a company can run inventories very high relative to sales in a quarter, as they prepare for the big Christmas rush, for example. Wouldn't want too few moon boots going into mid-December, right? So, inventories may be seasonally inflated (or deflated) in anticipation of great oncoming demand. And accounts receivable may be a tad high simply by virtue of when a company closed out its quarter. Perhaps the very next day, 75 percent of those receivables will arrive by wire transfer. Here, the calendar timing of its quarterly announcement hurt your company. Rising payables can also be a very bad thing. If the company is avoiding short-term bills because it can't afford to pay them, look out! Finally, flow ratios can run high for all the reasons listed above.

Having qualified our assertions, we still believe that the best businesses have such high ongoing demand that inventories race out the door, product distributors pay for the merchandise up front, the company has enough cash to pay off payables immediately but doesn't, and future growth hasn't been compromised by present borrowing. Look to companies like Coca-Cola and Microsoft to find these qualities fully realized.

WHAT YOU WANT TO SEE ON THE INCOME STATEMENT

Once again we turn to our friends at Messages Inc. to investigate what we should hope to find on the income statement of any company whose stock we're considering.

MESSAGES INC. INCOME

(IN THOUSANDS)	2002	2001	CHANGE
INCOME			
Revenue	97,000	50,000	94%
Cost of sales (goods)	46,500	21,000	121%
GROSS PROFIT	50,500	29,000	74%
OPERATING EXPENSES			
Selling/general/administrative	27,500	12,000	129%
Research/development	4,500	6,000	(25%)
TOTAL OPERATING EXPENSES	32,000	18,000	78%
INCOME FROM OPERATIONS	18,500	11,000	68%
Interest income	1,080	1,000	8%
Income before taxes	19,580	12,000	63%
Income taxes	6,700	4,100	63%
NET INCOME	12,880	7,900	63%

Here's what you should be looking for . . .

1. HIGH REVENUE GROWTH

You'll want to see substantial and consistent top-line growth, indicating that the planet wants more and more of what your company has to offer. Annual revenue growth in excess of 8–10 percent per year for companies with more than $5 billion in yearly sales is ideal. Smaller companies ought be growing sales by 20–30 percent or more annually. Messages posted 94 percent sales growth for 2002. Outstanding.

2. COST OF SALES UNDER WRAPS

The *Cost of sales (goods)* figure should be growing no faster than the *Revenue* line. Ideally, your company will be meeting increasing demand by supplying products at the same cost as before. In fact, best of all, if your company can cut the cost of goods sold during periods of rapid growth, bravo! It indicates that the business can get its materials or provide its services cheaper in higher volume. In Messages' case, cost of goods sold rose by 121 percent in 2002, outpacing sales growth. A red light just blinked from the income statement.

3. GROSS MARGIN ABOVE 40 PERCENT

We prefer to invest in companies with extraordinarily high gross margin—again, calculated by (a) subtracting cost of goods sold (cost of sales) from total sales, to get gross profit, then (b) dividing gross profit by total sales. That line was a brainful, eh? OK, let's check out Messages.

Sales	$97 million
Cost of goods sold	$46.5 million
GROSS PROFIT	$50.5 million
GROSS MARGIN	_____

Getcher calculator buzzing! Divide gross profit by total sales to get gross margin. For Messages, you'll end up with 52 percent. This indicates that there is only moderate material expense to the Messages business. It's a "light" business. We like that.

Not all businesses are this light, of course. Many manufacturing companies have a hard time hitting this target, as do many retailers. Does that mean you should never invest in them? No. Does it mean you should have a slight bias against them in favor of higher-margin companies, all other things being equal? Yeah.

4. RESEARCH AND DEVELOPMENT COSTS ON THE RISE

Yep, we actually want our companies to spend more and more on research every year, particularly those in high technology and pharmaceuticals. This is the biggest investment in the future that a company can make. And the main reason businesses spend less on R&D one year than the last is that they need the money elsewhere. Not a desirable situation to be in. Look for R&D costs rising. Of course, though, not all companies spend much on R&D. A kiss is still a kiss, a Coke is still a Coke.

Generally, the best way to go about measuring

R&D is as a percentage of sales. You just divide R&D by revenue. You want to see this figure trend upward, or at least hold steady.

5. A 34 PERCENT–PLUS TAX RATE

Make sure that the business is paying the full rate to Uncle Sam. Due to previous earnings losses, some companies can carry forward up to a few years of tax credits. While this is a wonderful thing for them, it can cause a misrepresentation of the true bottom-line growth. If companies are paying less than 34 percent per year in taxes, you should tax their income at that rate, to see through to the real growth. Messages paid a 35.5 percent tax rate on earnings in 2002. Brush by this one, then.

6. PROFIT MARGIN ABOVE 7 PERCENT AND RISING

How much money is your company making for every dollar of sales? The profit margin—net income divided by sales—tells you what real merit there is to the business. We prefer businesses with more than $5 billion in sales to run a profit margin above 7 percent, and those with less than $5 billion to sport a profit margin of above 10 percent. Why go through all the work of running a business if out of it you can't derive substantial profits for your shareholders? In the case of Messages Inc., net margin is running at 13.3 percent ($12.88 million earnings ÷ $97 million in sales = 13.3%). Excellent.

Another way of thinking about this is that in a capitalistic world, high margins—highly profitable businesses—lure competition. Others will move in and attempt to undercut a company's prices. So companies that can post high margins are *winning;* competition is failing to undercut them. As with gross profits above, some industries do not lend themselves to a high profit margin. Costco, for example, is unlikely to ever show high profits, but it remains a wonderful company.

WHAT YOU WANT TO SEE ON THE CASH FLOW STATEMENT

The most important thing to find out from the cash flow statement is whether the line dedicated to *Net cash provided by (used in) operating activities* is positive or negative. If a company is cash flow negative, it means that these guys are burning capital to keep their business going. This is excusable over short periods of time, but by the time companies make it into the public marketplace, they should be generating profits off their business. If a company you are studying is cash flow negative, it's critical that you know why that's occurring. Perhaps it has to ramp up inventories for the quarter, or had a short, not-to-be-repeated struggle with receivables. Some companies are best off burning capital for a short-term period, while they ramp up for huge business success in the future. But if the only reason you can find is that their business isn't successful and doesn't look to be gaining momentum, you should steer clear of that investment.

You now have a fine checklist of things to look for (and hope for) on the balance sheet, income statement, and statement of cash flows. Few companies are ideal enough to conform to our every wish. The best businesses show financial statements strengthening from one quarter to the next. For smaller companies with great promise and for larger companies hitting a single bad bump in the road, shortcomings in the financial statements can be explained away for a brief period. But when you do accept these explanations, be sure you're getting the facts. You want to thoroughly understand why there has been a slipup and do your best to assess whether or not it's quickly remediable.

All of that noted, let's practice on some calculations. In the next chapter, we'll begin digging in closer toward valuation. You'll note that, up until now, we've merely outlined the ideal characteristics, without ever putting a price tag on them. That's coming. But first, let's make sure you've nailed down our basic concepts.

Quiz: Basic Concepts

1. Assume that the S&P 500 rose 10.29% last year. Which of the following would you expect to be the performance of average managed mutual funds for the year?

a. 12.49%
b. 19.42%
c. 10.34%
d. 9.11%

2. Which of the following situations is preferable?

	CASH	LONG-TERM DEBT
a. Otter World	$145 million	$11.4 million
b. Jefe Airlines	$891 million	$3.9 billion
c. Orangeblood Beachwear	$11 million	$4.6 million
d. Hoop-It-Up Inc.	$321 million	$0

3. What is Orangeblood Beachwear's gross margin?

Sales	$85 million
Cost of goods sold	$35 million
Gross profit	$50 million
Gross margin	_____

4. Calculate the flow ratio for Hoop-It-Up Inc.

Cash	$321 million
Current assets	$853 million
Short-term debt	$0
Current liabilities	$615 million
flow ratio	_____
Is that good?	_____

5. What is the sales growth for Otter World?

	1999	2000
Sales	$584 million	$618 million

Sales growth from 1999 to 2000 _____ %

6. Given the size of Otter World, is that sales growth substantial enough to put you up on your office desk, cheering?

Yes   No

7. Take a look at Otter's growth in research and development. Is this a good trend?

	R&D Expenses
1996	$9.4 million
1997	$12.5 million
1998	$22.4 million
1999	$34.5 million
2000	$51.3 million

Yes   No

8. Calculate Otter's net profit margin for 2000.

Sales	$618 million
Cost of goods sold	$246 million
R&D expenses	$51 million
SG&A expenses	$237 million
Total operating expenses	$534 million
Total operating income before taxes	$84 million
Provision for taxes	$31 million
Net income	$53 million
EPS	$0.58
Shares outstanding	91.4 million
Profit margin	_____

9. In question number 8, do you understand every single term?

Yes   No

10. If you knew that Otter's gross margin in 1999 was 46.4%, what would you be thinking while looking over the 2000 statement?

a. Gasp, gross margin has remained the same, and that's not a good thing.
b. OK, so we're making more money here. Good job!
c. I haven't a clue what you're talking about, Fool.
d. I'm not happy about this; gross margin is falling.

Without being too preachy, if you got any of these ten questions wrong, you should work your way back through this chapter. It will take you only an hour or so, and it might result in a substantial difference in your savings ten years from today. Here are your answers: 1. *d* 2. *d* 3. 58.8% 4. 0.87, Yes 5. 5.8% 6. No 7. Yes 8. 8.6% 9. Yes 10. *d*

And if you nailed them all, Fool on. Let's go fishing for some companies! Afterward, we'll start talking about some other ways to evaluate companies.

CHAPTER 8

LOCATING WINNING STOCKS

Remember when we sent you searching through your refrigerator and your neighborhood, looking for great businesses? Well, of course that's the first place we search for *market-beating companies*—among those businesses that sit all around you. Giant consumer businesses that provide us with the stuff we need in our daily lives often make wonderful investments. Campbell Soup? That was a great investment over the last twenty years. The Gap? Another great long-term investment. Coca-Cola? Perhaps the greatest business and greatest investment of the twentieth century. Truly, most of the greatest investments you'll make in your lifetime are no more than an arm's length away.

For this reason, it bewilders us that so many Americans rely on hot tips from phone-calling brokers and cocktail party experts, that so many people invest in obscure mining companies or shady limited partnerships. They've been misled into thinking that obscurity, not simplicity, is the mother of ingenuity. Pshaw! Among Warren Buffett's key holdings at Berkshire Hathaway are Coca-Cola, Gillette, and American Express. Buffett did not create his holding company empire by searching for obscure businesses about which he knew very little, hoping to

get lucky. Instead, he looked around at the products and services he knew something about, used simple mathematical principles to help him evaluate the merit of the business, and treated investing as a life-long endeavor. Want a reason to get out your calculator and do a little homework every time one of the companies that you encounter every day catches your eye? Berkshire Hathaway, essentially an insurance corporation that provides funds for investment to Buffett, is valued at over $110 billion as of this writing. Let's see how we can follow this example.

WHAT SHOULD YOU BE LOOKING FOR?

1. CONSUMER BRAND

The first question you'll need to ask yourself is, Is this a name-brand company? There are literally hundreds of products and dozens of companies that provide you with brand-name stuff—from soda to antifreeze, from newspapers to personal computers, from cold medicine to dairy products. You'll want to start by listing the favorite products you use, much as you did here previously. In addition, please note the parent company of the product. Here are five examples. After them, list six of your own.

Product	Company
Doritos	Pepsi
Windows XP	Microsoft
Chicken McNuggets	McDonald's
American Express card	American Express
Saturn	General Motors
_____	_____
_____	_____
_____	_____
_____	_____
_____	_____
_____	_____

looking for the largest threat to the entire business. In that case, Coke is it.

Please list what you consider to be the largest competitor to the businesses you've listed.

Company	Competition
Pepsi	Coca-Cola
Microsoft	IBM
McDonald's	Diageo (Burger King)
American Express	Citigroup
General Motors	Ford
_____	_____
_____	_____
_____	_____
_____	_____
_____	_____
_____	_____

2. BEST IN THE BUSINESS

Now we're going to ask you to make a qualitative judgment call. Are the companies that you've listed above the best in their business? Possibly you have no idea. But guess what? That's the second challenge facing you. For now, just list the lead competition of each of your companies. Do not worry about who competes directly with the product you like; instead, concentrate on the largest direct competitor of the company. What do we mean by that? Well, we started by listing Doritos. We then noted the company, Pepsi. But now we place to their right their most substantial competitor—Coca-Cola—which does not make any snack food products. We're

Now think through your list again. Do you think you have the premiere brand between the two? In *our* case, we're going to supplant Pepsi with Coca-Cola, even though we know that might make a lot of people unhappy at Pepsi headquarters in Texas. At present, Coca-Cola is the leading brand. Please circle only the six top brands on your list.

Now, heck, let's try to shorten our list even more.

3. REPEAT BUSINESS

From here you'll want to narrow your list down to account for only those companies that you regularly do business or come into contact with. What you will find is that typically the greatest businesses on the planet are those that constantly deal with their customers and repeatedly make a positive impression. The single greatest example of this is Coca-Cola, which gets free advertising each time you open up a big red can. Microsoft greets millions of people each day when they flip on their computer. You almost can't drive down the street without encountering McDonald's golden arches. And these have naturally been among the greatest companies to invest in. They make contact with their customers every month, week, or, ideally, day.

Please now shorten your list to include only those companies that meet your eye at least once a month. Cross off your list those that don't make it.

COMPANY

Coca-Cola
Microsoft
McDonald's
American Express
General Motors
_____
_____
_____
_____
_____

Now you have our five stocks and a collection of your own. Let's run a few numbers!

4. PROFIT MARGIN ABOVE 7 PERCENT

Aha, remember profit margin? Among these very large consumer businesses, we're going to demand profit margins of at least 7 percent. This means that, after taxes, they make 7 cents in earnings on every $1 of sales. We don't want to hitch our wagons to businesses that haven't figured ways to generate substantial profits. When a businessman buys a major-league baseball team, he wants the value of that team to increase as they sell more season tickets, more hot dogs and soda, more T-shirts and ball caps. The value of the team increases as the profits increase. So, too, with your investment in a public company. Let's make sure we have companies earning at least 7 cents on every dollar.

How? The best way, so that you can be sure of the source, is to calculate it for yourself. It's not hard, if you read the last chapter carefully (you did, didn't you?). Simply find the net income figure for the last twelve months and divide that by sales. You can find the data in the company's recent financial statements (remember to add up the last four quarters) or simply from the stock's profile on Yahoo!

Here's what we came up with for the first five—which will be out of date by the time you read this:

COMPANY	PROFIT MARGIN
Coca-Cola	16.1%
Microsoft	30.5%
McDonald's	12.5%
American Express	9.2%
~~General Motors~~	~~1.1%~~

_____   _____

_____   _____

_____   _____

_____   _____

_____   _____

Lookie there, GM with only 1.1% margin is scratched out, four of our five businesses are still alive. It almost makes you wonder if we knew the characteristics in advance of our submissions! OK, so how many companies remain from your original list?

5. MORE CASH THAN DEBT

We also don't want to invest in companies that are forced to shoulder loads of long-term debt to fund new ventures. This is perhaps the trickiest of all our demands, since in many cases, larger companies can borrow money at very low rates. Additionally, there are instances where companies borrow billions of dollars to maximize future growth, feeling very strongly that carrying the debt won't be difficult. McDonald's is a case in point. It felt that it could afford to carry a large debt load, since it has the assets to do so and the free cash flow to pay it off when it needs to. It may well be right, but that debt may put McDonald's at some risk in a serious economic or brand downturn.

So it almost seems unfair to cross McDonald's off the list, just because they have more debt than cash. But you know what, we're looking for the strongest consumer businesses on the planet. In most cases, they have so much cash saved up that they don't have to borrow. We're going to stick to our guns and save for consideration only those large consumer businesses that have more moolah than debts outstanding.

And how do you determine how much cash and how much debt your selections have? Follow the same steps suggested above: check a recent balance sheet from a 10-K or 10-Q, or check Yahoo! OK, excellent, you got the information. Draw a line through any companies that don't meet the criterion of more savings than borrowed money.

COMPANY	CASH	DEBT
Coca-Cola	$2.7 billion	$1.4 billion
Microsoft	$31.6 billion	$0
~~McDonald's~~	~~$440 million~~	~~$8.6 billion~~
American Express	$11.8 billion	$7.7 billion

_____   _____

_____   _____

_____   _____

_____   _____

_____   _____

6. PAST PERFORMANCE

This final one is truly contrary because we live in a world where legal disclaimers must state that "past performance is no guarantee of future results." It seems some corporate executives got a little bold with their predictions for growth and some activist shareholders felt that was unfair, and some enterprising lawyers found ways to profit off the debate. The consequence has been an ever-so-slight move away from believing that great companies often get greater over time, while weak businesses often weaken. We think it makes a good deal of sense to know exactly how well companies have performed when you invest in them.

Certainly, there are damaged businesses that, after a difficult decade, turn everything around. But a good general point of reference is how well the company has done over the past ten years. We like to see market-beating performance.

So how do you figure how well your companies have done over the past ten years? You can look in your local library's edition of *Value Line,* the thick and imposing green book full of business and investment statistics for thousands of corporations. You can also call the company and ask. You can look at a bunch of different sources on the Internet, including the company's website or Fool.com. For a general impression, there are some charts on the Internet that will show you a decade's return. You got the numbers already? Great. Fill 'em in!

COMPANY	10-YEAR TOTAL PERFORMANCE
Coca-Cola	+ 230%
Microsoft	+ 1,280%
American Express	+ 380%
S&P 500	+ 230%
_____	_____
_____	_____
_____	_____
_____	_____
_____	_____
_____	_____

We do not think it's a good idea to cross companies off this list unless they've dramatically under-performed the S&P 500. Chances are, the stock price has bounced up and down over the years. In fact, as of this writing, Coca-Cola—the one company on our list that has not beaten the market over the past ten years—had not appreciated at all in the last five years, which let the market catch up on Coke's big lead. So, past-ten-year performance is important just to provide you with some context. It's not a must.

CONCLUDING THOUGHTS ON MARKET-BEATING GIANTS

Let's take a look at the final three stocks that made it through our gauntlet: Microsoft, Coca-Cola, and American Express. Each of these businesses is familiar to almost every American; each of them is best of breed in their industry; each has frequent and repeated contact with its customers; each has a healthy profit margin; none has more debt than cash; and all have performed remarkably over the last five years.

The reason these are great stocks and great companies is that the principles outlined above make sense. These companies generate extraordinary earnings by serving people across the planet on a regular basis. If any stock on your beginning list made it through the gauntlet, think very seriously about doing more research on that business and adding it to your portfolio for the long run, if it passes muster. The very best place for you to start—and possibly finish—as an investor in common stocks is with those companies that you and everyone know, that you believe provide useful products and services, that are fiscally responsible, and that have been successful.

With a bit of money in an index fund and a bit of money in large-cap consumer heavies, we don't necessarily think you need anything else in your investment portfolio. With these, you'll be invested in the five hundred companies on the S&P 500 Index and you'll have a handful of name-brand giants pumping out growth for you across the globe.

RULE MAKERS

The qualities we just mentioned provide a good first screen for companies that we have dubbed "Rule Makers." This type of company is the king of the hill, the largest, most powerful company not only in its sector but also in the world. We have made Rule Maker investing a central tenet of Foolishness, both in an online real money portfolio with the same name and in our best-selling book (hint, hint) *Rule Breakers, Rule Makers*. The Rule Maker strategy is built upon the idea that individuals should have at least a portion of their portfolio dedicated to rock-solid companies that they plan not to sell for five to ten years or longer. This buy-and-hold model limits the commission, tax, and opportunity costs of investing.

The quintessential Rule Making company is one that manufactures products and provides services bought every day or every week by tens of millions of people the world over. This repeated sale of the same profitable item results in the methodical accumulation of a mother lode of cash on a Rule Maker's balance sheet. But a Rule Maker is more than just an industry leader. Certain industries don't yet (and may never) offer the sort of company that would attract smart investment money. For instance, to an investor, the leading maker of sewing machines is likely far less attractive than America's third-best pharmaceutical business. Some industries will create no Rule Makers, while others may house a half dozen. Finding Rule Makers is more about finding the appropriate business model for long-term investment than it is about picking the leaders in each category.

There are ten characteristics that we consider for a worthy Rule Maker investment candidate.

1. AT LEAST ONE SUSTAINABLE COMPETITIVE ADVANTAGE—AND THE MORE, THE BETTER

A company with a sustainable competitive advantage has differentiated itself in such a way that it's sheltered from competition. Brands, trade names, patents, de facto standards, consumer monopolies, and superior distribution systems are just a few examples of sustainable competitive advantage.

2. GREAT MANAGEMENT OF UNQUESTIONABLE INTEGRITY, WITH A TRACK RECORD OF EXCELLENCE

When making an investment, no matter how much research you do on a particular company, it's just plain impossible to know everything. Therefore, the best way to minimize the risk and maximize the opportunity of what you don't know is to buy a company with best-of-class management.

3. EXPANDING POSSIBILITIES THAT WILL ALLOW THE COMPANY TO HAVE A FUTURE SWEETER THAN THE PRESENT

We want to invest in businesses that can be bigger and stronger five or ten years from now than they are today. That leads us to ask such questions as: Will the company be more, or less, relevant in the future than it is today? Does the company compete in an industry that will support growth? Does the company have lots of options to grow?

4. ANNUAL SALES GROWTH OF AT LEAST 10 PERCENT

Sales growth is the most fundamental indication of an expanding business. A company with growing sales has either rising customer demand or pricing power—or perhaps both. We're looking for companies that are growing sales (a.k.a. revenue) by at least 10 percent per year, which is a decent clip for large-cap Rule Makers.

5. GROSS MARGINS GREATER THAN 50 PERCENT

Gross margins are a reflection of how expensive it is to manufacture a product relative to the price at which it can be sold. Ideally, a Rule Maker has a product that costs very little to manufacture but that can be sold dearly. Thus, we would like to see gross margins ringing in above the very lofty perch of 50 percent.

6. NET PROFIT MARGIN OF AT LEAST 10 PERCENT

The net margin tells us how much profit a company is making after every cost has been subtracted from sales revenues. The calculation is net income (after all expenses, including taxes, marketing and administrative expenses, and the like) divided by sales. Thus, we're looking for companies that earn at least a dime of profit on each dollar of sales.

7. CASH KING MARGIN GREATER THAN 10 PERCENT

The Cash King Margin is similar to the net margin, except that instead of measuring profits with net income from the income statement, we use free cash flow from the cash flow statement. The advantage of measuring profits with free cash flow is that cash flow isn't as easily manipulated as net income. The calculation here is free cash flow divided by sales. We're looking for Rule Makers that generate lots of the green stuff, and thus we want to see a Cash King Margin of at least 10 percent.

8. CASH NO LESS THAN 1.5 TIMES TOTAL DEBT

The best Rule Makers sport little or no debt and plenty of cash. If we want to invest in a company that's going to thrive for ten to twenty years or more, we don't want short-term profits at the expense of long-term survival and success. No, no . . . we prefer to find companies that grow their business out of profits from operations and, thus, don't have substantial interest payments to make to banks in the years ahead. Therefore, we require that a

company's cash be at least 1.5 times greater than its total debt (including both long-term and short-term debt).

9. EFFICIENT WORKING CAPITAL MANAGEMENT, AS MEASURED BY A FOOLISH FLOW RATIO NO GREATER THAN 1.25

One of the most important attributes of a Rule Maker is efficient use of cash. We want our companies to bring money in quickly, but to pay it out slowly. We can measure how well a company does this with our Foolish Flow Ratio. This is the ratio of current assets less cash, divided by current liabilities less short-term debt. We go in search of flow ratios that run lower than 1.25.

10. A REASONABLE PURCHASE PRICE THAT ALLOWS FOR THE CLEAR POSSIBILITY OF 2X/5Y

This last one is an investment criterion. With Rule Makers, our goal is to buy at a price that allows us to have a good shot at doubling our money (2x) over the course of five years (5y)—that's a 14.9 percent annual return. The 2x/5y pursuit is not so much a matter of stock valuation, but rather of business *evaluation*. In order to assess the likelihood of a company's market cap doubling in the next five years, you need a solid understanding of the underlying business and its future prospects.

Now, as we mentioned in the last chapter, some industries do not lend themselves to the types of economics listed above. Costco is never going to have high gross or net margins. Tiffany & Co., an obvious Rule Maker, is always going to be hampered by the fact that its inventory requirements are enormous. The chance of 10 percent growth for many large companies is a thing of the past. Do not be discouraged if the company you are analyzing doesn't fit all of these criteria. But if the company fails *all* of them, well, you might be looking in the wrong place.

Now that you've got Rule Makers, the class of their industries, why go anywhere else? Well, of course . . . to learn more and to seek even better opportunities. From here, that will mean smaller companies with substantially greater risk but greater possibility for reward. Beyond this point lie trapdoors and treasure chests. Proceed at your own risk.

RULE BREAKERS

The Rule Breaker strategy is built upon the idea that experienced investors should have at least a portion of their portfolio dedicated to high-risk, high-reward stocks. Investing like a venture capitalist is exciting, stomach churning, and potentially very profitable. It's also intentionally *very* risky.

The strategy is appropriate for skilled and knowledgeable investors prepared to take such risks—and the disappointments that inevitably come with such risks. Among The Motley Fool's online portfolios, the Rule Breaker Portfolio has had more bomb investments perhaps than all the others combined. It has also outperformed all the others. If you cannot stomach the thought of one of your stocks being a complete loss, you might think about using a different strategy. Even if you are willing to take these kinds of risks, we do not believe that it is Foolish investing to have a portfolio comprised *only* of Rule Breaker stocks. We wouldn't feel right about omitting fair warning, but at the same time, to us there is very little in investing more exciting than correctly predicting the best participant in an exciting emerging industry.

The quintessential Rule Breaking company is one that has the potential to change the world. We want our companies to be brand names or have brand name products that are familiar to virtually *everybody*. We believe that true sustainable advantages come from brand and visionary management, not necessarily from technological advantage.

We pay little or no attention to traditional valuation metrics, and neither do we pay much attention to market history. Since we buy young companies, we find far more value looking through the windshield than the rearview mirror.

We divide our criteria into two groups—business criteria and stock criteria—to recognize that while some *businesses* may well be Rule Breaking, we would not invest in them due to one or more restraints imposed by our *stock* criteria. Finding Rule Breaking businesses is the most important part of our analysis, however, since they will likely remain strong while the stock criteria may fluctuate. We'll keep a Rule Breaking business on our radar until it becomes an attractive buy.

BUSINESS CRITERIA:
THE BUSINESS SHOULD . . .

1. Be in an important, emerging industry. Important, emerging industries are the areas with huge growth curves. Emergent industries come from invention, reinvention, or adaptation of existing technologies. An important industry has lasting relevance, deep consumer reach, and expanding possibilities.

2. Be the top dog and first mover *with gusto* in that industry. Top dogs draw the best talent, form the best partnerships, and have the best growth rates. They do not always win, however. Companies that first realize the industry's potential and attack the market with gusto, through aggressive sales and marketing and smart partnerships, can claim top-dog position.

3. Have a sustainable advantage. Rule Breakers are usually too young to have demonstrated sustainable advantages, but we look for short-term protections that can give the company an early competitive boost. These advantages come in the form of business momentum, patents, visionary leadership, or inept competition.

4. Have good management and smart backing. Great management is the key to success for a Rule Breaker. It must be daring, visionary, flexible, savvy, accountable, communicative, and adaptive. We pore over the company's mission statement, its conference calls, in-depth news articles, and track records to try to gain as much understanding of management as we can. We also look for financial backing from smart investors or corporations.

5. Have strong consumer appeal. We look for companies with strong consumer appeal. All else being equal, a company that imprints its logo in the minds of the public stands a better chance of surviving than one that does not. A strong brand serves to attract, to habituate, to profit, and to protect.

STOCK CRITERIA: THE STOCK SHOULD . . .

1. Have a relative strength of 90 or better. (We'll get to more about relative strength soon.) Contrary to conventional "buy low, sell high" market wisdom that would have you searching for "beaten-down" stocks, we like to find Rule Breakers that have displayed strong price growth over the last twelve months, relative to the stock market as a whole. When it comes to Rule Breakers, we think past market strength is a good indicator for future strength, too.

2. Have the potential to appreciate tenfold in five years. We take a lot of risk by investing in unproven, often unprofitable companies, so we seek a high return—ten times appreciation in five years. That's a very ambitious goal. It means that we have to consider carefully the profitability potential of our purchases. We won't be precise in our estimates, but we will form a quantified vision of our expectations.

3. Have been called overvalued by a significant constituent of the financial media. Great companies with enormous potential do not often, if ever, look undervalued by traditional measures. The market values companies by their future, not their past. We try to exploit the financial media's tendency to value companies by their past. To that end, we look

for companies that the market likes but the media calls overvalued.

Remember that Rule Breakers are *risky*. Not all of them succeed in the long run. They're for more experienced investors who are comfortable taking on risk. Rule Breaker stocks should make up only a part of any portfolio. And if they make you uneasy, know that you can enjoy a fine and profitable investing career without investing in Rule Breakers.

SMALL-CAP GROWTH STOCKS (FOOLISH 8)

You're a glutton for this stuff, eh?

One of our favorite dishes happens to be investing in smaller companies. Of all nations, America most champions the start-up entrepreneur and the small business. Small businesses in America continue to create more jobs than conglomerates ("upsizing" in the face of so much downsizing), and the growth in new technologies has only increased the desire to build better mousetraps and solve the various problems that face us every day—among them, pollution, hunger, disease, despair, and complacency.

Large companies have a way of plodding on with automatic business models, aspiring to monopolize control far more than concerning themselves with designing solutions for a better world. That's the responsibility of their smaller brethren. Dynamic bantamweight companies in the United States pop up to build new technologies, provide services at less expense, and create innovative products that no conglomerate would bother with. It is these smaller companies that have historically provided the strongest investment returns on the U.S. markets, as they can exhibit a rate of growth in earnings that blows away larger companies. Small-cap businesses, however, bring with them the ongoing possibility of disintegration and bankruptcy. But they also are many investors' favorite fare, because if you find the right one or two small companies, your portfolio can explode on the upside. America Online, an absolute monster stock for the Rule

Breaker Portfolio appreciated over 10,000 percent in seven years, growth that did extraordinary things to our initial investment of $5,000. How did America Online—now AOL Time Warner—do it? It started with a small base of sales and profits and exploded them, by attracting millions of new subscribers.

But finding great small companies that turn into great big companies isn't easy. It often feels like looking for your best friend among seventy-five thousand screaming fans at the Super Bowl. If you haven't been given any clues about where to search, you'll be embarking on a nightmare journey. Ahh, but here we aim to provide you with some of those clues. Thankfully, many of the same principles that turned up the greatest large companies (consumer familiarity, profitability, past performance) hold true for superior small-caps. But other qualities become more important: How big is too big? How fast should sales be growing? What indications are there that management is solid? These and other questions are critical.

To help answer them, we use a few simple screens to narrow the field of over ten thousand public companies to a few dozen with the potential to blast out their business reach. Throughout this section, we'll be using Messages Inc. to examine what to look for, and we've left space for you to start evaluating companies of your own choosing as well. We'll be using eight filters, or screens, known as the *Foolish 8*. Again, the aim is to help your eyes focus in on what counts and to narrow the field of ten thousand fillies to just a few powerful steeds.

SCREEN #1: MARKET CAP UNDER $1 BILLION

Small-cap investing looks for certain preliminary features in a company that make it *just right*—not too big and not too small. Too big, and the potential for significant return on investment may have passed. Too small, and the company may not have the critical mass to stay competitive and grow. This first screen is all about market capitalization—or total company value—which we presented earlier.

Refer back there to see if you got all of the quiz questions right! For you slackers, market cap is simply the stock price multiplied by the total number of outstanding shares. You can get this last number from the company's income statement. Here are the numbers for Messages. Perhaps you'd like to try this out with one of your own companies, too.

	SHARE PRICE	TOTAL SHARES	MARKET CAP
Messages Inc.	$24	12 million	$288 million
Your company	_____	_____	_____

What we're looking for here is stocks with a market capitalization under $1 billion.

SCREEN #2: SALES BELOW $500 MILLION

To further keep us among the properly sized public businesses, we look to companies with sales below $500 million per year, which are therefore generally undiscovered by Wall Street. Because institutional investors have so much money to invest, they can't buy shares of smaller companies without either buying the company outright or putting their eggs in so many different baskets that they can't keep an eye on 1 percent of them. Thus, smaller investors have a chance to get in before the big fellas do. And if their instincts and research are right, these companies will continue to grow until the institutions can buy as well. When that happens, you have the simple principles of supply and demand at work: huge money pours in, the purchasable shares remain the same, and the price will rise—sometimes dramatically.

	2002 SALES
Messages Inc.	$97 million
Your company	_____

SCREEN #3: SHARE PRICE ABOVE $7

Two-dollar stocks can seem awfully attractive. After all, you can buy more shares! The reality is, of course, that no matter how many shares of stock you buy, you'll have made the same dollar investment. And if you have 1,000 shares of a $3 stock that falls to $1 per share, that's far more painful than holding 150 shares of a $20 stock that falls to $15. The total dollar investment is what matters most.

So, why avoid companies with stocks trading under $7 per share? Because many of them are trading there for a bad reason—they dropped! While *real* businesses are churning out steady cash profits, many of the nickel-and-dimers are busy promoting their stocks, trying to lure newbie investors into taking a chance on their dubious business prospects. And because brokers get paid based on how many trades they make and how many shares they trade, they love to pitch the penny stocks to you.

The majority of such companies are low-grade promotional businesses. It's estimated that three quarters of the companies trading under $5 per share end up worthless. And almost all of these businesses are unfamiliar to you. Avoid this group forever and we think you'll be better off.

	SHARE PRICE
Messages Inc.	$24
Your company	____

SCREEN #4: EARNINGS AND SALES GROWTH OF AT LEAST 25 PERCENT (QUALITY SCREEN)

Across the spectrum of ten thousand public companies in America, you'll find sales growing at all kinds of rates. Some companies will see sales declines, while others will more than double their revenue; but look closely and you'll see that most companies' sales are growing at a rate of 5 to 10 percent annually. Since we're specifically looking for those smaller companies at the strong end of the spectrum, we like to study companies with at least 25 percent growth in *sales* over the past year. (There is some reason to think that the bar should be raised even higher, to study only the highest-growth businesses.)

Additionally, we like to find operations whose *earnings* off those sales are growing at comparable rates—ideally, faster. Earnings growth that outpaces a very rapid climb in sales is an excellent situation; it indicates that while the company is selling truckloads of more product, it is—simultaneously—finding ways to do so more profitably.

	SALES GROWTH	EARNINGS PER SHARE GROWTH
Messages Inc.	94%	35%
Your company	____	____

While it isn't ideal to see earnings not keeping pace with sales, if both are rising rapidly enough, we'll choose to overlook the decline in the rate of profitability—or at least find out *why* this is happening before dismissing a prospect. Messages' earnings growth looks frightening, though, compared to sales growth. Why is it happening? Part of the problem is that some costs are increasing faster than revenue, but another important part is that the company has issued more shares, thus diluting each owner's share of the earnings. Both do serious damage to the value of your shares.

SCREEN #5: NET PROFIT MARGIN OF AT LEAST 10 PERCENT (QUALITY SCREEN)

Companies with profit margins in excess of 10 percent are a rare breed. But that's precisely what we're looking for when we go out in search of the limited group of smaller companies that warrant our investigation. If they are earning 10 cents for every dollar of sales, these smaller companies may be taking market share away from larger companies while generating healthy profits. Look especially for companies that are also driving already high margins higher. Profitability drives the value of the overall company, and thus the stock price. As a shareholder, you'll always be rooting for the earnings growth rate. We don't think you should accept any small business as a potential investment unless it's maintaining these high margins. You're too good for the rest!

	MESSAGES INC.	YOUR COMPANY
Revenue	$97 million	_____
Net income	$12.9 million	_____
Profit margin	13%	_____

SCREEN #6: CASH FLOW POSITIVE

The next of our filters is based on the cash flow statement. All we're looking for here is that companies have positive cash flow from operations. This is simply a check to see if the company is making money, rather than burning it.

	NET OPERATING CASH
Messages Inc.	− $4.62 million
Your company	_____

Yikes! This is the unfortunate sign that we talked of earlier when discussing Messages' levels of receivables and inventory. Negative cash flow is excusable only in companies ramping up into phenomenal growth. Unless you have a good reason to believe that your company is burning cash to fuel a growth spurt, you should discard it and hold to your standards!

SCREEN #7: RELATIVE STRENGTH OF 90 OR MORE

Investor's Business Daily offers a statistic for every public company that we find extremely useful. It's called *relative strength,* and it works just like the grading system used on you in high school. A 95 is smashingly excellent, a 25 is a dreary disappointment. What do the numbers mean? They speak to how well a particular stock has performed relative to the rest of the market. A number of 95, for example, means that the company has outperformed 95 percent of all public companies traded on all U.S. exchanges over the past year. The number 25 would indicate outperformance of a mere 25 percent of the companies; this company has lost badly to the general stock market.

Our screen requires that a company have a relative strength ranking of 90 or higher. Why? Because the cream usually congregates at the top. Typically, those small-caps that have succeeded in the past have the greatest chance of further success. Trying to buy very small companies that have gotten hammered by the market is, we think, an extremely dangerous game. So, buy a copy of *Investor's Business Daily* and search out stocks with relative strength of at least 90; make your search easier. (Oops! Look at Messages Inc.!)

	RELATIVE STRENGTH
Messages Inc.	42
Your company	____

SCREEN #8: INSIDER HOLDINGS OF 10 PERCENT OR GREATER

Knowing that management holds a significant stake in the company's stock is an added assurance that they care enough to do their best and that they have confidence in the company's future. Look for at least 10 percent of stock to be held by insiders.

While it's a little difficult to find up-to-date owner-ship information, fairly accurate data is found in the company's annual report (SEC filing 10-K) and the accompanying proxy (DEF-13A). You can also look in the *S&P Stock Guide*. These figures are on the Internet as well. Finally, you can call the company directly and ask them for an ownership profile.

	INSIDER HOLDINGS
Messages Inc.	56%
Your company	_____

INSIDER BUYING AND SELLING

If you were the CEO of a company and had three kids to put through college, two mortgages, and an un-paid second honeymoon, where would you most likely get the money to pay for it all? Very likely, you'd sell some shares of the company you own. What's more, you'd probably do this somewhat often, even though you might not really want to—after all, you believe in the company, but you've got to pay those bills. Then again, when the stock happens to hit a low point, it makes sense to buy it on the cheap, since you may know that the company's doing well and the share price will improve. For these reasons, the Foolish investor pretty much ignores insider sell-ing. We do pay attention to insider buying, which says more about management's sentiment than their selling. Selling can occur for too many reasons to draw any solid conclusions from it. Buying occurs for only one reason.

CONCLUDING THOUGHTS ON SMALL-CAPS

Unfortunately for Messages Inc., the company failed two of the critical screens that we use to limit the enormous number of small public companies we consider buying down to just a few. Status as cash flow negative and a stock performance that has out-performed only 42 percent of the market over the past year are both unacceptable. As many things as there are to like about Messages—rapid sales and earnings growth, a great business concept (those messages are tasty, if you've never had one), strong management ownership—their balance sheet is far too unstable for us, and perhaps that's why Mes-sages has outperformed only 42 percent of all stocks in the past year.

But that's not going to stop us from trying to value its business fairly. We'll close by asking you:

Is there a present value for Messages' business? If so, name it:

$ _____ million

You don't have a clue? Well then, it's valuation time!

CHAPTER 9

PUTTING THE NUMBERS TOGETHER

All right, now that we've found some interesting companies, let's look a little bit more at their financials. We've gone through each of the financial statements on its own, but we're not done with them yet. We've seen that balance sheets give us a decent picture of the basic financial health of the company, determining if it's got enough cash to cover its upcoming bills, if it's managing its working capital well, or if it's swimming in a pool of debt. We've used income statements to give us an idea of the level of profitability the company attains, calculating if it profits over and above its cost, if it's increasing its revenue currently, or if it's funding research to increase future revenue. We've also found that cash flow statements tell us exactly how much money is coming into the company each year from operations, investing, and financing activities.

Those are important points on their own. Now we need to think about how the financial statements work together, in order to get the *big* picture of the company. We want to ask some questions about the relationship between one aspect of a company's business and another. How does the management of working capital balance with revenue and costs? How much income does the company earn off the assets it owns? How much does it earn on share-

holders' investments? For that matter, how much does the operation earn on *all* its sources of funding? After all, we don't want to put money in a company if it is not going to produce a return of its own that is better than the cost of the money it raises. That would be throwing good money after bad. It's a well-kept secret in investing that companies can be profitable long after they've ceased to be good investments. How would one find this out? Why, by not concentrating on just one of the three sheets in the financial statement, that's how, Fool! Learn this one lesson and the moment you begin investing you already have an advantage over millions of other people in the stock market.

So let's put on our thinking caps and start considering how well our company is managing its resources. We're going to start building out a few of the tools we use to track the economic performance of our companies.

CASH CONVERSION CYCLE

The cash conversion cycle is a combination of three independent calculations that tell us about how well a company is handling its working capital. (You remember working capital, right? It's the stuff contained in current assets and current liabilities, the components of day-to-day operations.)

ACCOUNTS RECEIVABLE AND DAYS SALES OUTSTANDING

At first it might seem a good thing to have a lot of people out there owing you money. But if you aren't charging interest on that money—as is the case with receivables at many companies—it is definitely a bad thing. Rising accounts receivable may indicate softness in product demand, since companies are selling their stuff but allowing buyers to pay for it later. This can inflate sales and earnings, since the purchase goes into revenue numbers even though no money has been paid, but it harms cash flows substantially, resulting in the misstatement of profitability. The difference between profitability and cash flows is no small thing. Think about this: A company has bills to pay. If it has no cash on hand, can it just send over a receivable? No. Cash is the fuel of commerce. A company that manages its cash poorly by giving its customers generous amounts of time to pay may be headed for trouble.

There is a simple equation called *days sales outstanding* that helps us determine how many days of receivables the company is carrying. Go back to the financial statements for Messages Inc. that we used in earlier chapters to get some real numbers from, well, OK, a fake company.

Divide revenue for the year ($97 million) by 360 days. This tells you how much the company sold in a day. (If you were doing this exercise quarter over quarter, you'd use ninety days. Four quarters totaled up equal 360 days—just ignore the extra five or six days.) Now, to find out how many days' worth of receivables the company has not yet collected, divide accounts receivable at the end of the quarter ($34 million) by a day's worth of sales. The equation looks like this:

$$\frac{\text{Accounts Receivable}}{\text{Revenue} \div 360}$$

Your answer is _____. Yes, 126 days of receivables. That means that it takes Messages 126 days to collect all its receivables—whoa! That seems like a long time. Messages may be misstating sales and earnings—what is called "stuffing the sales channel" with product that customers aren't paying for in four months. Flashing red light here.

This is something to follow up on, but there isn't really a target number of days that is "right." Different industries have different standards for selling on credit. To use days sales outstanding, then, you'll need to compare Messages' days outstanding with other companies in its industry. You will also want to track its receivables over time, which means making the same calculation for its previous years. You can get a company's previous years' financial statements on a site like freeedgar.com or on the company's website, or you can call up their Investor Relations department and ask 'em to send them to you. If more and more days of sales keep building up, it may mean that demand for the company's products is weakening. That's not good.

Now that you've gotten the hang of days sales outstanding, we're gonna throw you a curve: to get a more accurate read for the pace of sales outstanding over the entire year, you'll want to use *average receivables*, rather than just the figures from the end of the year. The point is that the receivables number on the balance sheet represents only the amount on the last day of the year, so it doesn't give you an idea of how receivables were managed over the course of the year. To get a slightly better idea, we average the numbers from one year to the next.

To calculate average receivables, take the receivables from last year, add it to this year's number, and divide by two. For Messages, the numbers look like this:

$$\frac{(34{,}000 + 14{,}000) \div 2}{97{,}000 \div 360}$$

That's an ugly-looking calculation, but it's pretty simple. Take some time to work it out. Finished? OK, here's what we get:

$$\frac{24,000}{269.4} = 89$$

That makes things look quite a bit better, but it's worth noting that the state of receivables was worse at the end of the year than at the beginning. Now we want to figure out the change since 2001. We can do it by going back to last year's 10-K to find the balance sheet numbers for 2000, so that we can use average numbers. It turns out that receivables stood at $8 million at the end of 2000, so our equation looks like this:

$$\frac{(14,000 + 8,000) \div 2}{50,000 \div 360}$$

That works out to seventy-nine days sales outstanding, meaning that it rose 12 percent between 2001 and 2002. That's not the way we would like to see the trend moving.

INVENTORY—DAYS INVENTORY OUTSTANDING

We prefer companies that don't have to carry much inventory. Products should race out the door and fly off the shelves, lickety-split. One way to measure this is to study the company's total number of days of inventory. It's a simple calculation, but it involves a few steps. First, take the *Cost of sales* line from the income statement (the inventory value of sales for the year) and divide it by 360 (the number of days in the year). Next, divide total inventory in stock by the result of the first calculation. This amounts to the company's inventory turnover. The equation looks like this:

$$\frac{Inventory}{Cost\ of\ sales \div 360}$$

Let's check Messages Inc. Here are the numbers you'll need:

Cost of sales during the most recent year: $46.5 million

Inventory: $20 million

So, we divide $46.5 million by 360, and come up with _____. Yes, $129,166. That is the cost of sales per day in a year. Now we divide our inventory by that number, in order to see how many days it will take for Messages to clear out its stockpiled messages at the current rate. We divide $20 million by $129,166 per day, and we get about 155 days. Messages turns over its inventory every 155 days. Was that clear? We hope so.

What we want here is for a company to turn its inventory as fast as it can. This means that the product is hot and that the company speedily rolls new inventory out the door. As with days sales outstanding, however, there isn't really a target number of days that is "right." The reason is the same: different industries keep product in inventory for different periods of time. Compare Messages' inventory turnover with that of other companies in its industry, and track it over time to see if it's increasing.

As with accounts receivable, we want to acknowledge that the last day in the year is not the be-all of inventory management for the year. To compensate, we think it's better to use numbers averaged over the course of the year. Again, then, we'll add inventory numbers from 2002 and 2001 together and divide by 2.

Cost of sales in 2001: $21 million

Inventory in 2001: $10 million

Here's the equation:

$$\frac{(20,000 + 10,000) \div 2}{46,500 \div 360}$$

Race ya! Tap, tap, tap . . . got your answer yet? We have ours: 116 days. That's better than our straightforward 2002 calculation, so it looks like inventory management also got worse from the start of the year to the end.

To get a better comparison, though, we'd better check the average days inventory outstanding for the previous year. A quick check of the 2001 10-K shows inventory at $6 million at the end of 2000, so our equation looks like this:

$$\frac{(10,000 + 6,000) \div 2}{21,000 \div 360}$$

That equation produces days inventory outstanding of 137 in 2001. That means that Messages actually *cut* the time that its products sat in inventory between 2001 and 2002 by twenty-one days—good news! But don't break out the champagne yet; we're far from done.

ACCOUNTS PAYABLE— DAYS PAYABLES OUTSTANDING

This one runs contrary to our thoughts about short-term debt in your *personal* finances—where it can be an extremely bad thing, because you'd pay a high interest rate on that debt, 16–18 percent for most credit cards. But this isn't true in the business world, where having accounts payable does not penalize the company with meaningful interest payments. Actually, there is a parallel in personal finance. You aren't really charged interest on your phone bill, for example, and some people like to try to squeeze out a few extra cents of interest from their banks each month by waiting until the last possible moment to pay. Miss that deadline, though, and *pow*!!!—interest and penalties start piling on. Business contracts tend to work the same way. They will include provisions for the number of days companies can put off payments. The best businesses can put off these payments for many days.

Think about payables in much the same way as receivables and inventory, except that we want the days payables outstanding to *increase* rather than decrease over time. The first step is to figure out how

many days payables outstanding the company has. That requires an equation similar to those we've used already:

$$\frac{\text{Accounts payable}}{\text{Cost of sales} \div 360}$$

Messages' payables were $6.5 million at the end of 2002. With cost of sales at $46.5 million, how many days were its payables outstanding? If you got about fifty, you're on the right track. Remember that you'll want to see the number *rising* in the case of payables, as opposed to *shrinking* in the case of receivables and inventory.

Now let's figure out the average numbers year over year. Accounts payable in 2001 were $3.2 million. We don't need to write out the calculation, since it's second nature to you now. Average payables divided by 2002 cost of sales per day (which you figured out already for inventory), and wham! You get _____. Oh, you got thirty-eight days, too? Excellent!

Finally, we'll calculate the days payables outstanding in 2001, for comparison's sake. Payables in 2000 were $2.4 million, so our equation looks like this:

$$\frac{(3,200 + 2,400) \div 2}{21,000 \div 360}$$

Out of that equation pops forty-eight days payables outstanding. Whoops, that's not the direction we want to see things trending—payables were down in 2002 relative to 2001. We want payables to *rise* over time.

Looking at it broadly, the company has $34 million in receivables and $6.5 million in payables (money yet to go out) in 2002. Hey, this must be good—$27.5 million more comes in than goes out. Ah, but the company has already accounted for that $34 million in profit even though it hasn't received it yet, so there's no upside here. Additionally, because interest is not being paid on either, the company is in a disadvantageous position here. Red lights are blinking all over the place.

PUTTING IT ALL TOGETHER: THE CASH CONVERSION CYCLE

Let's put all these numbers together in the *cash conversion cycle*. The cash conversion cycle represents the number of days it takes a company to purchase a raw material, convert it into a finished good, sell the finished good to a customer, and receive payment for that product. It puts together all three of the "days outstanding" numbers we've calculated above.

It's a simple number to calculate. Simply add the days receivables outstanding (we'll use the average numbers, since they are more representative of the whole year's performance) and the days inventory outstanding, then *subtract* the days payables outstanding. So that you don't have to look back, we'll repeat the numbers here:

> Days receivables outstanding (89) +
> days inventory outstanding (116) −
> days payables outstanding (38) = _____

All finished? This is not hard stuff. You should have come up with 167 days. That means that it takes Messages 167 days to buy materials, make messages, sell 'em, and receive payment.

We hear you ask: Is 167 days a long time? Well, it *seems* like a long time, but some industries have a long cash conversion cycle. We need to compare Messages' to the cash conversion cycle in 2001. Hey, we've already figured out the components, so let's just plug them in!

> Days receivables outstanding (_____) +
> days inventory outstanding (_____) −
> days payables outstanding (_____) = _____

C'mon, now, don't wait for us to give you the answer. Plug the numbers we calculated before into this equation. Done? All right, here's what we got. In 2001, Messages had sales outstanding for 79 days, inventory outstanding for 137 days, and payables outstanding for 48 days. That gives us a cash conversion cycle of 168 days.

Messages' cash conversion cycle essentially stayed level from 2001 to 2002. It wasn't exactly the same, however. While there was a marked improvement in inventory management (down to 116 from 137), there was a significant *worsening* in payables (down to 38 from 48—remember, we want this one to *rise*) and a change for the worse in accounts receivable (up to 89 from 79). Now we know where the problems lie: payables and receivables. We will want to keep a close eye on them.

RETURN ON ASSETS (ROA)

The cash conversion cycle tells you how well a company is managing its short-term assets and liabilities. Investors also want to know the return that a company generates on its fixed assets, like property, plant, and equipment—the largest component of assets at many companies. The main question is: how much value does the company create with the cash investors have given it? There are a few ways of approaching this question, which is what we'll spend the rest of the chapter discussing. Let's start with *return on assets* (ROA).

ROA is a pretty straightforward measure of profitability: it illustrates how much a company earns on its total asset base. The equation for calculating it is pretty simple—in fact, would you like to guess at it? How would *you* figure out how much a company makes from its assets? What would you divide by what?

You're every bit as smart as you look (you do look smart, right?): ROA is simply the company's earnings over the last twelve months divided by *average* total assets—we love to use average numbers, as you know, since they give us a more representative figure for the course of the year.

$$\frac{\text{Trailing 12-month earnings}}{\text{Average total assets}} = \text{Return on assets}$$

Now apply the equation to Messages Inc. at the end of 2002. You remember that net income for the company in 2002 was $12.88 million, but you may have forgotten that total assets were $90.3 million in 2002 and $50.2 million in 2001. That makes the calculation:

$$\frac{\$12,880}{(\$90,300 + \$50,200) \div 2}$$

And the answer? It's 0.183—or, expressed as a percentage, 18.3 percent. We hope that you got that; this is not rocket science. So, is 18.3 percent good? You can probably answer this one for yourself, too: there isn't really a "right" or "wrong" answer. (Well, there is in some cases—a company with a negative ROA is pretty squarely in the "not good" camp.) More important is how the number compares to Messages' past performance and the performance of its closest competitors. Let's figure out the average ROA for Messages in 2001 (its total assets for 2000 was $31.6 million):

$$\frac{\$7,900}{(\$50,200 + \$31,600) \div 2}$$

Go on, pick up your calculator. We won't be there to do your calculations for you, once you leave the pleasant confines of this workbook. You have to practice. Got your answer? It should be 0.193, or 19.3%. That means that the trend is negative; ROA dropped 1 percentage point from 2001 to 2002.

It's useful to know what is driving the change in ROA. All you math students out there will recognize that we can break the ROA equation into two parts:

$$\frac{\text{Net income}}{\text{Average total assets}} = \frac{\text{Net income}}{\text{Sales}} \times \frac{\text{Sales}}{\text{Average total assets}}$$

The first part should be familiar to you: it's called *profit margin* (net income ÷ sales), which we dis-

cussed last chapter. The second part is known as *asset turnover* (sales ÷ average total assets), which tells you how many times the company creates revenue off its assets. For Messages, it was 1.38 times ($97 million in sales and $70.25 million in average total assets) in 2002, and 1.22 times ($50 million in sales and $40.9 million in average total assets) in 2001. That's an improvement in asset turnover. So, how did ROA get worse? It was from the shrinking profit margins that we saw before.

RETURN ON EQUITY (ROE)

Return on equity (ROE) in our opinion is one of the best barometers of management excellence. If you look at the return on assets calculation above, you may notice one very important financial component that is not being taken into account. Yep, you guessed it: *debt*. If a company has a small asset base and wants a higher ROA, it could always just add some debt. Remember our discussion of equity? Don't panic if you don't; we'll remind you what we said:

> Shareholders' equity is simply total assets minus total liabilities. It is the owners' piece of the business's assets, after it pays off the debt (long-term and short-term) and other bills that it owes in the form of liabilities. Think of equity in a house; it is the value of the house (the asset) minus the mortgage still owed on it (the liability). When the house is sold, the debt is paid, and the rest of the proceeds belongs to the owners.

Equity is what belongs to the owners, not the debtors, of a company. It's like the amount of money you have in your house. There's a mortgage, or a debt, but then everything else between that debt and the amount the house is worth is equity. Whenever a company generates profits—that is, has money left over after the bills are paid—there are four main things it can do with that moolah. It can pay shareholders a dividend, pay down debt, buy back shares of the company stock, or reinvest in operations. That reinvested money shows up on the balance sheet as equity. *Return on equity,* then, reveals how effectively reinvested earnings—and capital that shareholders originally invested in the company—are used to generate additional earnings. For example, profits might be used to acquire another company. Or a new factory might be built, upping the firm's output and sales. So what we want to know is this—how much profit is being generated based upon the amount of equity in the company?

$$ROE = \frac{\text{Trailing 12-month earnings}}{\text{Average shareholder equity}}$$

Technically, ROE is a measure of how much in earnings a company generates in four quarters compared to its average shareholder equity for the period. Like ROA, it's measured as a percentage. For instance, if XYZ Corp. made $1 million in the past year and has shareholder equity of $10 million, then the ROE is 10 percent. Consider General Electric as another example. It earned $7.3 billion and had shareholder equity of $31.1 billion. Divide 7.3 by 31.1 and you get an impressive ROE of 0.23, or 23 percent.

Some use ROE as a screen to find companies that can generate large profits with little in the way of capital investment. Coca-Cola, for instance, does not require constant spending to upgrade equipment—the syrup-making process does not regularly move ahead by technological leaps and bounds. In fact, high ROE companies are so attractive to some investors that they will take the ROE and average it with the expected earnings growth in order to figure out a fair price-to-earnings (P/E) multiple. This is why a pharmaceutical company like Merck can grow at 10 percent or so every year but consistently trade at twenty times earnings or more.

You want your company's ROE to be as high as possible. You also want it to be better than that of its competitors. Mainly, though, you want to know what is driving ROE up or down. To do that, you have to look at its parts.

DUPONT ANALYSIS

As we did with return on assets, let's break down the ROE equation to see what components it contains. This is called a DuPont analysis. (Insert goofy chemical pun here. Oooh, those chemical puns always do come in handy.)

$$ROE = \frac{\text{One year's earnings}}{\text{One year's sales}} \times \frac{\text{One year's sales}}{\text{Total assets}} \times \frac{\text{Total assets}}{\text{Shareholder equity}}$$

Because the sales and the assets are in both the numerator and the denominator of the entire equation, they cancel one another out. (For those too stunned by the algebra to fully comprehend the above, you'll have to trust us.) When you do that, you're left with the simpler earnings-over-equity ROE formula we gave earlier.

Look closely and you'll see that earnings over sales is *profit margin,* sales over assets is *asset turnover,* and assets over equity is the amount of *leverage* (a fancy-schmancy way of saying "debt") the company has. Looking at it this way, you can see which components are dragging ROE down or boosting it up. You can see how changes in any of the measures will affect ROE. Nifty, eh?

Look even more closely and you'll notice that two of the three equations in ROE are also part of return on assets. The one that's different is the leverage equation—assets divided by equity. It deserves a little explanation.

LEVERAGE

Remember that the balance sheet balances assets on one side against liabilities and equity on the other side. If a company has no liabilities—no debt, no payables, nothing—then you know that all the assets came from shareholders. Nothing was given to the company to use as assets by creditors or suppliers or unpaid employees. Leverage will be 1, and ROE will be the same as ROA.

Add some liabilities in there, however, and you start to get more leverage. Say some suppliers allow sixty days for a company to pay for goods. That money will show up on the asset side of the equation in the form of inventory, but it will also show up on the liabilities side in the form of accounts payable. Say, too, that the company borrows $2 billion from Orangeblood's Big Bank. That money shows up on the assets side in the form of cash and on the liabilities side in the form of debt. (Accounting trivia: this is why our system of accounting is known as "double-entry bookkeeping." Be sure to use that little piece of knowledge at the next party you go to.)

If you calculate return on assets, the return is based on total assets. It includes all the money that creditors and suppliers and shareholders have given it. ROE, on the other hand, uses only the shareholders' money—equity equals assets minus liabilities. The advantage to that is that it tells the owners how much the company earned (through whatever other financing) on their dollar investment. It's a much more precise level for quantifying return.

The potential downside is that it rewards leverage. If a company can maintain profit margins and asset turnover, then ROE will improve as leverage increases. In the normal world, that's OK. In order to maintain profit margins when interest payments go up, the company has to make more money on operations. In order to maintain asset turnover after increasing assets by borrowing money, the company needs to turn assets faster. But in the real-life world of accounting, it is not unheard of for a company to take on leverage at strategic moments in order to make its ROE for a given period look better. It's also possible for a company to take on enough debt that it hurts profit margins but improves the leverage ratio enough to drive ROE up nevertheless.

It's always a good idea, therefore, to break ROE into its individual components, so that you know what's driving it up or down. If the company is leveraging itself to the hilt while hurting margins and turnover, that's not a good sign. If the com-

pany has taken on more debt but margins and turnover have gone up, that's good. We want our companies to borrow money if they can invest it in the business and earn more than the cost of that debt.

Ready to calculate Messages' ROE? We sure are.

	2002	2001	2000
Shareholder equity	65,800	37,000	21,200
Net income	12,880	7,900	

What will the return on equity equation for 2002 look like? It should be something like this:

$$\frac{12{,}880}{(65{,}800 + 37{,}000) \div 2}$$

Don't wait for us—punch those calculators. You should get something like 0.25058. Turn that into a percentage by multiplying the number times 100, and you get 25.1 percent. Now do the same for 2001 to find out whether Messages' ROE is improving or declining.

Messages' ROE for 2001: _____

Did it get better, or worse? _____

You should have come up with 27.1 percent. Uh-oh, it looks like Messages' ROE is declining, meaning that it is earning less of a return on the money its shareholders have contributed to the company, in terms of primary investment and earnings that the company retained rather than returned to owners. That's not great news, but in raw terms, 25 percent is not a bad return. It means that for each dollar that shareholders contribute, the company earns 25 cents in a year. It will take four years to return shareholders' investment. Not bad.

Still, we'd rather see the ROE going up than going down. What is driving it down? In the return on asset section, we saw that asset turnover improved from 2001 to 2002, but we knew that profit margins had fallen from 15.8 percent in 2001 to 13.2 percent in 2002. How did the leverage ratio change? Simply divide total average assets by average shareholder equity.

	2002	2001	2000
Assets	90,300	50,200	31,600
Equity	65,800	37,000	21,200

Leverage equation for 2002:

$$\frac{(90{,}300 + 50{,}200) \div 2}{(65{,}800 + 37{,}000) \div 2} = \frac{70{,}250}{51{,}400} = \underline{\qquad}$$

Leverage equation for 2001:

$$\frac{(50{,}200 + 31{,}600) \div 2}{(37{,}000 + 21{,}200) \div 2} = \frac{40{,}900}{29{,}100} = \underline{\qquad}$$

Have you filled in the blanks? Well done! That calculator sure is getting a workout. So you've found that Messages' leverage ratio was 1.367 in 2002 and 1.405 in 2001. It's down a little bit, meaning that the company had slightly lower liabilities last year. The difference isn't very significant, however. That's not surprising, since Messages doesn't have any debt. It seems that the lower profit margin is the element responsible for driving down ROE in 2002.

RETURN ON INVESTED CAPITAL

We've looked at return on assets, which tells us how much a company's business returns on all the money, or capital, that it has in it during the year—equity, debt, working capital (current liabilities), everything. Then we looked at return on equity, which tells us how much a company made just on the equity in it. Now we're going to move on to one of the most fundamental financial metrics, return on invested capital (ROIC). *Invested* capital means money that has been invested in the business—basically debt and equity. We're also going to define *return* a little differently this time, to get to the real cash a company is generating. This is the most essential return equation, because it spells out clearly what the company gets out from the money it has put in.

Despite its importance, it does not receive the same kind of press coverage that earnings per share, return on equity, and the price-to-earnings ratio get. That's a crying shame. The concept is fundamental for measuring how much value a company creates. This is the measure of profitability that we really want to get right, so we're going to have to work harder to get to a satisfactory answer.

Calculating ROIC isn't too complicated for normal folks like us; it just takes a little more time and thought. Rather than using canned numbers from the income statement and the balance sheet, you're going to have to think about the cash *behind* the numbers.

We do not exaggerate when we say that ROIC is to most people the most difficult component of corporate performance to calculate. If you find yourself struggling at the outset, earmark this section and come back to it. Do not despair! Don't worry if it fails to make sense right away! In fact, before we get started, go make a sandwich or something. You know, get a little brain food in the ol' system!

Back already? Great.

So, what exactly is ROIC? It is defined as the cash rate of return on capital that a company has invested. It is the true measure of a firm's cash-on-cash yield and how effectively it allocates capital.

$$ROIC = \text{net operating profits after taxes} \div \text{average invested capital}$$

Sheesh, after chapters and chapters on financial statements, we present you with two terms you've never heard before that you need to calculate the best measure of profitability. Well, don't blame us. Accounting conventions don't call for companies to state these important numbers explicitly, so they don't. But they are to be found in the numbers they *do* present.

NOPAT

Net operating profits after taxes (NOPAT), the numerator, defines how much *cold, hard cash* the company made from its operations. It is better than net income because it drills down to operations but excludes items such as investment income, goodwill amortization, and interest expense, which don't represent actual cash coming in from business activities. It's very similar to cash flow from operations, which in some cases is a fair proxy for NOPAT if you're in a hurry.

To calculate NOPAT, you start with pretax operating income. By starting there, you skip interest income and extraordinary items the company may have, like onetime restructuring costs and gains from discontinued operations. To that number, add back depreciation and amortization, which are noncash charges to operations. You should take depreciation and amortization from the cash flow statement (instead of the balance sheet) to make sure you use the right totals. Then you're going to have to tax the earnings—there is no getting around Uncle Sam. The tax rate will vary by company. You can get a general sense of what your

company pays on operations by figuring out how much it actually paid last year—just divide the tax paid by pretax income. Generally, the marginal tax rate will be around 35 percent. You'll want to multiply your adjusted operating income by 1 minus 0.35, in that case, so that you're left with 65 percent of the pretax total. The equation looks like this:

$$NOPAT = (\text{pretax operating income} + \text{depreciation and amortization}) \times (1 - \text{tax rate})$$

INVESTED CAPITAL

We talked about how equity represents the money that shareholders have given the company, in the form of seed money, public offering proceeds, earnings that they have allowed the company to retain, and the like. That is not all the capital that has been invested in the business, however. Creditors, too, have given the company money to work with. Both the creditors and the equity holders expect operations to provide a return on their investment—that's what we're here to calculate. Later, we'll figure out whether the future return should meet *our* investment expectation. Right now, we're figuring out what the *business's* return on investment has been in the past. To do that, we need to figure out how much money has gone into the business.

There are two ways to get to invested capital. The first starts with total assets. From that, deduct current liabilities, except for those that the company has to pay interest on—usually called short-term debt or notes payable. The reason is that accounts payable and accrued expenses don't represent money invested by debt or equity holders to fund operations. It may have the effect of doing so, but it doesn't expect a return on the investment. Short-term debt, however, does, so we need to include it in invested capital.

You'll probably want to deduct most of the company's cash from invested capital, because it is not money invested in the business—it hasn't been deployed yet. A company like Microsoft may carry lots of cash for an extended period of time without using it for operations. We like to see cash, because it protects the company from big downturns in business, but we're not investing in a company for the money it makes on its cash investments. If we want investment returns from cash instruments like Treasury bonds, we'll buy cash instruments.

We don't take *all* the cash out of invested capital, though, because the company does need *some* to handle its day-to-day operations. To figure out how much to take out, look at working capital. Will the company need cash to pay off its big accounts payable? That's the case with Amazon.com—it has a lot of cash, but it needs a lot to pay off huge payables after a strong selling season. For most companies, a prudent rule of thumb is to take all but about 5 percent of total annual (not quarterly) sales out of invested capital.

All right, we're zeroing in on the equation for invested capital.

$$\text{Invested capital} = \text{total assets}$$
$$- \text{ current liabilities} + \text{short-term debt}$$
$$- (\text{cash} - [\text{sales} \times 0.05])$$

Now we can rewrite the entire ROIC equation.

$$\text{ROIC} = \text{net operating profits after taxes}$$
$$\div \text{ average invested capital}$$

$$\text{ROIC} = \frac{(\text{Pretax operating income} + \text{depreciation and amortization}) \times (1 - \text{tax rate})}{\text{Total assets} - \text{current liabilities} + \text{short-term debt} - (\text{cash} - [\text{sales} \times 0.05])}$$

It may sound complicated, but it's just seven items from financial statements. Inevitably, of course, when you get down to running your own calculations, you'll run into company-specific issues. The tax rate and the question of how much cash to exclude from invested capital are among them (though the general guidelines of a 35 percent tax rate and 95 percent of cash can provide a pretty good rule of thumb). You may find the process a bit frustrating at first. Just keep at it. Like all things, learning how to invest takes time and practice. ROIC will provide you with a valuable tool in the long run, so stick with it.

Let's start practicing with Messages Inc. First, we'll calculate its NOPAT for 2001 and 2002. To estimate the tax rate, we looked at Messages' past tax rates. With minimal investment income to cause deviation, the rate has been about 34.2 percent. Here, then, are the numbers we'll need:

	2002	2001
Income from operations	18,500	11,000
plus Depreciation	1,200	800
Pretax net operating profit	_____	_____
times 1 minus tax rate	0.658	0.658
NOPAT	_____	_____

See, it isn't that difficult. People have climbed Mount Everest, walked across hot coals, peered into deepest space, and sat through entire Carrot Top concerts, for goodness' sake. You can do this. It didn't take much effort at all to come up with $12,963 in 2002 and $7,765 for 2001. That is the amount of cash earnings that the company made from operations.

On to invested capital! We'll figure it out for 2002, 2001, and 2000, then we'll use annual averages.

	2002	2001	2000
Total assets	90,300	50,200	31,600
minus Current liabilities	24,500	13,200	10,400
plus Short-term debt	0	0	0
Invested capital *plus* cash	___	___	___
Sales	97,000	50,000	32,500
times	0.05	0.05	0.05
5% of sales	___	___	___
Cash and equivalents	24,000	20,000	13,000
minus 5% of Sales	___	___	___
Deductible cash	___	___	___
Invested capital *plus* cash	___	___	___
minus Deductible cash	___	___	___
Invested capital	___	___	___

We'll let you fill in all those blanks on your own, but the final answers should be:

2002	2001	2000
$46,650	$19,500	$9,825

Now it's a fairly simple matter to calculate ROIC. We just need to divide NOPAT by average invested capital.

For **2002:**

$$\frac{12,963}{(46,650 + 19,500) \div 2}$$

For **2001:**

$$\frac{7,765}{(19,500 + 9,825) \div 2}$$

Given the general degradation of Messages' performance when we calculated everything else, it's not surprising to see that ROIC fell from 53 to 39 percent in 2002. That's a big drop. Still, earning 39 cents in 2002 from every dollar invested is not bad.

WEIGHTED AVERAGE COST OF CAPITAL

ROIC is a useful metric on its own, indicating how much money the company earns on a dollar. It's also informative to note the direction ROIC is trending from year to year. In Messages' case, that's the downside. You'll also want to note the difference between the *return* on capital and the *cost* of capital. No investment in a company comes for free. Debt costs the rate of interest that is owed on it. If Messages had raised all its money from a bond that paid 9 percent annually, then its cost of capital would be 9 percent, right? Well, close. Remember that interest payments are deducted from taxable earnings, driving the cost of debt lower. If the tax rate is 35 percent, then 35 percent of the cost of capital will be returned to the company in the form of taxes that otherwise would have been paid. At 9 percent, that's 3.15 percentage points. The cost of capital on a bond that pays 9 percent, then, is 5.85 percent.

The trickier cost is equity. Even though the cost of equity does not show up on a company's income statement, it is not free. Investors also expect some return for their investment, and it's usually higher than the cost of debt, since stock investors generally demand a higher return than bond investors. Otherwise, they'd buy an asset-backed bond rather than stock. What's more, the cost is not tax deductible. If investors expect an 11 percent return from the market, then that is the cost of its equity capital. For a particular stock, which may be more risky than the general market, investors may expect some extra return. The common practice for measuring the additional risk is to multiply the expected market return by the company's *beta*. Beta is a measure of the volatility of a company's stock price relative to the market. You can find it in a company's profile on Yahoo! or in the snapshot on MarketGuide.com. To use beta, simply multiply it by the expected market return—call it 11 percent.

Another word of warning is due here. We really, really don't like beta. Not because it's done anything bad, of course—beta's just a number. But too many people use beta as an exact statement of risk. It isn't; it's just a statement of volatility. Enron, for example, never had a huge beta, but as we all now know, it was carrying some massive risks. You can use these approximations to calculate a cost of capital, but *by no means* should you treat low-beta stocks as being less risky. Again, learn the difference and you will have an advantage over most market participants.

Most companies are funded by both debt and equity, so it's necessary to put the two costs together to find the cost of capital. Once you've determined a company's invested capital, you need to determine how much comes from equity funding and how much comes from debt funding. If you find that debt makes up 40 percent of invested capital and equity 60 percent, then you need to weight the costs accordingly. The result is called the *weighted average cost of capital* (WACC). So if we have a situation where debt at 6 percent accounted for 40 percent of invested capital and equity at 11 percent times a beta of 1.2 made up 60 percent, then the WACC equation will be:

$$WACC = (6 \times 0.4) + ([11 \times 1.2] \times 0.6) = 10.32\%$$

This is how much the capital cost the company to obtain on an annual basis. By subtracting that from ROIC, you'll find out how much the company returned on capital after paying the cost of capital. In Messages' case, where there was no debt, the cost came entirely from equity. If its beta is 1.5, then its cost is 16.5 percent. Subtract that from the 2001 ROIC of 39 percent, and Messages returned 22.5 percent on capital in 2002, after accounting for cost.

Beating cost of capital is essential to running a growing business. It's a sign of competitive advantage. If competitors can enter the same business without impediment, prices will fall and returns will shrink, until finally it reaches the cost of capital. Then the business will cease to offer economic value to shareholders. That's a pretty heavy concept, which is why it's critical for potential investors to work through a company's ROIC and WACC. It may save you from some big problems.

Quiz Time!

Since this has been a tough chapter, it's gotta have a comprehensive quiz. This is important stuff. We're going to give you a hypothetical set of financial statements for Messages' 2003 fiscal year and ask you to discern the profitability trend through the various metrics we've discussed. Remember to use average numbers!

MESSAGES INC. BALANCE SHEET—YEAR 2003 COMPARED TO 2002

(IN THOUSANDS) ASSETS	2003	2002
CURRENT ASSETS		
Cash and equivalents	30,000	24,000
Accounts receivable	60,000	34,000
Inventory	40,000	20,000
Prepaid expenses	2,000	1,500
TOTAL CURRENT ASSETS	132,000	79,500
FIXED ASSETS		
Property, plant and equipment, net	18,500	10,800
TOTAL ASSETS	150,500	90,300
LIABILITIES		
CURRENT LIABILITIES		
Short-term debt	0	0
Accounts payable	8,000	6,500
Accrued expenses	23,000	18,000
TOTAL CURRENT LIABILITIES	31,000	24,500
Long-term debt	0	0
TOTAL LIABILITIES	31,000	24,500
SHAREHOLDER EQUITY	119,500	65,800

MESSAGES INC. INCOME STATEMENT—YEAR 2003 COMPARED TO 2002

(IN THOUSANDS) INCOME	2003	2002
Revenue	180,000	97,000
Cost of sales (goods)	100,000	46,500
GROSS PROFIT	80,000	50,500
OPERATING EXPENSES		
Selling/General/Administrative	55,000	27,500
Research/Development	5,000	4,500
TOTAL OPERATING EXPENSES	60,000	32,000
Income from operations	20,000	18,500
Interest income	1,500	1,080
Income before taxes	21,500	19,580
Income taxes	7,300	6,700
NET INCOME	14,200	12,880
Earnings per share	$0.95	$1.07
Basic shares outstanding	15,000	12,000
Diluted shares outstanding	15,000	12,000

MESSAGES INC. 2003 STATEMENT OF CASH FLOWS

(IN THOUSANDS) CASH FLOW	2003	2002
CASH FLOW FROM OPERATING ACTIVITIES		
Net income	14,200	12,880
ADJUSTMENT TO RECONCILE NET INCOME TO NET CASH		
Depreciation	1,800	1,200
EFFECTS OF CHANGE IN OPERATING ASSETS AND LIABILITIES		
Accounts receivable	(26,000)	(20,000)
Inventory	(10,000)	(10,000)
Accounts payable	1,500	3,300
Accrued expenses	5,000	8,000
NET CASH PROVIDED BY OPERATING ACTIVITIES	(13,500)	(4,620)
CASH FLOW FROM INVESTING ACTIVITIES		
Purchases of property, plant, and equipment	(7,700)	(3,000)
Purchase of investments	(8,000)	(10,000)
Sale of investments	13,000	12,500
NET CASH PROVIDED BY INVESTING ACTIVITIES	(2,700)	(500)
CASH FLOWS FROM FINANCING ACTIVITIES		
Proceeds from debt	0	0
Payments of debt	0	0
Proceeds from sale of stock	26,700	11,620
NET CASH PROVIDED BY FINANCING ACTIVITIES	26,700	11,620
NET CHANGE IN CASH	10,500	6,500

1. Determine the cash conversion cycle.

	2003	2002	2001
a. Days sales outstanding	_____	89	79
b. plus Days inventory outstanding	_____	116	137
c. minus Days payables outstanding	_____	38	48
d. Cash conversion cycle	_____	167	168

e. Was this better, or worse, than last year? _____

f. Is this a good trend? _____

g. What were the causes of the change? _____
_____

*Answers: a. 94 b. 108 c. 26 d. 176 e. Worse f. No
g. Shrinking payables and rising receivables*

2. Calculate Messages' return on assets for 2003

	2003	2002	2001
a. ROA	_____	18.3%	19.3%

b. Is Messages' ROA trend positive, or negative?
_____

c. What is driving the trend: profit margin or asset turnover? *(You can determine this by looking at each separately.)* _____

_____

Answers: a. 11.8% b. Negative c. Profit margin. It shrank from 13.3% to 7.9%, even though asset turns increased to 1.49

3. Calculate Messages' return on equity for 2003.

	2003	2002	2001
a. ROE	_____	25.1%	27.1%

b. Is Messages' ROE trend positive, or negative?

_____

c. What is driving the trend: profit margin, asset turnover, or leverage? *(You can determine this by looking at each separately.)* _____

_____

Answers: a. 15.3% b. Negative c. Declining profit margin. Leverage did not change by much and asset turn actually increased.

4. Calculate Messages' return on invested capital for 2003 (tax rate remains 34%).

	2003	2002	2001
a. NOPAT	_____	$12,963	$7,765
b. Invested capital	_____	$46,650	$19,500
c. ROIC	_____	39%	53%

(Remember to use average invested capital.)

d. Is Messages' ROIC trend positive, or negative?

_____

e. What is driving the trend? _____

Answers: a. $14,388 b. $98,500 c. 19.8% d. Negative e. Invested capital base is increasing, but NOPAT is growing slowly.

5. If Messages' weighted average cost of capital is 16.5%, is it beating its costs?

Yes   No

Answer: Yes, but only by a small amount. With the trend running the wrong way, the situation does not look good for next year.

CHAPTER 10

VALUING YOUR COMPANY

Now you're ready to start buying stocks. Congratulations. It's a fascinating, stimulating, and—hopefully—enriching step.

To start this chapter, let's head straight to the dictionary for a refresher in the meaning of the word *investing*. OK, maybe you don't want to get up, jog into the den, and lug that fun-filled volume off the shelf, so we'll look it up for you, courtesy of Merriam-Webster: "To commit money or capital," it reads, "in order to gain a financial return."

Read the second part of that sentence again: "in order to gain a financial return." You invest, in other words, by committing money or capital with the expectation that someone, someday, will buy whatever asset you purchased for more than you paid for it.

It's simple enough to understand when stocks are involved. You buy a stock with the hope that it will go up in value, right? Right. But as we'll discuss here, that's a bit of an oversimplification.

Let's say you woke up tomorrow morning, found $1,010 in cash under the bed, spent $10 taking us to McDonald's for breakfast and enjoyed your meal so much you decided to spend the other $1,000 on McDonald's stock. Flush with cash and hash browns,

you surf over to your online broker and place an order for as much McDonald's stock as you can buy for a grand.

Investing, are you? Sure, since you hope you'll be able to sell those shares someday for more than $1,000. But here's our question for you: what makes you think you will? That brings us to valuation, which, put simply, is the practice of trying to figure out how much a stock is worth. Once you've done that, you can decide how much you are willing to pay for it—and wait for your price to come along.

Let's amend the Merriam-Webster definition of *investing,* if we may be so bold. We find the above definition to be a bit broad, because it would cover a great many activities that we do not consider to be investing. After all, putting all your money down on 33 black at the roulette table is "to commit money in order to gain a financial return," right? So is playing the horses or the lottery, but we dare say those activities are well outside what we define as investing. Let's define it this way: "Investing is the informed deployment of capital with a reasonable expectation for financial return."

Now, we've jimmied with the old dictionary enough. Let's get down to pricing stocks.

LOOKING FORWARD AND LOOKING BACKWARD

There are two main ways of examining a stock's valuation: by looking backward and examining real results and numbers that have already been reported, and by looking forward, making assumptions about how a company is likely to perform down the road.

Both methods have their place in an investor's tool kit, but it's important to understand the distinction between the two. Historical performance is very useful—in large part because the numbers are real, and therefore don't require any guesswork or assumptions about what they mean. But if you are considering a stock purchase, you are in essence making a statement about what a company is going to do in the future.

Unfortunately, as anyone knows who's ever tried predicting the future—using tarot cards, tea leaves, Ouija boards, whatever—it's pretty much impossible to perfectly forecast anything. (That's why The Motley Fool suggests you stay away from short-term trading and market timing: whatever tools you may have, they won't turn you into Nostradamus—who was still wrong a heck of a lot more than he was right.)

But every time investors buy a stock, they're making the statement—even unconsciously—that they think a stock's price is lower than the present value of all the cash flows a business will be able to generate. We say "present value" to take into account something called the "time value of money," which essentially means that a dollar delivered today is worth more than the mere promise of a dollar tomorrow. You dealt with a similar concept last chapter with return on invested capital.

The predictive part of an investor's job is pretty tough, certainly tougher than blowing bubbles and eating strawberries. (Welcome back from your bubble-blowing, strawberry-eating break! Did you really try to do those things at the same time?) That's why, although backward-looking valuation measures are useful, they can take you only so far. Unless you just made a time machine out of a DeLorean, you're not buying a stock because of what it did yesterday, or even today. You're buying it for what you believe it can do tomorrow, the next day, and hopefully, the next few decades.

But to do that, you need to be able to make assumptions about how a company will perform in future periods. Again, unless you're neighbors with Doc Brown from *Back to the Future*, you can see the inherent difficulty—we might even say impossibility—in doing this with scientific precision. (Then again, if you're neighbors with Doc Brown you've got other, bigger problems to deal with—like the plutonium he keeps sneaking into your trash can.)

Luckily, scientific precision isn't what we're shooting for. "Good enough" is something that can work quite well in investing. We'll explain why a bit further on, but first some nuts and bolts. In order to get you comfortable with the concept of looking into a company's crystal ball, let's talk about growth rates and forecasts.

UNDERSTANDING GROWTH AND GROWTH RATES

Investors, generally speaking, gauge a company's worth by looking at its profits. This comes from the notion that when an investor buys shares of a company, he is buying the right to a—you guessed it—*share* of the profits that business is able to generate. In practice, this isn't the case. A company isn't going to write investors a check equal to the sum total of its profits at the end of this year—that's just not the way companies work. And as a long-term investor, you wouldn't want that anyway.

That's because when you buy shares of (for example) a restaurant operator, you want that eatery to make more and more money, to expand, to attract more customers. And to do that, the company must do the types of things that allow it to raise prices and boost profit margins—like teasing you with huge baskets of bread to start the meal, then putting five shrimp in your cocktail instead of six.

These things cost money. The company needs to reinvest profits, dropping that money into new stores, more waiters, advertisements, nonstick bibs, and so on. The company's betting that they'll bring in more money than will be needed to make that happen. It's the concept of *operating leverage,* which suggests that profits can grow more quickly than revenues or costs.

If the restaurant's plans work, profits will increase even further and the company will be able to grow even more, and so on and so forth. (When the restaurant chain finally starts to hit a time when it can't grow as quickly as it once could, that might be a good time for it to start paying you a dividend to compensate for the slowed growth potential.)

Quiz: Which Type of Company Would You Rather Own?

- One that consistently posts better earnings and whose stock plows steadily higher?

or

- One that has made the same amount of money for six straight years, has little sense of enterprise, and has a stock that is trading at the same price it was ten years ago?

OK, that wasn't particularly difficult. Not all quizzes are; after all—this is a workbook, not an inquisition. Obviously investors should want to own companies that can grow profits consistently and more rapidly than their competitors, which helps explain why a stock's value is tied so closely to its profits and its profit growth. But simple concepts are essential to beating the market. (There actually is a third option here. If a company made the same amount of money for six years but was *(a)* profitable and *(b)* disciplined in paying hefty dividends back to investors, this might be a better choice. These companies are harder to find, but in such situations, a no- or low-growth company may actually be OK.)

You want to find companies that have legions of customers starving for their products, and that have a systematic approach to generating profit off that demand. And if you understand these companies' growth rates, you're one step closer to being able to make educated guesses about their future.

A company's earnings growth rate is much like a child's. Infants double in size during their first year. The chances of a fifty-two-year-old man doubling his height next year, though, are pretty slim. (If you need a break from all this heavy thinking, check out F. Scott Fitzgerald's short story "The Curious Case of Benjamin Button," about a man who is born elderly and lives his life in reverse.)

But much of what we're going to do here has, as its direct analogy, the growing rate of your ten-year-old daughter or son. If your child grows from sixty inches to sixty-six inches next year, he will have grown by 10 percent. We'll be making a similar calculation when studying the growth in profitability of public companies.

Generally, investors like to look at one-year, three-year, and five-year growth rates to get a sense of the short-, intermediate-, and longer-term performance of, and expectations for, a company. Let's use our old friend Messages Inc. as a guinea pig—it doesn't mind.

MESSAGES INC.'S GROWTH RATES

Two years ago, Messages Inc. posted earnings per share of $1.05. Last year, the company improved earnings nicely, reporting $1.27 in net income per share. What was the company's one-year growth rate? You figure it by taking this year's number, dividing it by last year's number, and subtracting 1.

$$\text{Growth rate} =$$
$$(\$1.27 \div \$1.05) - 1 = 1.21 - 1, \text{ or } 21\%$$

To express your mastery of the calculation you just ran, please stand up in your chair and tell the world, "Messages Inc. grew earnings by 21 percent last year." (Turn off the ceiling fan first.)

Now sit down again. You should have told us that you were reading this instead of paying attention in class. Ready for the next challenge? OK. Let's say this year the company managed to churn out $1.41 in earnings per share. What's the total growth from two years ago? This stuff is cake.

Growth rate =
($1.41 ÷ $1.05) − 1 = 1.34 − 1, or 34%

Expressed in English, "Messages Inc. grew earnings by 34 percent over the last two years."

Got it? Now it's time to step up the most difficult growth rate calculation we'll force you to make. While knowing a company's growth rate over time is useful, even more important to us as investors is its compound annual rate of growth.

Before we proceed to the compound annual growth rate (some annoying people abbreviate this as CAGR), though, we're going to force *another* acronym on you. We generally hate acronyms, but over time some of them even actually stick, making it easier for lazy authors. So henceforth, when referring to earnings per share, we'll often be using "EPS."

Armed with your new acronym, let's return to Messages Inc.

EARNINGS PER SHARE

2002	2001	2000	1999
$1.41	$1.27	$1.05	$0.87

What we're searching for now is the compound annual EPS growth rate. To find it, we'll need to put our first root into play. Yep, you've come a few hundred pages in this workbook using nothing but fifth-grade mathematics. Now it's time to push things up a year or two, and force a cube root on you.

To get the smoothed-out, annual growth rate over a given number of years, follow these steps:

1. Divide the most recent number by the earliest.
2. Take a root of the resulting number, using the root that matches the number of years measured (for example, a square root for two years, a cube root for three years).
3. Subtract 1.

Let's try our example. With Messages, we must divide 2002's number by 1999's. Then, because we're looking at a three-year period—we're counting the number of years *elapsed* here—we must take the cube root of that number. Then we subtract 1. OK, so what was Messages Inc.'s compound annual growth rate between 1999 and 2002?

Step 1. 1.41 ÷ 0.87 = 1.62

Step 2. Cube root of 1.62 = 1.18

Step 3. 1.18 − 1 = 0.18 = 18%

In other words, Messages grew its EPS at a compounded rate of 18 percent annually between 2002 and 1999. (We generally won't try this for anything less than three years, and the more the better. If only one or two years have elapsed, you probably don't have enough data to really justify the smoothing-out effect this operation creates.)

That covers the three-year growth rate. To do the five-year or any other, all you have to do is replace the cube root with the fifth root or whatever root is appropriate. *Voilà!* In truth, you should definitely consider three-year, five-year, or even longer periods when analyzing stocks to see how a business is developing, rather than honing in on short-term results.

Why not try out your newfound knowledge on a quick exercise? A note, though: unless you're Vulcan, chances are you'll need a scientific calculator to do the roots. (Your computer may have one installed, or you can make a spreadsheet to do it for you.) Several websites, including, of course, Fool.com, have compounding calculators that do all this fun work for you—but don't cheat just yet. Try some out so you get familiar with the math at work.

CALCULATING GROWTH RATES

Good luck with these, Fool.

	First Earnings	Latest Earnings	Years Elapsed	Annual Growth Rate
Messages Inc.	$0.87	$1.41	3	18%
Mr. Software	$0.56	$0.71	2	13%
Tatooland	$2.00	$2.92	2	a.___
Gino's Games	$0.20	$1.43	3	b.___
Pennsylvania Steel	$17.21	$21.23	2	c.___
Alfonso Lucky's	$1.57	$1.92	1	d.___
FoolMart	$0.89	$1.32	2	e.___
PG's Putters	$2.20	$4.17	4	f.___
Young Programmers Co.	$0.36	$3.21	9	g.___
Just for Dogs	$4.98	$6.12	1	h.___
Just for Automobiles	$19.68	$23.12	2	i.___
Nightlights Co.	$0.75	$1.25	2	j.___

Answer key: a. 21% *b.* 93% *c.* 11% *d.* 22% *e.* 22% *f.* 17% *g.* 28% *h.* 23% *i.* 8% *j.* 29%

Great job!

PROJECTIONS

That should give you a pretty good idea about how to examine a company's past earnings growth. As we've said, however, investors should be more concerned with what a company *will* do—and coming up with useful projections can be tricky business.

One place you can go to get these numbers is Wall Street research. This comes in many forms, generally, put out by analysts at one of the big brokerages, but also by publishers like Value Line and Standard & Poor's, whose publications are available at your local library. You could also come up with your own estimates, using past financial information, company guidance, and your understanding of a business and industry to generate your own numbers. Truth be told, we like this kind of numbers best, but it does take a lot more work.

We can't give you detailed instructions on how to do that here—there's just too much going on, and we'd hate to oversimplify. What we can do, however, is give you a general idea about how analysts come up with their estimates so you understand some of the work that goes into forecasting financial results.

Wall Street analysts are paid to tell investors how much they think a company's earnings are going to grow in the future. In general, analysts will begin with the estimates put out by the companies themselves. Naturally, the company is a great place to start for insight into its own future performance. When a firm tells investors what to expect in coming quarters or years, it's called "guidance."

But management isn't always going to get things right, nor are most managers ever going to come right out and say, "Wow, we've seen the future, and it looks absolutely awful." And while you might think there's nothing riskier that an executive could do than speculate about specific aspects of his or her company's future performance, they do so constantly. For example, eBay's CEO once told investors what sort of revenues they could expect in 2005—even though it was only 2001 when she said it.

That was nice of her, but she doesn't really know what's going to happen between now and then. In the late 1990s, for example, telecommunications companies spent an aggregate $1.2 trillion on a communications revolution that never materialized. Ouch. Anytime you're using anyone's forecasts, keep in mind that they should always be taken with a grain of salt—and the further out the forecast looks, the larger the grain should be. (It grows exponentially, like our prize aluminum foil ball.)

And so, while there are limitations inherent in any earnings forecasting—which is why you shouldn't just take any analyst's number and consider it gospel—there are some safeguards against the numbers' fallibility.

First, there is usually more than one analyst covering a company. That's a good thing, because it allows you to collect a number of different viewpoints. There's some safety in numbers, after all. Second, if you can get a look at an analyst's full reports you can see the assumptions they used to come up with their earnings targets and either accept them, discard them entirely, or tinker with them to come up with your own projections. Just be absolutely sure to look at the assumptions and think about them.

Next-quarter earnings estimates should be fairly accurate because so much direct company input is factored in, and many times companies' sales cycles for the next quarter have already begun. (Remember those cash conversion cycles? Bingo.) In the end, however, we aren't really concerned with whether anyone can predict next year's, or next quarter's, earnings per share to the penny, or a company's quarterly revenue to the dollar. Close enough is good enough.

For stuff that looks further out we'd rather tinker with our expectations—incorporating company input, if available—to develop a range of scenarios that can help us guess at how a company might perform down the road under a variety of different cir-

cumstances. The exercise is useful because it makes you think, in a detailed fashion, about what really makes a company go.

Wall Street analysts sometimes use very acutely detailed forecasting models, while others use very simple ones or rely almost wholly on company guidance (particularly in the short term). What we hope to illustrate here is a very logical, but important, concept: the more variables an analyst considers, the harder his job becomes—but the more informed his output can become. And many times you will find that these analysts with their multivariabled models are absolutely precisely wrong in their projections, because they don't take into account something as basic as, well, the fact that economic conditions change.

THE MORE FACTORS, THE BETTER

Putting on our analyst hat for a moment—it's really just a dirty old University of Alabama baseball cap—let's use Franks Corp. (ticker: DOGG) as an example of what we mean. Franks Corp. has been growing sales at a compounded rate of 10 percent annually over the last five years, but the trend has been improving and the company has been able to get its products into more and more supermarkets each year.

Last year, the company performed thus:

MOST RECENT YEAR

Revenue	$100M
Gross profit	$50M
Operating expense	$15M
Operating income	$35M
Income tax	$11.9M (assumes a standard 34% tax rate)
Net income	$23.1M
Shares outstanding	20M
EPS	$1.16

If we assume, based on recent history and perhaps comments from the Franks Corp. CEO that the company can bump up sales 13 percent this year, the easiest thing to do might be to estimate as follows:

NEXT YEAR

Revenue	$113M ($100M × 1.13)
Gross profit	$56.5M ($113M × 0.5)
Operating expense	$17M ($113M × 0.15)
Operating income	$39.5M ($56.5M − $17M)
Income tax	$13.4M (assumes a standard 34% tax rate)
Net income	$26.1M ($39.5M − $13.4M)
Shares outstanding	20M
EPS	$1.31

Presto! We've made a very cursory EPS estimate for Franks Corp. based on 13 percent sales growth and the assumption that gross and operating margins won't change.

But there's a danger in simply extrapolating trends from the past into the future. For one thing, few companies grow smoothly. A young company that's growing rapidly may see sales grow 30 percent one year, then 55 percent the next, and so on, before maturing as a company and slowing down. Had trends stayed the same as they were in the 1970s, for example, we would all be using Polaroid cameras, drinking four gallons of Tang a day, and neckties would currently be approximately three and a half feet wide.

Meanwhile, it can be hard to grow a large company quickly, for any number of reasons. Disappointments always happen. No company can outperform every year, just as no investor should expect to have a perfect track record with every stock she buys. Even established, world-beating companies can't be counted on to reliably grow earnings by 15 percent every year. The economy changes, tastes change, and—as Hillary Flammond noted in the too little remembered film *Top Secret!*—hairstyles change.

Our example, meanwhile, was so simple that all we did was boost the revenue number by 13 percent and keep all the other margin figures the same. What's the chance of that happening?

ANALYSTS KEEP TINKERING

Analysts try to do better, and so can you. Let's say, for example, that we knew from reading the annual report that half the company's sales were from hot dogs and half the company's sales were from buns. And what if we noticed that over the last several years, the company had been selling more hot dogs, on a relative basis, than buns, and the company said hot dogs were more profitable than buns?

Let's say that gross profits on hot dogs are 55 percent, compared with 45 percent for buns. And let's say that next year we can expect Franks Corp. to get 60 percent of its sales from hot dogs, and 40 percent from buns. (Still there?) We can incorporate those factors into our model to make our estimate even better, even using that same 13 percent revenue growth estimate and leaving all the other numbers the same.

NEXT YEAR

Revenue	$113M ($100M × 1.13)
Gross profit	$57.6M ($113M × 0.60 × 0.55) + ($113M × 0.40 × 0.45)
Operating expense	$17M ($113M × 0.15)
Operating income	$40.6M (57.6M − $17M)
Income tax	$13.8M (assumes a standard 34% tax rate)
Net income	$26.8M ($40.6M − $13.8M)
Shares outstanding	20M
EPS	$1.34

As you can see, by tinkering with our minimodel we've improved the information it can give us by incorporating more data about the business and the way it operates. In order to make it truly useful, however, we'd need to go much further—but this, at least, should give you some idea of the thinking analysts do when making projections.

To improve on the above, an analyst might, for example, consider factors like changes in compensation and other costs, a changing tax rate, gains (or losses) from corporate investments, the potential cost of legal or labor issues, changes in the number of shares outstanding, fluctuations in the Amazon basin's monthly rainfall, the trend of bun manufacturing facilities relocating to Papua New Guinea, and so on.

Before we move on, let's do one more quick exercise, in which *you* come up with a new set of estimates for the company by adding a new variable. Let's raise operating expense by 2 percent as the company spends more on advertising and hires a few new people to handle the growth in the bun account, but keep the rest of the data the same as in the last example.

NEXT YEAR

Revenue	_____
Gross profit	_____
Operating expense	_____
Operating income	_____
Income tax	_____
Net income	_____
Shares outstanding	20M
EPS	_____

ANSWERS

Revenue	$113M ($100M × 1.13)
Gross profit	$57.6M ($113M × 0.60 × 0.55) + ($113M × 0.40 × 0.45)
Operating expense	$19.2M ($113M × 0.17)
Operating income	$38.4M ($57.6M − $19.2M)
Income tax	$13.1M (assumes a standard 34% tax rate)
Net income	$25.3M ($38.4M − $13.1M)
EPS	$1.27

Look at that! We tinker with the company's expenses a bit and suddenly our growth expectations are shaved by a few points.

You've no doubt figured out by now that the more variables you play with in your model, the more assumptions you are making and the more things you are setting yourself up to be wrong about. There are also always going to be unexpected events—layoffs, for example, or lawsuits, or CEO firings that require big payouts—that you can't predict and that will confound your predictions.

As a result, models and their outputs shouldn't be used with the idea that the more work you put into them, the better the chance you'll be closer to right. (You might even be more wrong if you are using bad assumptions or neglect important factors.) Instead, consider them a means of testing different situations and circumstances—a boom year, for example, or a couple of down quarters—to get an idea of the possibilities.

Now that you understand the concepts of growth rates, ratios, and projections, let's put those concepts to work on some basic valuation concepts. We'll start with the "dollar bill" of valuation—in other words, the number most commonly handed around—the price-to-earnings ratio.

THE PRICE-TO-EARNINGS (P/E) RATIO

You've probably heard a business-suited lady on her mobile phone in the airport gabbing about the P/E ratio of particular stocks she's studying. "I've been watching Mr. Software," she'll say, "and the company is trading at a P/E of 21. In the meantime, Messages Inc. is trading at 23 times earnings. I'm thinking of selling."

Don't get it? In just a few minutes you will.

The P/E ratio is just a quick way to compare a company's market value with the amount of earnings (or net income) it reported in a recent period. Most folks use either the latest full year or last twelve months, but it doesn't matter as long as you compare oranges to oranges. (Some prefer to use estimates for next year's earnings, a topic we'll discuss in greater depth later.)

There are two ways to generate the P/E: either *(a)* divide a company's share price by its earnings per share, or (b) divide its market capitalization (the total value of all its shares) by its total net income to get the same figure. We'll illustrate below, but first let's look at some numbers from the income statement in Messages' 2002 annual report:

Net income	$12,600,000
Shares outstanding	12,000,000
Earnings per share	$1.05 (or $12,600,000 ÷ 12,000,000)

Now, let's say the company's stock is trading at $24 per share today. How do you conjure up the P/E? Well, using method *b*, you could take the company's market capitalization . . .

Market capitalization =
$24 × 12 million shares outstanding = $288 million

. . . and divide that by its net income:

P/E = $288 million ÷ $12.6 million = 22.9

Or, using method *a*, you could simply divide the share price by the earnings per share:

P/E = $24 ÷ $1.05 = 22.9

Either way, you get the same number: a P/E of 22.9, or 23 if you're the sort who likes to round off your numbers. In investorese, you can now say with confidence that Messages Inc. "has a P/E of 23" or "trades at 23 times 2002 earnings." This is sometimes called the *trailing P/E* and is a very commonly discussed number.

EXERCISE

Before we start talking about the "forward P/E" and other ways we can use the P/E ratio to help us value stocks, let's calculate a few quick P/Es to get our juices flowing.

	Price Per Share	Earnings Per Share	P/E Ratio
Messages Inc.	$24	$1.05	23
Mr. Software	$8	$0.56	14
Tattooland	$67	$2.00	34
Gino's Games	$11	$0.20	55
Pennsylvania Steel	$143	$17.21	8
Alfonso Lucky's	$21	$1.57	*a.___*
FoolMart	$25	$0.89	*b.___*
PG's Putters	*c.___*	$2.20	34
Young Programmers Co.	$12	$0.36	*d.___*
Just for Dogs	$91	*e.___*	18
Just for Automobiles	*f.___*	$19.68	12
Nightlights Co.	$16	*g.___*	21

Answer key: a. 13 *b.* 28 *c.* $75 *d.* 33 *e.* $5.06 *f.* $236 *g.* $0.76

OK, dear Fool—question time. Why do you think Gino's Games, which makes games for your PlayStation, is trading at a much higher multiple of earnings than Just for Automobiles, which sells car parts? Why would the market value Gino's earnings much more richly than those of the auto company?

Think on this for a second. (You're done already?) Well, you were right: it could be a number of things. Perhaps the market expects Gino's earnings to grow more rapidly because the video game business is hot these days. Maybe Gino's has five consecutive years of strong performance under its belt, while a competitor has beaten the oil filters off Just for Automobiles for twenty years.

Or maybe investors simply like the fact that making software has profit margins a good deal better than hawking replacement oil filters. It's an investor's job to figure out the whys and decide whether they represent good opportunities.

The more tools you add to your repertoire, the better you'll be able to do this—so let's go get some more tools!

THE FORWARD P/E

Now that we've talked about the trailing P/E, let's talk about the forward P/E, which is shorthand for the price-to-earnings ratio of a company using *projected* future earnings as the *E* in the equation.

You figure the forward P/E the same way as the trailing: you take a company's share price (or market value) and divide it by that company's projected earnings per share (or net income) for a future period. Where do you get the projection? As we said before, you can come up with your own estimate, use an analyst's, or use a combination of the two.

The most commonly used *E* for figuring forward P/Es—which, like trailing P/Es, generally look forward one year or twelve months—is what's called the market's consensus estimate. (Users of the Value Line data service sometimes favor something called the "median P/E," which incorporates six months of trailing numbers and six months of estimates.)

Several firms, including First Call, Zacks, and I/B/E/S, regularly poll the analysts covering each company to find out what their estimates are, and then come up with a mean. These numbers are widely available online, at Fool.com and elsewhere.

So, if five analysts cover Franks Corp., and they have the following estimates for next year's EPS . . .

Analyst 1	$1.31
Analyst 2	$1.34
Analyst 3	$1.27
Analyst 4	$1.32
Analyst 5	$1.40

. . . then Wall Street's consensus estimate for next year is $1.33, since

$$(\$1.31 + \$1.34 + \$1.27 + \$1.32 + \$1.40) \div 5$$
$$= \$6.64 \div 5 = \$1.33$$

It's this one-year forward P/E—analysts will often have estimates going several years out—that is used in the most commonly accepted shorthand for valuing a stock.

USING THE P/E

Now we'll talk about ways you can put P/E ratios to work.

COMPARE IT TO GROWTH RATES

Let's return to Franks Corp., which we discussed not long ago, to explore this concept. Remember its forward P/E?

$$P/E = \$10 \div \$1.33 = 7.5$$

And what is next year's projected earnings growth rate?

$$Rate = \$1.33 \div \$1.16 = 15\%$$

What some investors will now do is compare the two numbers—the 7.5 to the 15 percent. The general thinking is that a company trading at a forward P/E equal to its projected growth rate is "fairly valued"—meaning that its shares are trading right about where they should be. But Franks Corp. is trading at a pretty nifty discount to its projected growth rate—about half—and might therefore be undervalued. (We're guessing that you can figure out "overvalued" for yourself.)

Comparing P/E ratios to growth rates can be significantly more useful than simply comparing two companies' P/E ratios. Why? Let's compare Franks Corp. to its old nemesis Beans Inc. (ticker: PNTO) to illustrate.

	FRANKS CORP.	BEANS INC.
Price	$10	$8
Last year's EPS	$1.16	$1.14
Projected EPS	$1.33	$1.14

Using the data above, we can see that Franks Corp.'s trailing P/E is 8.6, while Beans Inc.'s is just 7. Golly, why would we want to pay $10 for the former's earnings when we can get the latter's—the same amount, no less—for $2 off? (Say, we could even take that $2 to the hot dog stand across the street . . . a little ketchup and onions . . . Could be good.)

We wouldn't, necessarily. That chart also tells us that Franks Corp.'s forward P/E is 7.5, while Beans Inc.'s remains 7. Remember, we're more concerned with what Franks Corp. is going to do—keep growing, while Beans Inc. has apparently run out of gas—than what it has already done, and we don't want to pay nearly the same amount for no earnings growth as we would for a nice 15 percent pop.

THE PEG (FOOL RATIO)

The Motley Fool has also developed a simple tool an investor can use for a very quick picture of a company's valuation: the PEG, or Fool Ratio.

The PEG—price-to-earnings growth ratio—is really just about taking the work you've already done with P/Es and growth rates one step further. Remember when we generated Franks Corp.'s forward P/E (7.5) and projected earnings growth rate (15 percent)? The Fool Ratio simply compares the two numbers to each other to create a new number.

$$PEG = 7.5 \div 15 = 0.5$$

Though we don't recommend using the PEG as a be-all, end-all valuation measure, it can give you a framework for further research. How should you use the number? We're interested in learning more about companies with Fool Ratios below 1. The higher it gets, the more overvalued the stock may be.

COMPARE A COMPANY'S P/E TO THOSE OF SIMILAR COMPANIES IN SIMILAR INDUSTRIES

If you think about it, it's not really fair to compare Gino's Games to Just for Automobiles. Really, what's the point? The companies' goals, business outlooks, and market opportunities are so completely different that you wouldn't get much out of such an apples–to–VW Beetles comparison.

Instead, why not compare Gino's Games to companies like Selena's Software and Verve's Videogames? We did, and we found out the following:

COMPANY	P/E
Gino's Games	25
Selena's Software	30
Verve's Videogames	12

Look at that! Something's definitely going on here. Unfortunately, we can't tell what it is just from looking at these numbers. We do, however, now have a reason to look things over and try to figure out if Verve's Videogames is the steal of the century or if there's something so wrong with the company that Selena's and Gino's have left it in the dust.

WEAKNESSES OF THE P/E

Many investors are wary of the P/E ratio. One of the biggest reasons is the formula's reliance on net income, the *E* in the equation.

Net income is a notoriously unreliable number. Though it theoretically represents profits, over the years the pressure on companies to meet quarterly earnings estimates—in other words, to have quarterly EPS match up with, or beat, the Street's mean estimate—has led many executives to make "managing earnings" job number one. We hate this.

Such an approach, focusing as it does on short-term results and a few pennies of net income per share, has turned net income into more of a creation of accountants than a real measure of how much economic value has been created each quarter or year. Remember our previously mentioned stress on the balance sheet and cash flow statement over the income statement? In this section, we'll discuss a few things to look out for when examining net income so you can decide how valuable a particular company's P/E will really be to you.

1. EARNINGS AREN'T ALWAYS "REAL"

You'd think figuring a company's profits would be pretty simple, right? Take revenues, subtract costs and expenses, take out taxes, and there you are.

Unfortunately, it's rarely that easy. There are a lot of ways companies can muddy the earnings picture:

- **Pro Forma Earnings.** There are two ways companies can report earnings. They can use either pro forma figures or generally accepted accounting principles (GAAP). *Pro forma* means

"as if," and that's exactly what pro forma figures represent: earnings *as if* certain things were the case. Those "things" are often quite important, however. While Wall Street has often let pro formas stand as a company's earnings number, watch carefully for signs of trouble, including (but not only) extremely large write-offs, "onetime charges" that happen more than once, and so on. Pro formas have their place—with telecommunications firms, for example, that have lots of network assets that depreciate as they age—but investors should watch for abuse.

- **EBITDA.** Some companies like to turn investor attention away from net income and cash flow and toward something called EBITDA, or earnings before interest, taxes, depreciation, and amortization. Companies like it because it is in some ways a proxy for operating cash flow because it leaves out two non-cash expenses: depreciation of assets and amortization of debt. Unprofitable companies will sometimes point to EBITDA profits as an indicator of what net income might look like when they turn the corner. Unfortunately, EBITDA excludes important cash factors like capital expenditures and debt payments. Without considering those, we really don't know much about how a company is doing.

- **Exchange Rates.** Companies that do lots of business overseas are often affected by changes in exchange rates, particularly if they deal in more volatile currencies. This can be complicated, but in essence the changes in exchange rates can raise or lower profits as recorded in dollars. In the end, currency fluctuations are a cost of doing business overseas and investors should ignore it—and watch for companies that tend not to mention it in good times but complain about it in bad times.

- **Stock Options.** Giving employees stock as part of their compensation is a nice way to boost esprit de corps. But there's a downside, too.

Companies can defer taxation on compensation based upon options, which means that while compensation comprising cash or stock is taxed at market value, options are assumed to have zero value at issuance. As a result, the employee pays no tax and the company records no expense until the options are exercised. This, critics say, deflates corporate compensation expense in the near term, and severely distorts earnings.

- **Buybacks.** One of the easiest ways a company can boost its EPS is by buying back shares, which can have a significant impact on the P/E ratio. While there's nothing wrong with buybacks, especially if a company gets its own stock on the cheap, investors should still track changes in a company's share count, because repurchasing stock can help a company increase EPS without actually growing earnings.

- **Accelerate Depreciation.** All companies make capital expenditures in factories, computers, office furniture, and the like. All of these things eventually become worthless from an accounting perspective, and are thus subtracted from current operations on a schedule. One way a company can alter its EPS is by changing that schedule. Got a factory depreciating on a thirty-year schedule? Change it to forty!

2. COMPANIES AREN'T ALWAYS PROFITABLE

If you paid any attention to the stock market in the late 1990s, you noticed that there were an awful lot of people buying companies that didn't have profits. At all. That means either that they sold whatever they were offering for less than it cost to obtain or make, or that it cost them more to run the company than they could recoup in sales. (Sometimes both.) Was that a smart move?

Well, in a lot of cases it wasn't. These companies kept themselves afloat by selling stock and/or issuing debt to raise money in the hopes that by the time that money was spent, they could turn a profit. In-

vestors who bought those stocks despite their being in the red either hoped nobody would notice and the market would keep pushing the stocks up, or hoped that their business plans would pay off. It was a risky move, and in the cases where it didn't work, they usually ended up buying shares of diddly-squat.

Remember EBITDA, which we talked about not long ago? In some of these companies' cases, EBITDA profits weren't enough to keep them afloat as other cash costs sunk their ships. Only advanced investors should consider companies that operate in this fashion, because analyzing them requires so many broad assumptions in order to analyze that they are very tough to value.

Of course, flimsy dot-coms don't have a monopoly on unprofitability. It happens to the best of 'em. Plenty of solid, established companies fall on hard times for quarters or even years as business slows, costs rise, the economy shifts, or other unforeseen events occur.

When that happens, it's an investor's job to decide how likely it is that the company will get back above water, what it will look like at that point, and how much that company might be worth. For a company with a long history of growth and profits—and plenty of cash on its balance sheet—a few unprofitable quarters shouldn't necessarily be seen as the end of the world.

3. SOME STOCKS MAY ALWAYS SEEM "OVERVALUED" ON A P/E BASIS

We've discussed a number of ways to use P/E ratios to determine whether or not a company's shares are fairly priced. But what if you've researched a company thoroughly, love everything about it from its balance sheet to the CEO's golf handicap (high, since she spends too much time in the office), and when you get down to valuation its shares are nowhere near your target price?

Unfortunately, many companies rarely represent what might be called bargains. Why? Because they are leaders. They have the smoothest operations, the best management, the best TV commercials, the best track record—you name it. When a company has shown the ability to outperform the competition quarter after quarter, year after year, investors generally award it a higher valuation.

Most of the time this means you'll have difficulty buying these "top" companies at bargain prices. (We're sure Mercedes coupes would sell like hotcakes if they cut the price to $15,000 apiece, but that's not likely to happen in time for Christmas.) As a result, you have a decision to make: look around for other opportunities, pay up for a great company, or simply set your price target and wait patiently.

In the end, you may be best off establishing a wish list of companies you'd like to own, tracking their performance and their prices, and holding out for a price you're comfortable with. Even the best companies' shares can come down as market conditions change. Don't feel pressure to buy any specific stock at any given time. Another great one will come along, we promise.

OTHER "PRICE-TO" RATIOS

There are a few other ratios worth noting that are also useful indicators of a company's value and can be used to identify promising investment opportunities. We'll talk about a few of them—the price-to-sales and price-to-book ratios—as well as a few variations.

THE PRICE-TO-SALES RATIO

A fairly simple, easy-to-generate number many investors find useful is the price-to-sales (P/S) ratio. The P/S—if you haven't already figured it out—is derived by dividing a company's market capitalization by the total revenue it reported for the last twelve months or full year.

So if Hollandaise Corp. (ticker: SAUCE) has 20 million shares outstanding that are trading at $50 each and the company had $500 million in sales over the last twelve months, the company's P/S would be:

$$P/S = (\$50 \text{ per share} \times 20 \text{ million shares}) \div \$500 \text{ million in sales} = 2$$

Put another way, investors are awarding Hollandaise Corp. $2 in market value for every dollar of sales. Not too tough.

Ready to try a few?

	Share Price	Sales	Market Capitalization	P/S
Messages Inc.	$24	$97 million	$288 million	2.97
Mr. Software	$8	$97 million	$48.5 million	0.50
Tattooland	$67	$142 million	$394 million	2.77
Gino's Games	$11	$32 million	$452 million	14.1
Pennsylvania Steel	$143	$1.4 billion	$241 million	0.17
Alfonso Lucky's	$21	$549 million	$742 million	a.___
FoolMart	$25	$245 million	$643 million	b.___
PG's Putters	$78	$812 million	$1.9 billion	c.___
Young Programmers Co.	$12	$15 million	$54 million	d.___
Just for Dogs	$91	$140 million	e.___	3.41
Just for Automobiles	$241	f.___	$117 million	1.29
Nightlights Co.	g.___	$610 million	$430 million	0.70

How'd you do? *The answers: a.* 1.35 *b.* 2.62 *c.* 2.34 *d.* 3.60 *e.* $477 million *f.* $91 million *g.* unanswerable

Wait a second. Did we say "unanswerable"? Sure did. (If you caught us, good job.) We didn't give you enough information to answer that last one.

So now you're ready to put the P/S to work. Before you do, however, a word of caution: there are problems with the ratio as a valuation measure.

SALES AREN'T CREATED EQUAL

First, the P/S doesn't take into account that all sales, unlike all people, are not created equal. What do we mean by that? Well, revenues are nice, but profits are even better. Let's compare Hollandaise Corp. to Canadian Bacon Inc. (ticker: PORK) to illustrate.

	HOLLANDAISE CORP.	CANADIAN BACON INC.
Revenues	$1,000*	$1,000
Gross profit	$750	$500
Operating expense	$250	$250
Net profit	$500	$250

* numbers in millions

Look at that! Even though both companies had the same amount of sales and spent the same amount on operating expenses—things like product development, advertising, and administrative costs—it appears that the business of making Hollandaise sauce is a good deal more profitable than the business of making circular slices of ham. (Who knew?) As a result, Hollandaise Corp. generated twice as much net income as Canadian Bacon Inc. That's money investors hope will turn into free cash flow—money that can be used to fund growth, buy back stock, set up private golf courses for employ-

ees, or throw a lavish holiday party for employees, hint hint! Using nothing but price-to-sales ratios here would have left you hurting for important information.

DON'T FORGET CAPITAL STRUCTURE

This computation also ignores a company's capital structure—whether it funds its operations using equity (stock) or debt. If you're wondering why this is important, simply consider your credit cards: if you've got debt, you've got to pay it off—and that can really eat into a lady's paycheck.

To illustrate, let's compare our old friend Hollandaise Corp., Poached Egg Industries (Ticker: RUNNY), and English Muffin Ltd. (Ticker: NOOKS).

	HOLLANDAISE	POACHED EGG	ENGLISH MUFFIN
Sales	$100M	$100M	$100M
Gross profit	$75M	$40M	$40M
Operating income	$25M	$15M	$15M
Interest expense	0	$15M	$40M
Pretax income	$25M	0	($25M)
Taxes	$5M	0	($8M)
Net income	$20M	0	($17M)
Total assets	$200M	$200M	$200M
Net debt assumed	0	$150M	$400M
Market capitalization	$300M	$150M	$10M
PSR	3.0	1.5	0.1

On what did we base our assumed market cap? On a simple concept: investors just aren't going to value a company like English Muffin—where last quarter's operating income was completely devoured by interest payments and even a tax credit to cover its losses couldn't help—as highly as a company like Hollandaise, which has a squeaky-clean balance sheet, or even Poached Egg, where a smaller debt load took a smaller cut out of net income. (Notice that we used the same 10 percent interest rate for both companies' debt obligations.)

As a result, here's another example of a time when if you had done nothing but look at a company's P/S, you might have set your sights on shares of English Muffin—and been stuck with a company that doesn't even have enough sales or profits to cover what it has to pay its lenders each quarter. Yikes!

STILL VALUE IN THE P/S

Given all this, why would anyone use the P/S? Even Wall Street fell in love with the ratio in the late 1990s, using it as a proxy for earnings- or cash-flow-based measures when dealing with unprofitable companies. The flawed logic of many well-compensated analysts went like this: "Company A trades at a P/S of 50. Company B is in the same business as Company A, so it should have the same P/S."

As we've proven above, however, such a simple strategy makes about as much sense as taunting a boar.

Don't give up on the P/S completely, however. It can be a good starting point for further research. If you spot a company trading at a P/S well below that of its competitors, for example, you might consider looking at it more closely to find out the reasons why, examining such other business factors as capitalization, profit margins, and cash flow. You might find out that the lower valuation is deserved after all—or you might find a diamond in the rough.

You can also improve on the P/S by figuring something called the enterprise-value-to-sales (EV/S)

ratio. *Enterprise value* is simply a company's market capitalization *plus* its debt *minus* its cash, the latter two numbers found right on your friendly neighborhood balance sheet. It's meant to represent the amount it would cost to buy all of a company's stock and retire its debt, taking the value of its cash hoard into account.

To see how that would affect Hollandaise Corp., let's say the company had $100 million in cash on its balance sheet and $250 million in long-term debt.

$$\text{EV/S} = (\$300 \text{ million} + \$250 \text{ million} - \$100 \text{ million}) \div \$100 \text{ million} = 4.5$$

The difference between 3 and 4.5 may not seem huge, but that's a difference of 50 percent. Essentially, the market is valuing every dollar of Hollandaise sales significantly higher by virtue of its lack of any long-term debt. Moreover, this number takes into account the $250 million in cash on Hollandaise Corp.'s balance sheet.

THE PRICE-TO-BOOK (P/B) RATIO

"Book value" is a favorite number of so-called value investors, many of whom like to look for companies that are trading for less than the estimated value of their assets (the amount that the company might fetch if it were liquidated and its debt paid off). Such investors sometimes look for situations where pessimism about a company's business prospects has gotten so out of hand that investors don't seem to care about valuable assets—things like cash, factories and facilities, inventory equipment, and so on.

Book value is an accountant's number, in that it's impossible for most investors to know exactly what a company's assets are worth. It would be pretty tough to know the precise value of an office building, for example, though you could estimate it.

It's much easier to calculate the number using information from a company's balance sheet, which is done by taking total assets and subtracting total liabilities. (Both numbers should be clearly marked.) More conservative investors may want to subtract *goodwill,* if there is any, as well: goodwill represents the amount paid in an acquisition above the book value of the acquired company.

Value investors will often look for companies trading at a discount to their book value, so that market value divided by book value is less than one. Be careful, though! If a company trades for less than the value of its assets, it essentially means the market believes its business is destroying value. Advanced investors buy such companies only when they think either the market is dead wrong or a buyout is likely. Both strategies are risky, risky.

There are far more ways to value stocks than these. Some are complex and some are simple. Some are useful and some (yes, some people do use astrology to pick stocks) are preposterous. Any single measure is just a snapshot of one part of the elephant. No single measure tells you all you need to know, and no single measure will be better than any other in every company's case at every point in time.

Is there a magic number you can arrive at to determine *once and for all* whether a stock is undervalued or overvalued? No. And even if there were, it would probably change the next hour or the next day as the company being valued launched some new initiative, or announced disappointing results, what have you.

But just because there is no perfectly accurate magic arrow of valuation that will always hit your target, that doesn't mean you shouldn't be drawing from your quiver and nocking and firing as many arrows as you can. Quite the contrary. Investors who know a company's P/E ratio relative to that of its competitors, who know its financial statements well enough to assess enterprise value, and so forth, will be the savviest investors, most likely to buy and sell at the most appropriate times. If you want to dig deeper and explore advanced topics of stock valuation, come to our Fool School at Fool.com and visit the Valuing Stocks section. Here's a direct address you can plug into your Internet browser: http://www.Fool.com/school/howtovaluestocks.htm.

CHAPTER 11

SO MANY STOCKS, NOT ENOUGH BUCKS

You've managed to get this far in our tome. Did you find the secret scratch-and-sniff surprise on page 47? No? Neither did we. But if you were scratching your head when you first started and now find yourself scratching your chin, you're doing great. No doubt you've been scribbling answers, reading and rereading when necessary, and occasionally dreaming about what you'll do with all your loot twenty years from now. Excellent! But now it's time to get practical. How much money do you have to invest? How much new money can you add each month or quarter?

Remember, you're not some Flying Spinelli circus performer who can work without a net. Any money that you will need in the next three years should *not* be invested in the stock market. The market is too volatile. People learned how true this was in 2000, when all of the "sure thing" stocks of the late 1990s suddenly collapsed, some losing upwards of 95 percent of their value. People who had invested money they needed in the short term were absolutely destroyed by the drop in the market. We cannot stress this enough: although the general trend of the stock market is up, it has in the past dropped precipitously, and it will again. And some stocks never ever recover.

If stocks only ticked higher, you would feel pretty well had by now, buying a workbook with "Buy now" written over and over, cover to cover. Nope. The market has its ups and downs and we have had many three-year periods in the market where stocks have fallen 50 percent or more. If that was money you were counting on for tuition, mortgage payments, medical purposes, or basic necessities next year, look out, Martha, the tree's going to fall. You aren't investing. You are gambling. Don't treat the market as a money machine, waiting for you to shake money out of it every few months or years.

The stock market is your long-term savings vehicle, your thirty-year depository that's built to last and outlast. Used correctly, it'll have you owning a minor-league baseball team in your retirement, or sailing on the *Fool-E-2*, or helping to rebuild a burned-out neighborhood in your city. Who knows? The next workbook might be yours! If you invest for decades to come, you'll recognize that it doesn't really matter how much money you start with, nor that you start *today*. What will matter is that you know what you're doing when you get in and that once you start investing, you never stop.

OK, so take a moment and flip back to your personal balance sheet. You know, at the beginning of the book. Please enter again here how much money you have to invest for more than three years and how much money per quarter you can add to the stock market:

Starting money $ _____

New money per quarter $ _____

Are you still comfortable with that? Great. Now let's determine how to smartly allocate it.

If you left the first line blank—what happened? If virtually all that you can save is already tied up in your company retirement plan, that's fine. That's great. You're like many people, just now wanting to take a more active role in shaping their financial future. However, as you're getting your fiscal house in order, you may find you have more to invest.

Where do you go from here? You've soaked in plenty in terms of possible investments. You have considered the steady index funds (the market equivalent of flicking on the autopilot switch). You have also begun a little independent research to line up a few consumer giants. And, yes, you even analyzed one or two small-cap companies. But now you have to figure how much money goes where. Remember that investing is not a one-time-only thing. You don't have to buy an entire portfolio all at once. In fact, most likely you'll buy a few stocks at a time, building your portfolio as money becomes available. So don't feel like you have to get all of your starting money into stocks *today*.

As you do add, you'll need to continually aim to maximize your investing potential while limiting your dependence on any one particular stock. It's one of the most common mistakes in investing—to dive in headfirst, buying the first stock that your dentist recommends. Many have done it, and most have lost their shirts. Investing can be fun, but it's not a game. This isn't Monopoly money you're playing with. It's the fruit of your labor, and the worst thing that you can do is fritter it away early on, when it can best form the base for future returns. Remember: an investor's greatest advantage is *time*. If you can remain patient and allow your money to grow steadily, rather than try to move it all into the latest, greatest thing, your chance of success is much, much higher. That doesn't mean that you should be timid. It means that you should be thoughtful, assessing at each step of the way what level of risk you are comfortable with, what kinds of investments fit your portfolio, and most important, what your limitations are.

If you're investing for the first time, it's a good bet that you aren't ready to invest intelligently in individual stocks. Even the largest, most dependable company is susceptible to sudden changes in fortune. Who would ever have thought that Polaroid, one of the "Nifty Fifty" stocks in the 1970s, with a great brand name and a history of innovation, would go belly-up? Seasoned stock watchers would have, but it takes time to develop an eye for disasters in the making. No, while you're getting your sea legs, it will be much more prudent to start with Ol' Reliable—an S&P 500 or a total stock market index mutual or exchange-traded fund.

For most people, index funds are the best long-term investment choice. They provide the lowest level of risk, since they are the most diversified single investment you can own. They are the foundation of the low-risk portfolio allocation strategy (along with bond index funds, depending on your investment horizon).

"Hey!" we hear the reader cry. "You just spent chapter after chapter telling us how to look at individual stocks. Now you're telling us to buy an index fund? No way!" It's an understandable reaction, one that most people have. We don't want to keep you from having fun. We just want to keep you from making the mistake that most investors make—getting in over their heads too quickly. All right, here's a compromise: buy an index fund, then select a group of stocks that you think you'd like to own, ones that fit your style of investing. Ah, ah, not so fast—don't buy 'em yet. Put them into a *mock portfolio* and track it for a year. Examine your companies' quarterly earnings announcements. Listen to their conference calls. Notice how the market reacts to news, so that you can determine what it thinks are measures of success. Most important, watch their financial statements develop, to find out which companies are becoming stronger, which are weathering bad times, and which don't have the competitive advantages you thought they had. You'll find that some will soar, some will sink, and some will stay the same. Don't mourn your losses from not buying the ones that shot up. There will be plenty more opportunities to buy good companies at great prices. Before you can do that consistently, however, you need to learn what good companies are and how to determine a great price. Until you really know that, you can't expect to outperform an index fund.

We learn by doing, so treat your mock portfolio as a chance to assess your ability and interest in stocks. Discover the level of risk you're willing to take. Determine the sectors you're interested in learning more about. Decide on the right time to take the plunge into individual stocks. If you're not ready to spend a lot of time on stocks, it's perfectly acceptable to stick with index funds. In fact, many people never get past this point. For these people, we can only say, "Congratulations!!!" Yep, you heard us. People who invest only in index funds will beat almost every other participant in the marketplace. In a sense, they've already won.

But once you feel comfortable with the idea, try adding a stock to your mutual fund base. You'll probably be better off starting with the market-beating giants, the Rule Makers, which are generally more stable than younger companies. Then, if you feel ready, add a Rule Breaker or a small-cap stock, which carries greater risk but also greater potential rewards that will allow you to beat the market, if it is selected well. After all, the greater your exposure to small-cap stocks, the more you'll need to know about financial statements, and the more volatility and short-term pain you'll have to be able to endure. But . . . you think you want to try other investments? Let's see if you should.

PICK *YOUR* ETERNAL FOOLISH ALLOCATION WITH M&M'S

To get a feeling for your Foolish Allocation preference, go to the kitchen and get four cereal bowls and a bag of M&M's. Count out one hundred of 'em. Now label the bowls according to the list above—Index Fund, Rule Maker, Rule Breaker, and Small-Cap Growth. Come on, grab a bag of M&Ms and a few bowls and do this. It's a neat way to approach this; it's worth it, we promise! There's a sweet reward at the end.

Before separating out the M&M's by bowl, bear in mind your preferences for safety and convenience. Consider how much time you have to give over to investing. Consider how able or unable you'll be to absorb high losses when the market gets punished. Consider your ability to refrain from wolfing some of those chocolate candies until the exercise is complete.

Can you hold your stocks through a market decline of 10 percent? Or 25 percent? How about 40 percent? If you remember the steep market losses of 2001, we probably don't have to remind you that stocks don't always go up. We hope the answer to all short-term-loss scenarios suits you because chances are the market will drop that much at least a handful of times more over the next few decades. But, if you want to minimize the amount of volatility and short-term drag, obviously you'll want to be either diversified inside an index fund or adding some large, stable consumer titans on your own.

OK, it's now time to break the hundred M&M's by bowl. We know this'll take some effort, but trust us, your eyes will be opened by doing so. Now, when you're done, first, you'll have your initial allocation. Maybe you have seventy M&M's in the index fund, twenty in consumer giants, and ten in small-caps, and you crossed out an entire category. Whatever you came up with, this is a nice starting point for how to spread your investing dollars out among your current choices, given your current interests and investing skills.

Only three steps left to this exercise.

With your M&M's allocated, translate the percentages into dollar amounts. You think those chocolate sweets have an *M* by accident? No way, that's *money* we're talking about. For example, if you've put seventy M&M's in your index bowl, that's 70 percent of your investing dollars. Multiply your total money to invest by 0.70, and there's how much you might choose to invest in the index fund. Repeat this for every bowl.

OK, now write down on a piece of paper the name of each of your companies. Drop those slips in their appropriate bowl—your heavy blue chips in one bowl, your promising upstarts in the other bowl.

And now for the final step. Look out over your bowls and ask yourself why you didn't just jot this out on paper. This entire exercise was a waste of time! Put all the M&M's in your two hands—don't worry, they won't melt—and begin munching them down, wondering how you got tricked into a silly exercise by Fools. The final step was designed to humble you! Hurry up, put the bowls away before anyone sees. Oh, and by the way, we can't believe we got you to stand up in public places and say things like, "Messages Inc. grew its earnings at a rate of 74 percent last year." That's *too* much! Wish we could have been there.

All right, enough fun. It's not like we're resisting being silly ourselves—just look at our book covers! Anyway, back to business.

The M&M's are simply a device to help you address the issue of risk in investing. It doesn't have to be accepted whole or achieved instantly. Even if you do put it into play, you'll need to reassess your allocation over time, as you add more money, as some of your investments thrive, and as others barely survive. Your first allocation should probably include no M&M's in the Rule Maker, Rule Breaker, or small-cap stocks bowls. Maybe you add some in a year. Or perhaps you invested in some small-caps early on but later realized you didn't have the time necessary to track them. Move M&M's out of the small-cap bowl as your portfolio grows.

A couple of notes before we leave this section. First, don't invest in too many companies at once. You don't have to be an index fund! Generally, *five to fifteen stocks is all that any Foolish portfolio will ever need.* And that's whether you have $6,300 to invest or $630 million. Any more stocks than fifteen and you won't have enough time to watch them all, you won't have enough money to invest significantly in them, and you'll probably start to dilute the effectiveness of your best investments. Remem-

ber, if you're buying individual stocks at all, you want to *out*perform the S&P 500, which you can duplicate just by buying the index fund on the cheap.

People sometimes get confused by this statement. "I hear that you shouldn't let one stock be more than 4 percent of your portfolio, it's just dangerous," they say. Poppycock! First of all, 4 percent maximum means that you own a minimum of twenty companies. Too many to follow. Second of all, that's an arbitrary number. In investing, arbitrary is dumb.

Let's make quick work of this and move on. We're going to name twenty companies:

Dell

Microsoft

Oracle

IBM

Hewlett-Packard

Sun Microsystems

Intel

AMD

Apple

Lexmark

Adobe

Intuit

Macromedia

Yahoo!

AOL Time Warner

Earthlink

NEC

Sony

PeopleSoft

Applied Materials

According to that 4 percent rule, this is a pretty well diversified portfolio. But is it? Heck no! All of these companies are in high tech, and can be expected to be, to varying degrees, influenced by the *exact same factors*. A portfolio containing these companies is in no way diversified.

Contrast this to a portfolio containing three companies:

White Mountains Insurance

Church & Dwight

Yahoo!

One company is in insurance, one is an Internet company, the third owns Arm & Hammer baking soda. With the exception of the fact that all three of these companies are in the pursuit of making money, they have very little in common. The second portfolio—though probably not one we would wholeheartedly endorse—is *much* more diverse than the first.

Finally, in this section and elsewhere, we've used the phrase *small-cap growth stocks*. However, as you may have already noticed, there are still plenty of mid-cap and large-cap companies with the same high-octane growth and the volatile price fluctuations of its smaller peers. They may lack a huge brand name or sell directly to consumers but if the potential upside is still huge, feel free to lump these candidates in your small-cap growth pool.

FOLLOWING UP ON YOUR INVESTMENTS

Stand up where you are and raise your hand if you think that *none* of the information you've collected about your company will ever change and that the stock will perform just as it has in years previous.

We'll hope that you didn't just stand up and raise your hand in public, and not just because it would have come on the heels of the embarrassing M&M's bowl episode. Truth is, nothing remains the same. Change is as inevitable on the stock market as it is in

life. Try to predict a few events in your life and those of your close friends and family, taking those guesses out a few years. You'll find that it's extremely difficult to match them up, and this is for something you really *know*, like your friends and family (at least we hope and assume that you know your family better than your stocks). Here, for the fun of it, let's make some predictions.

THE FOOLISH CRYSTAL BALL

Make a few predictions about what you think that you, your family members, and your close friends will be doing five years from now. Mark down where you think everyone will be, what they'll be primarily focused on, and whether or not they'll have read our money books by then!

You: _____

_____

_____

Your _____: _____

_____

_____

Your _____: _____

_____

_____

Your best friend_____: _____

_____

_____

Your other best friend_____: _____

_____

_____

Return back here in five years, and we think you'll see that it's extremely difficult to predict events and interests over a sixty-month period! Sure, we predicted that the 2001 World Series would have three amazing come-from-behind-in-the-ninth-inning games, but we did that the week before it started. Again, uncertainty is why we have markets that move in the first place, and just as you couldn't predict that your best friend and your other best friend would hook up in real life come 2007, the same thing is true of the stock market. Even if your company continues to do well, there's no guarantee that another business won't come in and do it better. And there's no guarantee that the market for your company's products will continue to flourish. When was the last time you bought an eight-track cassette? Horse and buggy, anyone?

So what does that mean for you?

It means that periodically you'll need to check on consumer giant and small-cap businesses that you've invested in. Are they beating Wall Street expectations? Are they pleasing their customers, driving profits ever higher, and sitting on a stock that has consistently beaten the S&P 500?

How often should you track your companies? Ideally at least four times a year, each time a company's earnings reports are released. This is when you get the best information on how they're spending money, executing their business plan, and meeting the challenges of the competition. You needn't live in a vacuum between statements. Read the paper, watch TV, go to the store, and keep an eye on news that may affect your company's fortunes. And thanks to the power of the Internet, where grassroots investing finds that the whole world is your lawn, you will find a countless number of like-minded investors who are, no doubt, writing articles about the stocks you're invested in both as we type this and as you read it.

Keep in mind that not all news or every opinion requires action. Even bad news shouldn't have you calling your broker a minute after the market opens. If it's that bad, the stock will have already taken the hit, anyway. Take the time to see how your company responds to the new climate. It's one thing for a company to blunder; it's another for a company to encounter a new challenge. A drop in the stock price may be simply the market's panicked guesstimate of how the news will affect the company. We expect that you picked good, strong businesses for the long run. Don't panic at the first sign of bad news. What you're looking for is continued growth on calm seas, and strong, clear-sighted navigation through stormy waters. So, before you buy stocks, take your time. And when you're holding them, well, taking your time works great then, too.

IS IT ALL OVER YET?

This said, investing is about more than just making your original selections. Your goal as an investor is to maximize your investment returns. Once a company you've invested in has achieved the goals you set for it—and doesn't appear to still have the growth potential it once did—why not say good-bye and jettison it out of your portfolio? Of course, here it's important to have new investment opportunities waiting in the wings. Don't stop investing your time just because you have no savings left to invest. Your adventure into common stocks can proceed without capital.

A Short To-Do List

1. Put the companies you own into a manila folder. Mark down the months that they'll be announcing earnings (you can call the company and ask, find the information online, or just go with the date of the last report and assume they will be at the podium every three months) and jot those dates in your business calendar.

2. In another folder, place the names of companies you looked at but decided not to own. Note their prices when you considered them. Plan to review them every year.

3. Start a third folder, for new companies or industries that you'd like to investigate and research. When you have new money to invest, return to this folder and begin your next search mission.

STARTING AND MANAGING YOUR OWN ACCOUNT

You are now ready to set aside money for investing over the long haul, you've designed an allocation model for yourself, and you've committed yourself to doing a bit of stock research each month. We're so proud of you that these very pages are blushing. Can't you see that pinkish hue just starting to come out? Well, despite the temptation to fire up the old jalopy, race over to the New York Stock Exchange, and place your orders *today*, we'd like to hold your attention for a few moments longer and discuss stockbrokers and market mechanics. We think we can make these otherwise drearily gray topics interesting. Give us a shot!

GETTING READY TO BUY STOCKS

Contrary to all the action taking place on the stock exchange floors, or on Nasdaq trading terminals all over the country, most investors never need to go farther than their telephone or their computer to communicate their buy and sell wish lists. That's where a brokerage house comes in. While we are extremely skeptical of the commission-frenzied financial industry, a broker is necessary to facilitate the order process and see to its fulfillment. You'll be best served by finding a deep-discount broker—if not the cheapest, at least a cost-conscious one that can compete with the least expensive one yet provide what you will require servicewise.

Thumb through any financial magazine, and you'll see ads for brokers. Dozens of 'em. Sometimes these magazines run feature stories where they compare various discount and full-service brokers—always a worthwhile read, even if their leading advertisers always seem to win the comparison game! The ultimate wine taster, however, is you. You should probably round up a few attractive brokerage candidates—from names that friends have recommended to online and offline advertised brokerage houses. Call them, request information and an application, and start asking a lot of questions online and at your investment club (if you're not in an investment club, well . . . join an investment club).

THE DIFFERENT SORTS OF BROKERS

Like a scoop of ice cream, brokers come in all flavors and sizes; finding what works best for you is critical.

Full-service brokers are usually the most anxious for your business. These brokers, oddly enough, are compensated based on how many trades they make in your account. This is why brokers call you during dinner (and breakfast and lunch) pitching you the next big winner. When you buy or sell stocks or mutual funds with a full-service broker—poof!—they collect a transaction fee, often a very stiff one. Ask about a low-cost, no-load index fund and they might be inclined to steer you into a high-load managed mutual fund. For this reason, we avoid the big investment firms and their brokers. More than just a telemarketing nuisance, they usually underperform the market's average returns. Why? Because they're focused on getting you to trade, not on buying the highest-quality companies and not trading for a lifetime. Doing the latter would turn their collective stomach—not to mention ruin their business.

There are definitely quality full-service brokers out there, but even though we recognize that the full-service industry has been trying to clean up its act, we still can't recommend the field as a whole with any kind of enthusiasm because it *has been an act* for so long. Few full-service brokers take the time to educate their clients, because they realize that if you teach someone to fish they won't need to come back to your fish store.

If you've been listening, you've probably narrowed your list to *discount brokers* and will have a few informational brochures heading right for your mailbox if you haven't surfed through their online sites. While the commissions they charge will weigh heavily on your opinion, don't forget to look at the entire picture. What is the minimum investment? What services do they offer? Are they open around the clock? Do they pay competitive interest rates on your money? Compare additional fees, too. Some may charge a postage and handling fee on top of every commission (ugh). Different brokers will charge different fees for services like transferring stock or wire transfers. In essence, find a company that offers the most cost-effective solution to serve your particular needs. While we have an excellent discount broker center area at broker.Fool.com, it should be one of your many online destinations in finding the right broker for you.

MAKING YOUR FIRST INVESTMENTS

Once you've actually set up your brokerage account and funded it accordingly, you're ready to make your first few investments. Huzzah and welcome!

While your local newspaper will publish the closing prices for common stocks, there are actually two share prices for every company at every point in time. There is the *bid*, which is the price you'll get when you *sell* a stock. And there is the *ask*, which is the price you pay when you *buy* a stock.

Quiz Time!

Think about it for a second. Will the bid price, or the ask price, always be higher?

Bid   Ask   Neither

We'll answer this in a jiffy.

Let's look at an example. While the final trade of the day for Microsoft may have been $65.85 a share, there were two other prices at the time. In this instance, the bid price was $65.75 and the ask price was $66.

If you wanted to *buy* Microsoft, the best price available to you was $66 per share. You could buy 100 shares for $6,600, plus the broker's commission. On the flip side, the best price you could get were you to sell shares of Microsoft was $65.75 per share. Were you to sell 100 shares of Microsoft here, you'd take in $6,575, minus your broker's commission.

The difference in these prices is known as the *spread*. And this spread in prices is how market makers make a living. Who are market makers? They're the folks who take and carry out the orders you give to your discount or full-service broker. Unlike the broker, these market makers keep an ongoing inventory of numerous stocks. However, sometimes your broker might be the market maker or affiliated with the market maker. The market makers play banker in the process, and they expect to be compensated for the risks involved in holding a ton of stock for you to buy from. Naturally, the more obscure the stock, the thinner its trading volume, the more risky it is for the market maker to hold it, and thus, the wider the spread in pricing. Sometimes you'll stumble across stocks bidding $10 and asking $11. That 10 percent difference is substantial. Were you to buy $10,000 worth of that stock, the spread alone would cost you $1,000. Yowch!

Ultimately, for the long-term investor, giving up 10 or 15 cents in the spread to buy an attractive stock, as well as paying a reasonable broker's commission, will be insignificant. However, it is indeed important to recognize that these trading costs exist and know that you'll want to keep them to a minimum.

Oh, in answer to our original bid-ask question. The asking price will always be higher than the bidding price. You'll always get less money back for selling than you'd get buying it at the same time. If the reverse were true, ask yourself what would happen!

RUNNING A SAMPLE TRADE

Let's follow a single trade.

Below is a confirmation slip, probably similar to the one you will receive when you buy or sell a stock. On it, you'll find the name of the stock you bought or sold, how much of it you bought, at what price you bought it, and how much in full you paid for it. Take a look at this one.

	BOUGHT	PRICE	COMMISSION	TOTAL
Pink Hair Inc.	500 shares	$25.25	$29.99	$12,654.99

Pretty self-explanatory stuff, eh?

SO YOU'RE ANXIOUS ABOUT PLACING THAT FIRST ORDER?

Maybe you think you might sound stupid phoning in an order or that you'll click on the wrong button, placing an online transaction. Maybe you're wondering if it really is such a good idea for you to take your financial future in your own hands, to become master of your own destiny. Wasn't it nice before when a broker could screw things up for you, you could blame him, struggle on with your life, and do so with the smug satisfaction that comes from passing the buck? No, it wasn't! But, there's certainly no need to ever rush. Let's take a minute here, tap into someone's cellular phone with our scanner (they thought these conversations were private!), and listen in on a stock order.

"But I really *do* love you, Homer . . ."

Duh! Wrong channel. Let's try this again.

"Hi, I'd like to place an order to buy some stock."

"Your account number, please."

"It's 92-22-3231."

"Name, please."

"Abby Normal."

"Yes, Ms. Normal, what order would you like to place?"

"I'd like to buy 200 shares of Messages Inc., ticker symbol M-E-S-S."

"Messages is currently bidding $19.75 and asking $20."

"Yes, I'd like those 200 shares, but I'd like to place a limit order there at $20."

"Thank you, Ms. Normal. Let me read you back your order to confirm." (Reads it back while we tap

our desk.) "OK, we'll call you back when the transaction is completed. Anything else?"

"Hmm, I've been thinking about that volatile stock Tattooland Inc. Any thoughts on it?"

"As you know, Ms. Normal, since we're a discount broker, we don't offer any advice or recommendations. You can find a lot of reference material on our site, or even better, check out those really swell folks at Fool.com."

"Darn. OK! Well, I think I'll hold off on Tattooland for now. Thank you!"

"Thank you. I will add, by the way, since I'm parked all day at the Fool.com website without my boss knowing, that you really should conduct all your own research and make your own decisions. It's the only way, Ms. Normal, that you'll ever derive any real education or true satisfaction from your investments! But there, I've gone and said that on a taped and monitored line! Ah well, another blow for freedom in the Fool Revolution!"

And with that we'll click off our scanner and review what we just tapped.

The call began with the person stating her account number. Routine. Then the discount broker confirmed her name. Routine. Then Abby ordered 200 shares of Messages Inc., and spelled out the ticker symbol for the broker. (What was she thinking? Had she not studied the balance sheet?) Routine. But then she said something unusual. Abby said, "Yes, I'd like those 200 shares, but I'd like to place a *limit order* there at $20."

Huh?

Well, at present, Messages Inc. is bidding $19.75 and asking $20 per share. Abby placed a limit order at $20, setting her boundary line there. In doing so, she's directed the broker not to buy any shares above $20. And if the stock moves up between the phone call and the placement of the order, Abby may not buy any Messages. The logic behind setting a limit price is debatable. Too many times a stock you like at $20 hits $20.25, then $22, and never returns home to $20. In general, we think you should avoid limit orders and buy the company, not the one-day stock price, expecting that if things go well the quarter point won't make a difference. Consider just buying at the market price.

Trying to shave a fraction may eventually cost you a great opportunity. It's happened to us! We've learned.

Anyway, placing your order is that simple. Your broker will call you back once the order has been filled. Some brokers may just put you on hold for a minute, then come back with the confirmation of your market order execution. With online orders, you can check on the status of a pending order right at the broker's website to see if it has been executed. Then, a couple of days later, a confirmation slip will show up in your mailbox, buried underneath a few pounds of unsolicited junk mail—more trees wiped out for low-grade promotions. Ack!

But there's your confirmation slip! Congratulations, a holding is born.

A LITTLE JARGON

Here are some terms you might expect to hear or use when talking with your discount broker.

"Market order, please." A market order is one that will be executed at the current price, without limit if it rises during the purchase.

"I'd like a limit order at $20." Unlike market orders, a limit order has a price of the most that they are willing to pay for a stock or the least that they are willing to receive for the sale of a stock.

"I'll make that a good-till-canceled limit order, please." Also known as GTC, this is a request that a limit order remain active until it is executed. Abby's limit on Messages Inc. at $20 per share can sit there for weeks waiting to get filled, if it's a good-till-canceled order.

"Make it good for the day only." You guessed it. This limit order designation is good only on that trading day.

"Ten-4 Rubber Duck, Convoy spotted a Smokey." Remember when CB radio jargon was cool? This has no bearing on your stock market order. It may still save you a speeding ticket, however, so we figured we should include it. Right? If your broker tries to give you a speeding ticket, might we suggest that you switch?

THE FUTURE OF BUYING STOCKS, TODAY

Nowadays one can place stock orders without ever saying a word. We don't want to downplay Alexander Graham Bell's achievement, but for the many who prefer the convenience of placing stock orders without delay or chatter (there are other times to socialize), punching numbers on a telephone or computer keyboard is ideal. Today, you can do everything electronically, from entering your account number to selecting a stock to buy, to getting an update on your account balance.

Investors can now place orders around the clock. And the costs of doing so are falling substantially. Over the last few years we've seen discount brokerage fees fall from $75 per trade to just a few bucks a trade. This has allowed more people to buy into the stock market, and left more funds on the table for the private investor. Touch-Tone and online trading have helped lower brokerage overhead expenses, and consumers are the ultimate beneficiary.

The greatest growth is coming directly from online services, where hundreds of thousands of investors talk about their investments and place orders a mouse click away. Dozens of discount brokers are on the World Wide Web to provide services to their customers. Internet access opens up a more visual presentation of the transaction and account information, but far more important, it provides access to everything from current news items to earnings estimates to analyst reports to public debate on business and investing. When we wrote the first edition of this book, online brokers were revolutionary. Now they're downright quaint.

DIRECT-PURCHASE INVESTING

There's one final way to invest—and an extremely inexpensive way—that deserves mention here. Today, there are a growing number of companies that, in an effort to increase their base of long-term shareholders, offer opportunities for you to buy stock directly from them without having to pay transaction fees for each trade.

These programs are called *dividend reinvestment*

plans, or DRIPs—one of the worst acronyms in all human existence—though we regularly refer to them as direct-purchase plans. Their popularity continues to grow, as the plans are now offered by over a thousand different companies. A direct-purchasing investor would, for instance, buy shares directly from the Coca-Cola Company and have the opportunity to submit additional funds each month to increase her position. Many of these plans are provided for free, while some will even provide a discount on dividends used to automatically purchase new shares. By going directly through the company's transfer agent, these plans have made building investment positions cost-effective for investors with little initial capital. In many plans you can invest as little as $25 a month.

Individual investors like all of us are apparently beginning to matter more and more to public companies. In an era of focus on increasing shareholder value, these companies realize that one way to do that is by increasing shareholder satisfaction. By making it easier for someone to own and add to company stock through the years, these plans are creating long-term investors. That is also why some companies are rewarding their shareholders with perks. Every holiday season, Wrigley's sends free gum to their investors. Chomp, chomp. Other companies will send coupons or discounted products to their shareowners.

Now, a free chew, or a low-cost investment, is a terrible reason to buy a stock. However, if you have researched first, and then found that these attractive add-ons also exist, then sure, buy through the direct-purchase plan and chew that Doublemint gum to your heart's content. There is power in being an individual investor. Heck, use it.

SOME DRAWBACKS TO DIRECT-PURCHASE INVESTING

This manner of investing isn't for everyone. It isn't as perfect as a slice of cool Key lime pie from Nicky & Kevin's Diner on a salty hot afternoon. For starters, one cannot time one's additional investments. A company will purchase your stock for the plan on a monthly, sometimes quarterly basis, and the money must be sent to the transfer agent well before then. Additionally, some companies will send you your shares and you'll be responsible for keeping them safe in a file cabinet or safety deposit box, or with the transfer agent. And the administrative hassles can be a bear. Each time you add more money and each time your company pays a dividend that it reinvests for you, you'll have an entirely new purchase price that'll have to be recorded for tax purposes. Thus, your "cost basis" will vary every three months. Thankfully there are a slew of computerized financial programs that will track this for you, but it's still something worth considering. Using a discount broker is only slightly more expensive and they provide basic accounting and share-handling services that can save you *a lot* of time.

CONCLUDING THOUGHTS

And there you have it, a brief review of portfolio allocation and a walk through making your first trade. That wasn't too bad, was it? Well, after working through hundreds of workbook pages, you might be discouraged to hear this, but . . . we think *the single greatest mistake you can make from here on in is acting too hastily.* There's no rush to get fully invested, if many of those investments are in low-quality companies or are holdings that you won't have the time to track. Pull back the reins a bit as you roll through the final chapters of this book. In the world of common stocks, haste makes more waste than you can imagine.

As we enter this workbook's home stretch, we still have some loose ends to tie, as well as a few new topics to cover. Let's get right to it then, with a chapter on tracking your investment returns, when to hold and when to sell, and whether investing is bringing additional value to your life, beyond money, or eating up large blocks of your free time and interrupting your sleep at night. Read on, we've got pages to go before we sleep.

CHAPTER 12

PERFECTING YOUR PORTFOLIO

Let's see now. You have read—and reread—all of the chapters leading up to this section, right? Excellent! Let's further assume that you've either put together a portfolio of stocks on paper that you're monitoring closely or you've actually started building a portfolio of common stocks and are ready to evaluate how well (or not) you're doing.

One of the biggest mistakes that the authors of this book made in their teenage investment years was to buy into way too many different companies. Sure, placing stock orders is a whole lot of fun, especially when it's for stocks with funny ticker symbols like Y-U-M for Taco Bell, Pizza Hut, and KFC parent Tricon Global Restaurants, or F-U-N for the roller-coaster mavens at Cedar Fair. It's great to have something new to talk about at the next office party. However, if you ever get to the point where you start referring to your investments by their ticker symbols rather than their rightful corporate names, it's time to take a step back and scale down your holdings to a collection of stocks whose company names and businesses are familiar to you. Remember, anywhere between five and fifteen stocks is plenty. Trying to follow any more than that is like trying to water an acre of farmland with a medicine dropper.

But you know all that!

So, let's imagine that you've taken all our advice and assembled a stock portfolio. And since we've got your suspension of disbelief cooking, let's imagine that we built a really cool time machine and were able to go back and buy up these companies at the end of the year 2000. Here's what your portfolio would look like.

Company	Symbol	Number of Shares	Buy Price	Fee	Total Cost
Consumer Giants					
Coca-Cola	KO	100	$60.94	$29	$6,123
Wal-Mart	WMT	100	$53.125	$29	$5,342
Campbell Soup	CPB	200	$34.625	$29	$6,954

(continued)

(continued)

COMPANY	SYMBOL	NUMBER OF SHARES	BUY PRICE	FEE	TOTAL COST
SMALL-CAPS					
Messages Inc.	MESS	100	$25	$29	$2,529
Mr. Software	SIR	320	$8	$29	$2,589
FoolMart	FMRT	140	$24.75	$29	$3,494
TOTAL				$174	$27,031

Wow, that was fast! Now let's take a few moments looking over your brand-new yet completely imaginary portfolio. You drink Diet Coke as if it was water, so you went for the fizz king, Coke. As a thrifty yet open-eyed shopper, you have seen Wal-Mart grow over the years. And despite high sodium levels, you consider soup to be a healthy food staple and you see a trend in that direction. Those are, by your take, three solid blue-chip companies fetching reasonable prices. You have also purchased three small-cap companies: Messages because you read about it in this Fool book, Mr. Software because you heard it was going to be the next Microsoft, and FoolMart because you've been buying a lot of stuff in our online store and you're hearing good things about our 2003 spring fashion line collection.

There's your portfolio. Now let's consider some of the statistics, and, we promise, we won't make you reach for those M&M's again.

1. Consider the dollar and percentage breakdowns by category.

CATEGORY	PERCENTAGE OF PORTFOLIO	TOTAL DOLLARS
Consumer giants	68%	$18,419
Small-caps	32%	$8,612

2. The total commissions you paid on your portfolio is $174. That represents 0.64 percent of the total portfolio. The largest commission on any single position was the $29 on your $2,529 investment in Messages Inc.—totaling 1.1 percent of that investment.

3. You own six stocks. In terms of maintenance, your three consumer giants need checking only once every quarter, while your small-caps should probably be studied at least once a month due to the nature of the investment. It should be noted that, ideally, you know these companies so well that you're constantly de facto checking up on them, without even really thinking about it.

There are just six stocks to follow, inside the recommended five-to-fifteen range. While some folks may be able to artfully juggle as many as twenty positions, anything beyond that is tougher, for any portfolio up to $1 billion in cash. (Bill Gates, you can stop reading here.) The account isn't overweighted in small-cap stocks, but isn't absent them. And there's a nice selection of consumer heavies, selling stuff each day to consumers all over the world. And finally—and we think extremely important—no investment ran commissions above 2 percent, and the overall portfolio incurred commissions costs of less than 1 percent. Naturally it's easier to do this with larger amounts of money.

The allocation here looks solid to us. Now let's consider the performance first of Messages Inc. and then of your overall portfolio.

MESSAGES INC. IN 2002

Messages Inc. closed out the year at $16.50 per share, down from your purchase price of $25. This means that in a single year, your investment in this company has fallen $879, or 34.8 percent. Tough year, chum. You had this book—you even had this time machine thingy—and you still bought in. Don't worry, you weren't alone. Anyway, let's tap the numbers into a table here, and if you've made your first investment, you can enter the numbers into your very first tracking list.

FOOLISH STOCK TRACKING LIST	YOUR TRACKING LIST
Date: Today	Date: _____
Ticker: MESS	Ticker: _____
Shares: 100	Shares: _____
Current price: $16.50	Current price: _____
Current value: $1,650	Current value: _____
Purchase price: $25	Purchase price: _____
Purchase cost: $2,529	Purchase cost: _____

Why did Messages fall so dramatically in value? Did the company announce mediocre earnings? Was it hurt by currency hedging gone wrong on its Asian business? Did management make the blunder of spending inordinate amounts of time trying to correct its losing markets rather than plowing resources heavily into its winning markets? Or was it just a really bad year for stocks? Before we can answer those questions, let's take a look at the performance of your overall portfolio for the year.

YOUR PORTFOLIO IN REVIEW

Nearly a year later, come late November 2001, you check your stock quotes. You tap the prices into your computer spreadsheet or write them down in a notebook after quoting them in your local newspaper. It's been a difficult year, but you're still holding all of your stocks. You've kept abreast of the earnings reports of your consumer giants, and you've kept even closer tabs on your more volatile upstarts.

Here's what the first year of investing Foolishly has brought you.

OVERALL PERFORMANCE

COMPANY	NUMBER OF SHARES	BUY PRICE	TOTAL COST	PRESENT PRICE	PRESENT VALUE
CONSUMER GIANTS					
Coca-Cola	100	$60.94	$6,123	$50	$5,000
Wal-Mart	100	$53.125	$5,342	$55	$5,500
Campbell Soup	200	$34.625	$6,954	$30.50	$6,100
SMALL-CAPS					
Messages Inc.	100	$25	$2,529	$16.50	$1,650
Mr. Software	320	$8	$2,589	$5.75	$1,840
FoolMart	140	$24.75	$3,494	$24	$3,360
TOTAL			$27,031		$23,450

Talk about a waste of a time machine jaunt, huh? Five of your six stocks are down for the year. Messages Inc. has gotten mauled. Investors have been bailing on Mr. Software as well, and, hey, Coke and Campbell's were human, too. You scored well with Wal-Mart. Otherwise, everything else has lost you money. Either it's been a horrible year for the U.S. stock market or you've done a very poor job of picking stocks.

Let's look at your percentage returns for the year.

PERFORMANCE BY STOCK

COMPANY	TOTAL COST	PRESENT VALUE	PERCENTAGE RETURN
CONSUMER GIANTS			
Coca-Cola	$6,123	$5,000	− 18.3%
Wal-Mart	$5,342	$5,500	+ 3.0%
Campbell Soup	$6,954	$6,100	− 12.3%
SMALL-CAPS			
Messages Inc.	$2,529	$1,650	− 34.8%
Mr. Software	$2,589	$1,840	− 28.9%
FoolMart	$3,494	$3,360	− 3.8%
TOTAL	$27,031	$23,450	− 13.2%

So, through the first eleven months of 2001, your $27,031 in savings lost a little more than $3,500, falling 13.2 percent in the process. Messages Inc. has lost over one-third of its value; Mr. Software has fallen nearly 30 percent. Your large-cap losses were less severe, but it was not exactly a banner showing. That's a look at your individual stocks. Now let's take a gander at your performance by categories—consumer giants and small-caps.

PERFORMANCE BY CATEGORY

Studying your portfolio by category requires a series of calculations that will take but a few minutes and will give you a grounded sense of how you're doing and how well you're allocating your funds. Too often investors don't know how their small growth stocks are doing relative to, say, their company stock, relative to the one or two conglomerates they own. By breaking them down into groups, you may well learn that you've improperly allocated funds. Let's see what this portfolio looks like.

CATEGORY	TOTAL COST	PRESENT VALUE	PERCENTAGE RETURN
Consumer giants	$18,419	$16,600	− 9.9%
Small-caps	$8,612	$6,850	− 20.5%
TOTAL	$27,031	$23,450	− 13.2%

While each of your categories shed roughly $1,800, your consumer giants made up twice as much of your portfolio as their smaller brethren. So, on a percentage basis, the biggies held up better, this time. At first blush, it appears you've done an extremely lousy job of finding small companies to invest in while your larger companies haven't exactly been the kind of stuff to write home about. What's going on here? Investing is supposed to be about *making* money.

Well, as much as the numbers above tell us about *your* year, they don't tell us how your investments did relative to the performance of the entire stock market in 2001. If stocks were up 2 percent, you'd be forced to conclude that you had a miserable year. Of all your investments, only Wal-Mart could be considered a success. Conversely, if the stock market fell 30 percent in 2001, you'd even be able to call Mr. Software a winner. Without the context of the broader market's performance, you'll have little idea of how well or how poorly you are doing. While your pocketbook might only understand the weight of its contents, it's important to see where you stand relative to the market. You won't know whether to just move all your money into index funds, because you can't beat the stock market, or whether to just put all of your money into small-cap stocks because your financial analysis there has been awesome. Without a snapshot of the market's doings, you're lost. Relativity is a compass. Use it well, scout.

VERSUS MARKET PERFORMANCE

Below are the performance numbers for the S&P 500 and the Nasdaq in late November 2001. The S&P 500 is used to measure the overall performance of the U.S. market; the Nasdaq is used here to measure the performance of the smaller companies in the marketplace. Let's check them out before we use the two to measure the performance of our portfolio by category.

Market Index	2000 Close	2001 Close	Percentage Return
S&P 500	1320	1139	− 13.7%
Nasdaq	2470	1899	− 23.1%
Your Portfolio	$27,031	$23,450	− 13.2%

Well, it turns out your portfolio didn't have such an awful year after all. While nothing can beat the market's historical returns, you will always have years like 2001 wedged along the way. Despite all of your portfolio's warts, you manage to best the S&P 500 Index. You can also rest assured that you beat the majority of managed mutual funds in the United States in 2001 as well. Yeah, you can't eat relative performance, but keep beating the indices in good times and bad, and we flat guarantee that your performance in the stock market will be satisfactory to you, to say the least.

You'll also note that the Nasdaq market—which holds more small-cap issues than the New York and American stock exchanges combined—got absolutely crushed in 2001. The smaller companies fell a whopping 23.1 percent for the year. What you have, then, is a market where the most enterprising companies, the riskiest ones to invest in, got clobbered. The larger companies, with many different products and services, and with business across the world, fared much better. But even they declined!

It was an extremely difficult year for common stocks in the United States. But it wasn't an extremely rare one. Since 1970, the stock market has closed out eight years with negative returns. In five of those years, stocks lost more than 9 percent. Every investor in common stocks should be prepared for double-digit decreases in any given year. If you are investing $10,000, you may well lose $1,000 or more over the next twelve months. Be prepared. Be patient, but be prepared.

So your workbook portfolio is unfortunately down 13.2 percent, but you managed to stay ahead of the market, so you're fine. Yes, ideally you would have been down only 5 percent or 3 percent, or even on the year. Ideally, yes. But you're not. So let's figure what you should do from here.

ALL SORTS OF RETURNS

Now that you can compute the gain (or—horrors—loss) generated by your portfolio, and present it in the form of a percentage (otherwise called a portfolio *return*—as in the return on your invested capital), we should briefly look at different types of returns that you'll want to be calculating.

1. Annual Return. This is the total return measured over a twelve-month period. When you see an annual return reported at 10 percent, it simply means that the investment earned 10 percent over the last year.

2. Total Return. Total return represents the total of price appreciation plus dividends or interest derived from an investment. If you started with the sample portfolio and have come to the close of your first year, your total return is a negative: minus 13.2 percent. (In other words, your portfolio is worth 86.8 percent of its starting point.) If come 2002 your portfolio were to rise by 18 percent, what would your total return be? Let's figure it out.

$$1 = \text{portfolio value at starting point}$$

$$1 \times 86.8\% = 0.868 \text{ (value after first year)}$$

$$0.868 \times 118\% = 1.024 \text{ (value after second year)}$$

$$0.024 = 2.4\% = \text{total return}$$

3. Average Annual Return. This represents the total return result, expressed as what you would earn for each given year on average. This is another calculation that might, at first, seem complex. But it isn't. There is going to be some root taking, but we're not talking about drilling at any nerves below your teeth. Let's take an example. Imagine that your portfolio has risen 159 percent over an eight-year period. Here you would simply take the eighth root of 2.59. The number represents your original investment plus the rise in value (100% + 159% = 259% = 2.59). Type 2.59 into your calculator. Then take the eighth root of it, and you should get 1.126. Subtract 1, and you get 0.126. This indicates that your portfolio has grown at a rate of 12.6 percent per year over the eight-year period. To check that, multiply 1.126 against itself seven times and see if you come up with 2.59. Ahh, perfect.

4. Return Versus the Market. The final note we'll throw in here is that you should always calculate your annual, total, and average annual returns alongside calculations of the returns by the S&P 500. How are you doing relative to the overall market? If your stocks are up 26 percent but the market is up 41 percent, you're losing. And if the market is down 18 percent and you're down 11 percent, you're winning. Conventional wisdom hasn't yet caught up to these simple truths. We know better than that, don't we?

WHERE TO FROM HERE?

After a little more than one year, you'll have some easy and some difficult decisions to make. On the easy side of the mix, you have to see how much long-term savings you can add to your portfolio. While it's true that the magic of compounding will work just fine if your initial investment is also your last investment, the commitment to adding to your portfolio so it grows along with your long-term capital appreciation is significant. You want to always be on the lookout for new stock ideas, and having money on the sidelines helps motivate the search party.

OK, you've added cash. But before you begin looking at new stocks, consider your existing holdings. Start with the consumer giants. You've seen the last few quarterly reports and you probably wound up with a glossy annual report along the way. Did the CEO's letter to shareholders impress you? Has the company made fiscal promises that its financial health wasn't able to keep? Is Campbell Soup still growing sales, earnings, and at least maintaining profit margins? Is Coca-Cola paying down debt, holding off its accounts payable, and increasing its savings? How's Wal-Mart doing—four good quarters of earnings? Our suggestion here is that unless you have very serious concerns about the business of your consumer heavies, you continue to hold them. Granted, change is a business reality. Certainly, for at least one of your heavies, at some point you'll have serious concerns in your lifetime. Consider selling then. But if the company seems headed in the right direction and its financial position is sturdy, we think you should hold.

Your final step is to consider those small-cap stocks. Of your three holdings, two lost badly to the Nasdaq: Messages Inc. and Mr. Software. Sometimes the investing community has just blown it, overlooking a great value and selling off a stock well below its fair price. This actually does happen, but you have to be modest enough to detach your personal bias. Sometimes your stocks aren't laughing with you, but at you. You'll need to ask the following questions:

- Why did Messages and Mr. Software underperform the Nasdaq?
- Are their income statements and balance sheets stronger this year than last?
- Do I feel that these businesses might excel in the year ahead?
- What are the most difficult challenges that lie ahead of these companies?
- What are people saying about these companies at Fool.com?*
- Am I having trouble sleeping at night because of these investments?
- Are there better places for this money?

* You can join these online discussions at boards.Fool.com.

There are another dozen great questions to ask, but these seven should get you on your way.

Remember, just because a stock underperforms its category in a single year, that doesn't mean you should immediately take your money elsewhere. You're an owner of the company and you should evaluate the business, not the stock price. Check through the earlier reading and exercises on financial statements, attempt to determine what went wrong, and consider whether things will get worse or better for the business in the year or years ahead. If things don't look promising, sell and don't look back. Sell at a loss? Yep. Even the greatest investors are wrong from time to time. What makes them great is the ability to be introspective to the point of

cutting one's losses. If there's a better place for your money, and there usually is, it should be there.

Oh, by the way, we know you didn't pick Mr. Software and Messages. We forced them into your portfolio, knowing full well that they were duds. Our apologies. You deserve better. We'd include a stack of softballs with this book so you can heave them our way as we straddle the dunk tank, but hey, we've got some stock selling to do now.

SELLING A STOCK

So, your portfolio lost slightly to the market. You've scoped through your consumer heavies—Wal-Mart, Coca-Cola, and Campbell Soup—and while none of them had a particularly awesome year, you're content that they're on the right track. You believe people of every age will still continue to patronize discount department stores, that people of every age and nationality will still drink Coke, and that in the cold of winter, most people head for Campbell's chicken noodle soup—not the generic stuff on the next shelf. So, you're going to hold on to all three of those.

But here you are left with the prickly decision about your small-caps. After looking over Fool-Mart's year, you're reasonably happy. The company had some inventory problems in the fourth quarter, but you remain confident and accepted the company's explanation that these were onetime problems with three specific products (the jester-shaped fire log, the Tom and Dave mood rings, and the "How to Tie Your Shoes Without Blinking" online seminar) that are falling out of the mix in the year ahead. So, you're going to stick with FoolMart.

But what about that pair of barking dogs, those dachsunds of depreciation, Messages and Mr. Software? What's it going to be: buy, sell, or hold?

WHEN TO SELL

You've reached the most frustrating topic in investing. Everyone has an opinion on when to sell. But while there are a few key principles, generally you'll have to build a selling strategy that fits your personality. In *The Motley Fool Investment Guide,* we proposed just one sell rule: "When you find a better place for your money, put it there." This generally focuses you on the opportunities that lie ahead rather than the prior performance. Certainly the biggest mistake that investors make is hoping for one of their losers to "just get back to even." If the business looks weak, you should sell.

The Fool Ratio is around to help you pick exit points. Selling a stock when it reaches fair value is about as reasonable as it gets. But even there, sometimes you're better off holding a winner that is priced fairly or even overpriced temporarily. If the business is strong, then it will eventually catch up to and rush past the present valuation, pulling the stock up with it. We call that the Motorboat Principle. Why? Have you ever seen a great water-skier slalom outside of the wake, up next to the boat, then fall back into the wake behind the boat? During the fall back, the rope loses its tautness. The skier isn't propelled forward. But then, kapow! Once back far enough, the slalom skier is yanked forward by the motorboat. The stock prices of great companies can get ahead of themselves, but if the business truly is great, eventually it'll yank the stock price up with it.

So far we've offered two ideas—sell if you have a better place for the money and sell when the stock looks fairly priced and the business doesn't seem superior enough to pull it higher anytime soon. That's a decent start. But what other clues are out there? Try asking yourself these questions:

- Is the business stronger this year than last year?
- Does the company appear to be telling the truth to its shareholders?
- Do the reasons I bought the stock still hold true?
- For the large-caps in particular, is the Foolish Flow Ratio improving, or weakening?
- Are sales and earnings climbing at a good pace?
- Will I want Frosted Flakes or fruit-topped pancakes for breakfast tomorrow?
- Will I need this money in less than three years?

- Do I really know enough about this business to be invested in it?

We consider it critical that you ask the last two questions. If you're going to need the money in less than thirty-six months, it shouldn't be in stocks. Period. And if you don't really understand the business you invested in, sell out. On par, you'll do better in an index fund than in businesses that you don't understand. And the first five questions there will guide you to a method for selling. We'll leave you with one last suggestion: don't base sell decisions on your emotions. Just as we told you not to rush into making your purchases, be patient with your sell decision process as well. Take your time, be methodical, be Foolish, and recognize that naturally you'll make selling mistakes in your career. Your aim should be to improve a little bit each time around.

THE SELL GAME: DON'T LOOK NOW!

Since we are focusing on ways to help you sort out how you look at investing in stocks, we want to give you a way of reviewing your stock sales and learning from them. *The Motley Fool Investment Guide* describes a simple technique—a game really—that we call Don't Look Now! At the time you sell your stock, record the exit price and the closing price of the S&P 500 Index. Just jot it down, place it in a lockbox, and forget about it in the near term. Try not to look at the stock's price after you sell for several months. Six months from the date you sold, record the follow-up price for your stock and the S&P 500 Index.

Here's the way to score your results:

If the stock has risen 20 percent or more over your exit price, that's a *total defeat!* You shoulda held. (Score: − 5 points)

If the stock has risen less than 20 percent but is outperforming the S&P 500—that's a *marginal defeat.* (Score: − 2 points)

If the stock has fallen less than 20 percent but is underperforming the S&P 500, you guessed it—*marginal victory.* (Score: + 2 points)

If the stock has fallen 20 percent or more from your exit price, claim a *total victory.* (Score: + 5 points)

Keep a running score of your performance as a stock seller. After five years of investing, evaluate your performance. What's your total score? You may well find that you bail on your investments much too soon. Or possibly, you hold your losers too long. Or maybe you nail every sale just right. You go, Fool!

THE SELL GAME: TAKE TWO

If you're really angling for fun, and care to make Don't Look Now! more than a fraternity drinking game, take the process one step further. Track what you did with the proceeds from your stock sales.

We have said it plenty throughout this chapter: sell a stock if there is a better home for your money. Here we'll score you bonus points if you were right. Follow what you eventually bought with the money left over after your stock sale.

If the stock you bought outperformed the stock you sold, well done! (Bonus: + 3 points)

If the stock you bought underperformed the stock you sold, tough break. (Penalty: − 3 points)

If you can't track the proceeds because you took it out of the market and used it to fund a shopping spree at Nicky and Kevin's House of Cheese, what were you thinking? (Penalty: − 7 points)

Pop Quiz!

It's back to that simple true-or-false game that haunted you in high school science class. Is your no. 2 pencil sharpened and ready to go? Good luck!

1. Don and Dawn Arrington have doubled their money in the stock market over the past three years. They're planning to buy a house with that money in twenty-four months, and they believe they've found a way to double their money every few years. Given this, it's a good thing that they've decided to keep their money in stocks over the next two years.　　True　False

2. No matter what anyone tells you, if you lose money at the end of any twelve-month period of investing in stocks, you've blown it.　True　False

3. Most people should just pay management fees to a mutual fund and let the professionals take care of their money.　　True　False

4. The best investors sell out of their positions a lot.　　True　False

5. The Motley Fool says that to be properly diversified you should have at least fifty stocks in your portfolio.　　True　False

6. A lot of really weird people live in nudist colonies.　　True　False

7. You can begin investing with as little as $100.　　True　False

8. Unless your consumer-giant investments are beating analyst expectations, you should sell them.　　True　False

9. Most people have a better chance of winning at roulette than they do of picking investments that will make them money in the years ahead.　　True　False

10. Harry Potter is a huge Motley Fool fan.　　True　False

The answers to all questions but lucky number 7 are *false.* Number 7 is true—remember those dividend reinvestment plans. And as for questions 6 and

10, we have no evidence that indicates those are true, so we'll have to mark them as false. If, however, it would impresses your children that Harry Potter was indeed a fan of all things Motley, we invite J. K. Rowling to have the fictional wizard fitted for a Fool ball cap immediately.

ADDITIONAL THOUGHTS ABOUT YOUR PORTFOLIO

You're tracking your portfolio, maybe you've sold a position or two that wasn't meeting your standards, and you're starting to see some results. Over the last eighteen months you've whooped the market, and neighbors have seen you jaunting down to the grocer in—what's that?—a belled, motley cap! You're excited. But still, something seems to be missing. In an attempt to fill that gap, we're tossing out nine ideas for your consideration. Some of these simply flesh out points we have tried to make earlier. Others are new. Let's count.

1. IS THERE A BETTER WAY TO TRACK MY PORTFOLIO THAN ON PAPER?

You've got pencil blisters on your writing hand and you've been pounding away at your handheld calculator to the point that the numbers have started to wear off. There has to be a better way!

There is!

There are plenty of stand-alone financial software programs like Microsoft's Money and Intuit's Quicken that will quickly keep tabs on how your stocks are doing. They each pack plenty of bells and whistles that will do everything from helping you with your personal budget to helping you come tax time. Some programs are even bundled for free in computer systems so you have little to lose but time.

Of course, it bears noting that Fool.com has a My Portfolio area to track your holdings. If you have an online broker, odds are that they, too, have plenty of Internet-based tools to help you follow your portfolio. There are also plenty more financial sites out there on the Internet.

If you're still not convinced to find your way online or try your hand with financial software, fear not. Investors have been able to keep tabs on their holdings with little more than a pencil, a four-function calculator, and a sheet of paper. To that end, this workbook is full of worksheets to help you along the way. While it might take some more time and there is a greater margin of error in calculations going the old-fashioned way, it's still a capable means of tracking.

2. DO MY RETURNS REFLECT THE PERFORMANCE OF THE MARKET, OR OF MY INDIVIDUAL STOCKS?

If you have followed the stock market long enough, no doubt you've heard the dreaded euphemism *correction.*

Correction is the word used to describe what happens when the market loses ground. We have dips in the market all of the time. Even during the best of years, the overall market will have drops of 5 percent or more, and usually more than once. While these might be nerve-racking times, things could be worse. Bear markets awake from hibernation with a growl to produce prolonged corrections. More severe than a correction, and a marked downtrend that typically lasts six months or longer, bear markets are truly trying times for the investing community.

In 2001, seemingly sound technology stocks quickly shed more than half of their value while many notoriously overfunded Internet companies surrendered far more than that.

Given that the overall market can see fairly dramatic swings over any twelve-month period, you'll need to be absolutely certain that you study the performance of your investments alongside that of the broader market. Remember, your company may be making spectacular progress, but when macroeconomic factors come into play, your company's stock price will be racing upstream at half or quarter speed—possibly losing ground in a strong countercurrent.

It can be frustrating to see one of your companies do nothing—or worse—over a prolonged period of time. Rest assured that if you've picked a strong company at a reasonable price, over the long term things will even out.

Here are some of the factors that can drive the whole stock market and make the actual business fortunes of your companies virtually irrelevant to their share price movement over a short-term period:

- Government economic data, such as jobless rates or inflation
- Interest rate changes
- Election results
- International conflicts
- Guru predictions in glossy financial magazines
- A clear trend up or down in earnings reports by conglomerates
- The flapping of a duck's wing in Hunan

If you just happen to buy into a company before one of these broad-reaching events trashes the entire market, maintain patience and keep your sense of humor. Just continue to compare your stocks to the market's indices. You know how the market has fared historically. Keep up with it, or lap it, and you know you'll be doing well in the long run. Even though we've already defined and mentioned the following indices in the workbook, we consider these important enough to give them one last mention here.

The Dow Jones Industrial Average (the Dow) is the granddaddy of 'em all. You hear about this index every night on the news when the anchor looks blankly into the camera, winks, and says, "The Dow was up 25 points today." One nationally administered Fool finance class in high school and we'd all know that the Dow index tracks the movement of thirty of the largest blue-chip stocks in America and the world. And even the news anchor would then know that a 25-point Dow move is akin to a four-miler-per-hour breeze coming in from wherever. It's just not news.

Standard & Poor's 500 Index (S&P 500) is probably our favorite index, in large part because it tracks five hundred large "bellwether" stocks over the Dow's collection of thirty. The list also includes smaller names and is a more precise measure of the market's performance because it is weighted (larger companies have a larger impact on the index itself).

The Nasdaq Composite is the index that tracks all of the stocks traded on the Nasdaq exchange. Because this index specializes in smaller companies, many of the high-technology flavor, it is more volatile than the two prominent ones listed above.

The FOOL 50 is our own creation, started on the first day of trading in 2000. The FOOL 50 consists of fifty companies that we consider to be among the most important, most forward-thinking in the world today. Unlike the three indices listed above, the FOOL 50 contains both U.S.- and foreign-based firms. These are all huge companies, but they aren't the world's largest—just among the world's most innovative and important.

You need to use one of these averages, or a combination, as a milestone to gauge how your portfolio is doing. Indices are a very useful tool for placing your wee little investment skiff's performance in the context of the entire U.S. fleet.

One final thought. Remember that matching or beating the market over any short-term period involves a high degree of randomness. So don't become discouraged if your portfolio does not immediately beat up on Wall Street your first week, or month, or year. Unlike Wall Street, you have your eye fixed squarely on the long term. Over time, your position as a small investor will significantly increase your chances of beating the market.

3. HAS MY COMPANY'S STORY CHANGED?

You're now able to track your portfolio and analyze the performance of your individual holdings against the overall market. Simultaneously, it's important for you to score the performance of your stocks against your own expectations for each.

What did we just write?

Well, we spoke earlier of filling out a single-page report that highlights your own research and sets down some of the main reasons why you've found a good investment. This should include some numerical projections that enable you to directly compare a stock's performance versus your own plans for it ahead of time. This step will help you to assess, on a continual basis, whether or not this stock belongs in your account.

Numbers make your assessments easier to perform, but don't neglect the "story," either. Many different factors could cause you to reassess your company's story. A management change, new and larger competitors, slowing sales, delayed FDA approval—those are just a few of the many items that can change the overall prospects for a public company.

So, Whaddaya Think?

Jot down some thoughts about the management, competition, and strength in products or services of a company that you own (or all of the companies that you own, by Xeroxing this page).

Management: _____

Competition: _____

Products or services: _____

4. ADMITTING YOU'RE WRONG

It's easy to get attached to your stocks. It's easy to get attached to the reasons why you bought into a company in the first place. Sometimes you do all your homework and buy stock in what you believe to be a great company. You love the product and believe in the management. You track it against the market, follow up on all news releases, and dig through the financial reports as they come. Two years later, you still own the stock. Unfortunately, the story has changed, and for the worse. The stock has gradually fallen, and is now down perhaps 50 percent, cutting the amount you plunked down in half.

Given that the business is weakened and weakening, it looks like the marketplace is trying to give you a hint.

Face it, some investments just don't work out. The stock doesn't worry about you, and oftentimes the company doesn't worry about you, either—not nearly so much as you may have worried about them. If no end to this underperformance appears in sight, sell the dog. Be thankful that you learned so much about their industry, that you learned a good deal about losing investments, and that you're still in relatively decent health! Years later, if you've been diligent, the stock's bad performance will be outweighed by the lessons you took away from the experience and the money you made after moving that money out of the kennel and into a better investment! To paraphrase the 2000 canine classic, who let the dogs out? You. You you, you you!

5. WHO SHOULD I LISTEN TO OUT THERE?

As fate would have it, planet Earth is well stocked with self-proclaimed experts on every subject. Our financial markets seem to lure these people at an unusually high rate, particularly those who make ridiculous short-term predictions about individual stocks or the direction of the market in general. Turn on the TV. Click on to the channel with the tickers streaming at the bottom. Wait for an expert. Now, specifically ignore whatever this person has just said.

Most of their predictions are wrong. They don't make money from being right, they make money from just being there and being heard. The medium rewards style over substance, so if they can pound the desk and smile pretty for the camera there is no degree of accountability. For years, the big financial newspapers and magazines have printed the short-term predictions of experts without printing any follow-up reviewing the performance of those predictions.

What the reader is left with is puffery and self-promotion, aided and abetted by journalists who need a quote before their deadlines. While many traditional reads are touting that if you're not an expert you can't make money in stocks, subscriber-ships are declining. Intelligent readers have tired of all the price guessing that ate up the space better reserved for a thorough and objective analysis of business. This continues to stoke the dramatic growth in the popularity of online services, where many have discovered they have more to learn from one another than from yesterday's news.

So, to whom should you be listening for guidance on your money? You! Yes, you! Of course, reading up on investment books written by actual investors like Peter Lynch and Philip Fisher will help. For every worthwhile book you do come across, feel free to toss a dozen business magazines with cover headlines like "Sell Stocks Now!" or "The Seven Mutual Funds You Need to Own This Summer!" into the bonfire. None of those topical attention grabbers speak to what should be your underlying interest: the vitality or frailty of a particular business. "Where's the Market Headed Next Month?" Puh-leeze. Into the fire with you as well.

Another source of opinion is the thousands of knowledgeable investors you can meet online today, many of whom own the same investments you do, and some of whom know the company or its industry as well or even better. Sign up with an Internet service provider and surf around Fooldom to participate in discussions about the thousands of companies, taking place twenty-four hours a day. Don't worry, you won't have to dress up for the occasion.

While you're there, feel free to seek out articles about investment strategies, your big consumer giants, getting out of debt, you name it. All this is great, but again, the one person whose opinion you should value the most is you.

6. HOW MUCH RESEARCH IS TOO MUCH RESEARCH?

Yes, like asking for seconds—then thirds—on your mother's legendary apple crumb pie, there comes a time when too much of a good thing is just too much. Of course, you will want to keep records of the resources you use to make investment decisions. Articles. Magazines. Also, on occasion you'll want to sift through your various subscriptions and eliminate those that aren't helping much. Save a tree and free your mind up for other things—how much better can it get?

Naturally, alongside your reading of another investment book or two, you should begin to stock up on some other research materials at the outset. Go ahead and scour different publications and websites in your first few months of investing. Read skeptically, of course, as always. The answer to the question we just posed is that early on, no amount of research is too much research. As you become more experienced, however, you'll begin to know when to say when. You may want to check out our monthly Stock Advisor newsletter for research on individual stocks at www.Fooladvisor.com.

7. THE BEAUTY OF COMPOUNDED GROWTH

Worth repeating, perhaps the most important lesson we can leave you with in this workbook is the principle of long-term compounded growth—a growth that adds more money in years thirty through forty than in all the first thirty years toted up. Time is the critical component here—not timeliness, as in gurus making the right market call over the next six months. The amount of time you allow for your investments to grow will radically change the rewards. Let's say you double your money in the market next year—from $2,000 to $4,000—and then remove it altogether to spend on something else, just happy to have "gambled" and won. You'll be kicking yourself fifty years from now when you realize that that $4,000 compounded at 11 percent annual growth for five decades grows into $738,000. That's the reality of compounded growth.

In the simplest of terms, compounding capital is the money you earn on money you've earned in previous periods. Remember your first lemonade stand? You scraped together $1 and bought the lemonade mix. You added some water, set up your stand, and away you went. At the end of the hot afternoon, you may have had $2. Wow, you doubled your money at age eight without ever picking up an investment book! Well, the next day, you went out and bought two packages of lemonade mix and, with hard work and some luck, ended the day with $4. Then you bought more, opened up a second stand, diversified into fruit punch and diet lemonade—and maybe before the end of your life you were an old guy sitting on a porch pitching Country Time Lemonade to America. That's compounding growth off a growing base of capital. You learned it then. You know it now. Let's muse over a few more numbers.

	ANNUAL GROWTH RATE	NUMBER OF YEARS	PRETAX MONEY
$1,000	13%	70	$5.2 million
$2,000	13%	60	$3.1 million
$4,000	13%	50	$1.8 million
$8,000	13%	40	$1.1 million
$16,000	13%	30	$625,000
$32,000	13%	20	$369,000
$64,000	13%	10	$217,000
$128,000	13%	1	$144,640

As you can see once again, the early bird with the least money got the worm. You simply cannot start soon enough. Even if you're not loaded at the beginning, just show up. And, sorry to repeat this once more but hey, it's absolutely ludicrous that our

children are not learning the basics of investing and putting away a little bit of money today for their retirement. With so many years in front of them, they have the most to gain! To hammer that home, consider that in the seventy-first year of the $1,000 portfolio, a 13 percent return would yield more than five million dollars. An initial investment and patience. (To help a teenager you know get started investing, may we suggest giving them a copy of our new *Motley Fool Investment Guide for Teens*.)

The lesson: once you've paid down your debts, begin saving and investing today, no matter how little or how much long-term savings you have.

8. ON BECOMING A PAPER TIGER

Occasionally we can be absolute experts at contradicting ourselves, so with point eight, allow us to do just that. We do not think that you should begin investing today unless you're secure in your thinking. Why not hone your skills by practicing on paper before you begin your investing career? Then compare the results of your paper portfolio with those of an appropriate index.

There's no rush to investing. Yes, show up, but as much as we think you'll benefit from getting involved today, you will be hard-pressed to perform enthusiastically well if you don't understand what you're doing. You may even want to reread the workbook when you're done with it. After all, isn't that why you didn't mark this book up as much as we asked you to?

Take your time, despite the propaganda you may have read elsewhere. Your grandmother may have once told you that "a stitch in time saves nine," and smart lady she was. Get it right the first time and, my, what a beautiful quilt you'll weave.

9. ARE YOU HAVING FUN?

Education and Folly go hand in hand. Yes, investing is serious, but investors need not be. None of the tools provided in this workbook will have any real meaning if the destination means more to you than the journey itself (all the living you did to reach the point of being rich). Indeed, if portfolio performance becomes the be-all and end-all of your investing experience, things can go wrong. You might throw all of your money at a "hot" sector and forget what you have learned about diversification. You might subscribe to that "can't lose" publication that tells you how to double your money in thirty days. Finally, you might do well but overlook the importance of your family in the pursuit of your profits.

That's not what we're about, and we expect it's not what you're about. Compounded growth, patience, and the search for great businesses is all about not becoming obsessed with your stock portfolio. Don't ignore your family—unless they won't let you have the TV remote control, in which case, grab it and ignore them! Don't spend all of your free time hunched over a copy of the evening news, trying to read the agate type. No matter how much we'd like to see you clicking around our site for sixteen hours a day, we don't want you there if it detracts from living a full-blown life away from the management of your moolah.

Manage your portfolio. Don't let it manage you!

ADDITIONAL RESOURCES AT FOOL.COM

We hope you have enjoyed reading this workbook and that it has provided you with valuable and helpful information. Throughout the workbook, you have been pointed toward additional resources and services to help you invest your money. Fool.com offers many of these additional resources at your fingertips. Below is an abbreviated but helpful list of some of the key areas, most of which have appeared in this workbook:

DISCOUNT BROKER CENTER— BROKER.FOOL.COM

- Looking to start investing, to switch from a full-service broker to a discount one, or maybe to select a better discount broker? We can help you compare, choose, and use discount brokers, and even get started investing directly online.

FOOL SCHOOL—FOOL.COM/SCHOOL

- The Fool School area will get you started with the basics. Learn the 13 Steps to Investing Foolishly, the skinny on mutual funds, and some beginner investing strategies such as dividend reinvestment plans and index funds.

INDEX CENTER—INDEXCENTER.FOOL.COM

- Learn about stock market indices, why they are important to use in comparison to your portfolio's performance, and how you can earn their investment returns.

SHORT-TERM SAVINGS CENTER— SAVINGS.FOOL.COM

- Everyone needs a cash stash for emergencies. We'll help you determine how much you need and where to keep it.

MOTLEY FOOL STOCK ADVISOR— WWW.FOOLADVISOR.COM

- Whether you are just starting to invest or digging deeper into analyzing stocks, Tom and David offer ideas for you in the *Motley Fool Stock Advisor.* In this monthly newsletter, the Gardners present their outlook on the stock market, individual stock suggestions, and tips on the best ways to manage your personal finances and investing.

THE FOOL COMMUNITY—BOARDS.FOOL.COM

Join other members online to interact, learn, question, and exchange ideas. The Community offers:

- An opportunity to post messages to get your questions answered
- Staff-monitored discussions

To check out what other Fools are saying, take a peek with a 30-day free trial.

TMF MONEY ADVISOR—HTTP://TMFMA.FOOL.COM

TMF Money Advisor provides personalized, objective advice for all aspects of your financial life. With TMF Money Advisor you get:

- Access to an unbiased, unconflicted financial advisor
- An online tool you can use to create a personal financial plan
- A package of ten Motley Fool online seminars

And, as a special bonus for all our book readers, we offer a special discount for our TMF Money Advisor service. To get this special offer, go to http://TMFMA.Fool.com.

The Motley Fool's aim is to help you find solutions to the many and sometimes complex matters of money and investing. Whether you're looking for new investment ideas, home-buying tips, minute-by-minute stock quotes, or just a place to interact with other investors, Fool.com has all of that and more—available twenty-four hours a day.

ABOUT THE AUTHORS

David and Tom Gardner cofounded The Motley Fool, an Alexandria, Virginia–based multimedia company, in 1993. They started out publishing a modest investment newsletter for friends and family, started talking stocks online in the early days of AOL, then launched their own investment education Web site, Fool.com in 1997.

Tom graduated with an honors degree in English and creative writing from Brown University. David graduated as a Morehead Scholar from the University of North Carolina at Chapel Hill. With many ideas and no regrets, he quit his job writing for *Louis Rukeyser's Wall Street* newsletter in order to found The Motley Fool with his brother.

Today, The Motley Fool has grown into an international multimedia company offering financial solutions to millions of individuals worldwide seeking to make better financial decisions and improve their overall quality of life. Tom and David have coauthored four *New York Times* business bestsellers, including *The Motley Fool Investment Guide, The Motley Fool You Have More Than You Think,* and *The Motley Fool's Rule Breakers, Rule Makers.* In addition to writing bestselling books, the Gardners oversee a nationally syndicated newspaper column, which is carried by more than 200 newspapers, and host a weekly radio program on NPR. The Gardners, once voted "Interactive Age's Entrepreneurs of the Year 1996," recently hosted the award-winning PBS show "The Motley Fool Money-Making, Life-Changing Special."